Foundations of Western Literature

High School Course

By Meredith Curtis

Published by Powerline Productions/Kingdom Building Services, Inc.

Printed by CreateSpace, an Amazon Company.

All Photos and clipart © Sarah Jeffords, Sarah Joy Curtis, Meredith Curtis, Laura Nolette, and licensees/Used by permission/All rights reserved.

Thank you to Laura Nolette for the Beautiful Cover.

Thank you to Katie Beth Nolette for all the great questions and insight on literary analysis.

ISBN-13: 978-1534768321

Contents

How to Use This Course

Foundations of Western Literature is a one-credit high school course. It was created for use in at home or in a homeschool co-op. Each month you will read two books, starting with Genesis, the oldest book ever written. You will also write and rewrite papers.

Western Literature refers to literature written by European, Australian, and North American writers. The foundations of that literature were laid in the Middle East, Greece, and Rome. The Old Testament, New Testament, Greek literature, and Roman literature are the beginnings of Western Literature, as well as this course. You will notice that the plots, themes, and characters resurface over and over and in modern times. After all, a good story is a good story.

The course is laid out for a typical school year: September to May, but you can extend it, adapt it, or change whatever you want. After all, you are the teacher.

Classic Literature

You will read books from Ancient History like *Genesis, Gilgamesh, The Odyssey, The Iliad, The AEneid, Rhetoric,* and *The Art of War*. Early Western literature was either histories, how-to books, or epic poems (super, super long adventure poems). Next, we move on to *Gospel of Matthew, Acts, Plutarch's Lives, City of God, 1001 Arabian Nights, Merry Adventures of Robin Hood, Grimm's Fairy Tales, Collection of Fairy Tales by Hans Christian Anderson,* and Norse Myths.

 You will notice that all of these are books you have heard of, seen movies, or read/watched stories based on these classics. They have all influenced Western culture.

One thing to keep in mind: just because it's old doesn't mean it's clean and wholesome. In fact, the Norse Myths, the Odyssey, The Iliad, and the AEneid have inappropriate material, so I have chosen to recommend other versions. A.J. Church wrote versions of the Greek and Roman classics that *are well-written classic in and of themselves. For the Norse Myths, I chose D'Aulaires'* Book of Norse Myths, an easy read with gorgeous illustrations. This enables us to read several books this year. The hardest book students will read is *City of God,* but they have six weeks to read it.

Writing Assignments

Along with exposing students to the classics of Western Literature, this course takes students step-by-step toward literary analysis. Each assignment is designed to get them ready for their final paper on *Robin Hood*. I want to take students from success to success to success in their writing/analysis.

Foundations of Western Literature Course Requirements

This page gives all the basic info of the course with a list of book titles, a list of writing assignments, and grading requirements.

Foundations of Western Literature Syllabus

The syllabus is also a check-off list several pages long, divided by months and weeks. There are also boxes to check off at the beginning of each section throughout the year.

Foundations of Western Literature Course Hours

This chart is for those counting hours. I guarantee you will cross the 150 hour mark unless you are a speed reader.

Home & Class Weeks

Each month is divided into Weeks with Home and Class. Home is simply independent work. Class is for Mom to meet with student or a homeschool co-op class. It is important for Mom to meet with student for the class time where they can discuss class info and read papers aloud.

Crash Course in History

Since we are going way back in time, these sections are included to remind students of their Ancient History people, places, and events.

Background on Book

I try to give you background on each book read so that you can place it in the context of its time and place.

Bible Charts

There are three charts and directions are clearly given to fill them in. Each chart is a little different, so be sure to read the directions.

Book Club

Discussing a book with a group is awesome. This class is even better if a sibling and a parent read the books, too if you are working this course independently. We like to kick back, eat cookies and drink coffee while we discuss books, sitting in comfy chairs in the family room. This should be fun!

Peer Reviews

Peer Review are only for students taking the class together. They give input to one another after reading essays and assignments.

Grading Rubrics

Created to help Moms and Teachers grade papers.

Have a wonderful year and God bless you!

Meredith Curtis

Foundations of Western Literature Course Requirements

Literature

The Holy Bible: Genesis

Adam and His Kin by Ruth Beechick

Gilgamesh the Hero by Geraldine McCaughrean retelling of *Epic of Gilgamesh* (Mesopotamia 2100 B.C.)

The Iliad for Boys & Girls by A.J. Church—Amazing retelling of *Iliad* by Homer (Greek written circa 800 B.C., setting circa 1200 B.C.)

The Odyssey for Boys & Girls by A.J. Church—Amazing retelling of *The Odyssey* by Homer (Greek written circa 800 B.C., setting circa 1200 B.C.)

Aesop's Fables (Greek circa 600 B.C.)

The Art of War by Sun Tzu (Chinese circa 513 B.C.)

The AEneid for Boys & Girls by A.J. Church—Amazing retelling of *The AEneid* by Virgil (Latin circa 20 B.C., setting circa 1200 B.C.)

The Holy Bible: Gospel of Matthew (28 chapters)

Plutarch's Lives by Plutarch (Latin circa A.D. 100)

The Holy Bible: Acts

City of God by St. Augustine (Latin 426)

1001 Arabian Nights (Persian Middle Ages 700-1200)

The Merry Adventures of Robin Hood by Howard Pyle (setting circa 1200)

Grimm's Fairy Tales by Jacob & Wilhelm Grimm (German collected centuries old stories 1812)

Collection of Fairy Tales by Hans Christian Anderson (Danish 1838)

D'Aulaires' Book of Norse Myths by Ingri and Edgar Parin D'Aulaire

Works Used in Class

Rhetoric by Aristotle (Greek circa 350 B.C.) Parts 1-4

"Song of Roland" by unknown, an epic poem about Battle of Roncevaux in 788 (French circa AD 1000)

Writing Assignments

Genesis, Matthew, and Acts Charts

Gilgamesh the Hero Plot Evaluation Paper

My Character in *The Odyssey*

David and Goliath in Literature Project

Aesop's Fables Theme Analysis Essay

Rhetoric by Aristotle Commercial Analysis Project

God's Love Theme in the Prodigal Son Essay

Sower and the Seed Imagery and Symbolism Project

Parallel Lives Biography

Comparison Essay of Pliny the Younger's Description of Mt. Vesuvius & Jack London's Description of the San Francisco Earthquake of 1906

Turn Prodigal Son into a Blog Post

Characterization Analysis on *The Merry Adventures of Robin Hood*

Paraphrase a Fairy Tale

Write a Modern Fairy Tale

Grading

Grades should be 50% completing assignments and reading books, 25% for group discussion, and 25% for paper grades.

To get a **C** grade, you must read all books and complete all writing assignments adequately. You must participate a few times in group discussions and give/receive input about writing papers.

To get a **B** grade, you must read all books, complete all writing assignments sharing your ideas clearly with proper grammar and punctuation, participate regularly in book club discussions, and give/receive helpful input about writing papers.

To get an **A** grade, you must read all books, complete all writing assignments showing excellence and creativity, participate regularly in book club discussions, and give/receive helpful input about writing papers. You must show improvement in your writing this year and demonstrate insight into the books read.

Foundations of Western Literature Syllabus

Assignments	Comp.	Time took

August before Fist Class

Read Crash Course in Ancient History: God our Creator

Read *The Holy Bible: Genesis*

Fill Our *Genesis* People Chart

Read *Adam and His Kin*

Read "Crash Course in Ancient History: Early Civilizations"

September Class Week One

Book Club: Discuss *Genesis* & *Adam & His Kin*

Heroes from Genesis Introduce Themselves

Read & Discuss "Plot," "How to Write an Essay," & "Background to *Epic of Gilgamesh* "

Read & Discuss "How to Explore Plot" & "How to Write a Plot Evaluation Paper"

List Questions about *Gilgamesh the Hero*

September Home Week One

Read *Gilgamesh the Hero* & Answer Questions

Read "Our Pathway to Literary Analysis" & "How to Write Essay on Plot from *Epic of Gilgamesh*"

Come up with Thesis & Outline for Essay on Plot from *Gilgamesh the Hero*

September Class Week Two

Book Club: Discuss *Gilgamesh the Hero*

Read & Discuss "Words, Lovely, Words" & "Elements of Literature"

Share Plot Evaluation Thesis & Outline in Groups

September Home Week Two

Read *The Art of War* by Sun Tzu

Fill Out *The Art of War* Book Review

Write Plot Evaluation Essay

Read "Crash Course in Ancient History: Ancient Egypt to Early Greece "

September Class Week Three

Book Club: Discuss *The Art of War*

Read & Discuss "Setting," "Background to *Iliad*," & "Between a Rock & A Hard Place"

List Questions about *The Iliad*

Read Plot Evaluation Essays in Groups & Peer Reviews

September Home Week Three & Four

Read *The Iliad for Boys & Girls* by A.J. Church (Homer)

Re-Write Plot Evaluation Essay

October Class Week One

Book Club: Discuss *The Iliad* by Homer

Read & Discuss "Background to *The Odyssey*" & "Characterization in *The Odyssey*"

List Questions about *The Odyssey*

Read Re-Written Plot Evaluation Essays in Groups

Turn In Plot Evaluation Essays

October Home Week One

Read *The Odyssey for Boys & Girls* by A.J. Church (Homer) & Answer Discussion Questions

October Class Week Two

Read & Discuss "Sentences Make a Difference" & "Background on David & Goliath"

Participate in David & Goliath Classroom Project

October Home Week Two

Read "Crash Course in Ancient History: Assyria to Greece"

Finish Reading *The Odyssey for Boys & Girls* by A.J. Church (Homer)

Write Thesis, Outline, and "My Character in the Odyssey" Paper

October Class Week Three

Book Club: Discuss *The Odyssey* by Homer

Read "My Character in the Odyssey" in Groups & Peer Review

Read & Discuss "Let the Paper Flow," "Theme," "Between a Rock & Hard Place," "Aesop's Fables"

List Questions about *Aesop's Fables*

October Home Week Three & Four

Read *Aesop's Fables* & Answer Questions

Write Questions, Thesis, Outline, & "How Theme is Illustrated in My Aesop's Fable" Essay

November Class Week One

Book Club: Discuss *Aesop's Fables*

Read & Discuss "Background on Rhetoric by Aristotle" & "*The Aeneid* by Virgil "

Read "How Theme is Illustrated in My Aesop's Fable" Essays in Groups & Peer Review

November Home Week One

Read "Crash Course in Ancient History: Rome"

Read *The Aeneid for Boys & Girls* by A.J. Church (Virgil)

Read *Rhetoric* by Aristotle

Complete Rhetoric Assignment on three Commercials

Rewrite "How Theme is Illustrated in My Aesop's Fable" Essay

November Class Week Two

Read & Discuss "Trojan Horse in Modern Culture," "Aristotle & Logic," & "Logic in Essays,"

Read *Rhetoric* by Aristotle Assignments in Groups

Play Logic Games

Read "How Theme is Illustrated in My Aesop's Fable" Essay   in Groups

Turn In "How Theme is Illustrated in My Aesop's Fable" Essay

November Home Week Two

Read "Crash Course in Ancient History: Jesus"

Finish Reading *The Aeneid for Boys & Girls* by A.J. Church (Virgil)

November Class Week Three

Book Club: Discuss *The Aeneid* using Discussion Questions

Read & Discuss "Background to Matthew," "Prodigal Son," & "Prodigal Theme in Literature"

Brainstorm Thesis Ideas

November Home Week Three & Four

Read *The Holy Bible: Matthew* chapters 1-20

Fill Out Matthew Chart

Read "The Prodigal Son"

Write Thesis, Outline, & "How Love is Portrayed in the Prodigal Son" Essay

December Class Week One

Book Club: Discuss *The Holy Bible: Matthew* chapters 1-20

Read & Discuss "Background on Sower & His Seed," "Gospel Themes in Lit.,"

Read & Discuss "Symbolism & Read Prodigal Son Essay in Groups

Read "How Love is Portrayed in the Prodigal Son" Essays in Groups & Peer Review

Brainstorm for the Sower & His Seed Project

December Home Week One

Read *The Holy Bible: Matthew* chapters 21-28 & Fill Out Matthew Chart

Write Up "The Sower & His Seed" Project Symbols & Story Ideas

Rewrite "How Love is Portrayed in the Prodigal Son" Essay

December Class Week Two

Book Club Discussion: *Gospel of Matthew*

Read "The Sower & His Seed" Project Symbols & Story Ideas in Groups

December Home Week Two

Write The Sower & His Seed Project Story

Read *Plutarch's Lives*

December Class Week Three

Read & Discuss "Background to *Plutarch's Lives*" & "Parallel Lives Greek & Roman"

Brainstorm Parallel Lives that Fit Together

Turn In "The Sower & His Seed" Project Story

December Home WeekThree & Four

Read *Plutarch's Lives* by Plutarch & Answer Questions

Complete "How to Write Parallel Lives Worksheet"

Work on Parallel Lives Biographies

January Class Week One

Read & Discuss "Narrowing Down the Focus of a Biography" & "Pay Attention to Sources"

Brainstorm Parallel Lives Combinations

January Home Week One

Finish Reading *Plutarch's Lives* by Plutarch

Finish Parallel Lives Biographies

January Class Week Two

Book Club: Discuss *Plutarch's Lives* by Plutarch using Discussion Questions

Go over "Grammar Review," "How to Edit Parallel Lives in Groups" & "Background on *Acts* 1-14"

Complete & Share Grammar Glad Lib

Read & Edit Parallel Lives in Groups

January Home Week Two

Read *the Holy Bible: Act chapters 1-14 & Fill out* Chart

Rewrite Parallel Lives Biographies

Start Reading *City of God* by Saint Augustine

January Class Week Three

Book Club: Discuss Acts 1-14 & Acts' Impact on Literature

Read Re-Written Parallel Lives in Groups

Turn In Parallel Lives Biographies

January Home Week Three & Four

Read *The Holy Bible: Act* chapters 15-28 & Fill Out Chart

Read *City of God*

February Class Week One

Book Club: Discuss Acts 15-28 & Acts' Impact on Literature

Read & Discuss " "How to Write a Compare & Contrast Essay"

Read & Discuss "Background on St. Augustine & *City of God*""

List Questions about both National Disaster Descriptions

How to Use Circles to Compare & Contrast

February Home Week One

Read "Crash Course in History: Early Church to Vikings"

Read *City of God* by St. Augustine (Latin 426)

Read Pliny and London's Descriptions of Natural Disasters

Underline & Write in Margins of Descriptions according to Directions

February Class Week Two

Book Club: Discuss Ancient vs. Modern Descriptions of National Disasters

Go Over How to Write a Compare & Contrast Essay

Brainstorm Compare & Contrast Essay Ideas

February Home Week Two

Read *City of God* by St. Augustine (Latin 426)

Brainstorm & Answer Questions about Compare & Contrast Essay

Write Compare & Contrast Essay

February Class Week Three

Book Club: Discuss Republic of Rome vs. City of God

Read Compare & Contrast Essay in Groups & Peer Review

February Home Week Three & Four

Read *City of God* by St. Augustine (Latin 426)

Rewrite Compare & Contrast Essay

March Class Week One

Book Club: Discuss *City of God* by St. Augustine Using Discussion Questions

Read & Discuss :"Background on *Arabian Nights*" & "Review of the Writing Process"

Read & Discuss "Crafting Essays & "Turning Papers into Blog Posts"

Turn In Compare & Contrast Essay

March Home Week One

Read "Crash Course in History: Middle Ages"

Read *1001 Arabian Nights*

Read "Turn Prodigal Son Essay into a Blog Post"

Write a Blog Post

March Class Week Two

Play Word Games like Scattegories®

Read Blog Posts in Groups & Peer Review

March Home Week Two

Finish Reading *1001 Arabian Nights*

Re-write Blog Post

March Class Week Three

Book Club: Discuss *1001 Arabian Nights* Using Discussion Questions

Read & Discuss "Background on *Robin Hood* by Howard Pyle

Read & Discuss "How to Write a Literary Analysis" & "Characterization"

Read Re-Written Blog Posts in Groups

Turn in Blog Posts

~ 19 ~

March Home Week Three & Four

Read *Robin Hood*

Brainstorm some Questions for Literary Analysis of *Robin Hood*

April Class Week One

Book Club: Discuss *Robin Hood*

Read & Discuss "Background on "Grimm's *Fairy Tales*

Brainstorm about Characterization Analysis

April Home Week One

Read Grimm's Fairy Tales & Answer Questions

Read "Things to Remember about Literary Analysis"

Make Outline for Characterization Analysis

Start Characterization Analysis Essay

April Class Week Two

Lecture: Background to Song of Roland, Battle of Roncevaux in circa A.D. 788 (French)

Recite "Song of Roland" Aloud in Class

Brainstorm about Characterization Analysis

April Home Week Two

Finish Reading Grimm's Fairy Tales

Finish Characterization Analysis

April Class Week Three

Book Club: Discuss *Grimm's Fairy Tales* Using Discussion Questions

Read & Discuss "Hans Christen Andersen's Fairy Tales" & "How to Paraphrase a Fairy Tale

Read Characterization Analysis in Groups

Turn In Characterization Analysis in Groups

April Home Week Three & Four

Read Hans Christian Anderson Fairy Tales

Follow Step-by-Step Instructions to Paraphrase a Fairy Tale

Type up Fairy Tale Paraphrase

May Class Week One

Book Club: Hans Christian Andersen Fairy Tales

Read & Discuss "Background on Norse Mythology" & "How the Vikings Found Jesus"

Read & Discuss "Ingredients of a Good Story" & "How to Write Your Own Fairy Tale"

Read Fairy Tale Paraphrase in Groups

Turn in Fairy Tale Paraphrase

May Home Week One

Read *D'Aulaires' Book of Norse Myths* by Ingri and Edgar Parin D'Aulaire

Brainstorm for Your Own Fairy Tale Using Charts

Write Your Own Fairy Tale

May Class Week Two

Discuss Norse Mythology Influence in the Western Culture

Read Your Own Fairy Tales Aloud in Groups & Peer Review

May Home Week Two

Finish Reading *D'Aulaires' Book of Norse Myths* by Ingri and Edgar Parin D'Aulaire

Rewrite Your Own Fairy Tale

May Class Week Three

Book Club Discussion: *D'Aulaires' Book of Norse Myths*

Turn In Your Own Fairy Tale

Foundations of Western Literature Hours

Optional Check-Off Chart if you are logging hours.

August: Genesis

Foundations of Western Literature

1 Building Noah's Ark, Franzosicher Mister 1675

August Home Week Three

- [ ] Read "Crash Course in Ancient History: God our Creator"
- [ ] Read Genesis, Filling Out Chart as You Go
- [ ] Plan Your Dress Up and Act it Out Presentation
- [ ] Read *Adam and His Kin* by Ruth Beechick

Crash Course in History: God our Creator

Before the Beginning

"In the beginning, God..." (Genesis 1:1 NASB)

"In the beginning was the Word, and the Word was with God, and the Word was God. He was in the beginning with God. All things came into being through Him, and apart from Him nothing came into being that has come into being. In Him was life, and the life was the Light of men. The Light shines in the darkness, and the darkness did not comprehend it" (John 1:1-5 NASB).

Before time, space, and earth existed, there was the Lord God. He has always existed in three persons: Father, Son, and Holy Ghost. In perfect unity and love, they existed.

Creation

"In the beginning, God created the heavens and the earth" (Genesis 1:1 NASB)

"God, after He spoke long ago to the fathers in the prophets in many portions and in many ways, in these last days has spoken to us in His Son, whom He appointed heir of all things, through whom also he made the world" (Hebrews 1:1-2 NASB).

God the Father, Son, and Holy Spirit created the earth and heavens in six literal days.

God the Writer

Our Beloved Heavenly Father wrote his account of Creation in Genesis chapter one and two. Maybe Adam wrote it down. Or maybe, like the Ten Commandments, He wrote the account Himself.

God gave us a book, The Bible, to reveal Himself and His love for us. He wrote each line and chapter through men, inspired by the Holy Spirit.

God is a writer. Here are some of the kinds of writing He does.

Stories: From Genesis to Revelation, God's Word is filled with stories of all kinds. Though these stories are all true, they read like classic adventure novels, taking place in lion's dens, aboard arks, on battle fields, and crossing bodies of water.

Histories: This is nonfiction writing at its finest: the history of the Jewish Nation, the life of Jesus, and the early church. The Bible is full of facts, information, and genealogies. In fact, it even gives us a glimpse of the end of time, where history is comes to a close.

Poetry/Songs: The Book of Psalms is a song book filled with poetry and lyrics.

Prophetic Words: Faithful men penned God's prophetic words, often after speaking them to a rebellious nation. It is exciting to see all the Messianic prophecies in the Old Testament fulfilled in Christ in the New Testament.

Romance: From Sarah & Abraham, Isaac & Rebekah, and Ruth & Boaz to Mary & Joseph and Hosea's unfailing love for his unfaithful wife, the Bible is filled with love stories. Of course, the greatest of all love stories is the amazing love the Lord has for His people, His Beloved Bride.

Proverbs: Wise sayings that give us insight for successful living, King Solomon's proverbs still help God's people to grow up in their salvation and walk uprightly.

Parables: Better than Aesop's Fables, Jesus' parables reveal truth in an easy-to-understand way that helps people draw closer to God.

Essays/Inspirational Writings/Sermons: Everything you ever wanted to know about Christian living, theology, and sound doctrine is found in God's book.

Prayers: Scattered throughout the Old and New Testaments, prayers are written down so that we can use them as models when approaching our Heavenly Father.

Other Kinds of Writing: You will find descriptive writing, narrative writing, persuasive writing, informational writing, and inspirational writing in God's Book, the Holy Bible.

God the Storyteller

Our Amazing Lord Most High did not write a theology book or an epic poem. Instead, the Bible contains poetry and theology, but it is also filled with true stories about real people with real strengths and weaknesses. In fact, the Holy Bible and all of life is one grand story.

Setting: "And he carried me away in the Spirit to a great and high mountain, and showed me the Holy City, Jerusalem, coming down out of heaven from God, having the glory of God. Her brilliance was like a very costly stone, as a stone of crystal-clear jasper. It had a great and high wall with twelve gates" (Revelation 21:10-12 NASB).

Beginning: "In the beginning God created the heavens and the earth." (Genesis 1:1 NASB).

Ending: "Then I saw a new heaven and a new earth; for the first heaven and the first earth had passed away, and there is no longer any sea" (Revelation 21:1 NASB).

Action: "As He was praying, the appearance of His face became different, and His clothes became as white and gleaming. And behold, two men were talking with Him; and they were Moses and Elijah, who, appearing in glory, were speaking of His departure which He was about to accomplish at Jerusalem" (Luke 9:29-31 NASB).

Plot: "Just as He chose us in Him before the foundation of the world, that we would be holy and blameless before Him. In love He predestined us to be adoption as sons through Jesus Christ" (Ephesians 1:4-5 NASB).

"Among them we too all formerly lived in the lusts of our flesh, indulging the desires of the flesh and of the mind, and we were by nature children of wrath, even as the rest. But God, being rich in mercy, because of His great love with which He loved us, even when we were dead in our transgressions, made us alive together with Christ (by grace you have been saved), and raised us up with Him, and seated us with Him in the heavenly places in Christ Jesus" (Ephesians 2:3-6 NASB).

Climax: "When the thousand years are completed, Satan will be released from his prison" (Revelation 20:7 NASB)

Foreshadowing: "The LORD said to Moses, "Make a snake and put it up on a pole; anyone who is bitten can look at it and live." So Moses made a bronze snake and put it up on a pole. Then when anyone was bitten by a snake and looked at the bronze snake, he lived" (Numbers 21:8-9 NASB).

Flashback: "As Moses lifted up the serpent in the wilderness, even so must the Son of Man be lifted up; so that whoever believes will in Him have eternal life" (John 3:14-15 NASB).

Theme: "Therefore many other signs Jesus also performed in the presence of his disciples, which are not written in this book; but these have been written that you may believe that Jesus is the Christ, the Son of God; and that believing you may have life in his name" (John 20:30-31 NASB).

Let's get back to Ancient History.

Creation

On the first day of Creation, God created light and separated light from darkness. He declared light 'day' and darkness 'night'.

On the second day of Creation, God created the sky by separating waters above from waters below.

On the third day of Creation, God gathered the waters together to form seas and created the dry land. He also created all kinds of plants with seeds.

On the fourth day of Creation, God created the sun, moon, and stars. He gave them to us for signs, season, days, and years.

On the fifth day of Creation, God created swimming and flying creatures, including birds, fish, whales, dolphins, crabs, clams, lobsters, barnacles, and krill.

On the sixth day of Creation, God created all kinds of land animals including cattle, bears, tigers, elephants, bunnies, cats, dogs, insects, spiders, snakes, pigs, and lambs. He also created man on the sixth day. Wow! That is a ton of things to create. No wonder He rested on the seventh day.

God created man and woman to be extraordinary. They would somehow reflect God the Father, Son, and Holy Spirit. I know that sounds a little confusing. Men and women not only were made in God's image, but they would rule over all the earth and everything that lived in it for the Lord. What a special call!

God made the first man, Adam, in a special way.

The first thing Adam got to do was to name the animals. He had a big job to do in fulfilling his purpose to rule over the entire earth. He needed a helper. God created Eve, the first woman, to be a helper for Adam, the first man.

God also started the practice of marriage in the Garden of Eden. He laid down a command for all people who would come after Adam and Eve: a man and a woman should leave their homes, come together, and be married to begin a new life.

On the seventh day of Creation, God rested. He blessed the seventh day of the week, and made it a special day for men, women, and children to rest from their hard work and spend time with Him.

Life in the Garden of Eden

God created Adam to work the garden, to plant crops for food. The very first man was a farmer and gardener. There was no rain yet. Every morning a mist rose up to water the plants.

The Garden of Eden was beautiful. God chose the plants and trees to be good for food and beautiful to look at.

There were two important trees in the Garden of Eden.

The Tree of Life gave them the life and health they needed to live forever.

The Tree of the Knowledge of Good and Evil was forbidden. Adam and Eve were not allowed to eat from it.

The Fall of Man

2 Adam & Eve Leave the Garden by Providence Lithograph Company circa 1900 public domain

Eve listened to the lies sputtered by the serpent and sinned against the Lord by tasting fruit from the Tree of the Knowledge of Good and Evil. Adam listened to Eve's prodding and tasted the forbidden fruit, breaking God's command willfully.

God punished the serpent, Eve, and Adam. Life would no longer last forever. There would be death. Sin entered the world. How sad.

But even in the midst of such horror, God made a promise.

"And I will put enmity between you and the woman, and between your seed and her seed; he shall bruise you on the head, and you shall bruise him on the heel" (Genesis 3: 15 NASB).

God was making a promise that through the seed of a woman, the Messiah would come to defeat satan.

The LORD God also had to kick Adam and Eve out of the Garden of Eden, but first He made them clothes.

What a terrible day. Adam and his wife departed from paradise to travel toward an unknown destination. Angels assigned by God guarded the entrance to Eden, so that no one could again eat from the Tree of Life.

However, the Messiah would come and He would make a way for His Chosen People to eat from the Tree of Life again in Heaven.

Life Outside the Garden

Good news: Adam and Even had two baby boys named Cain and Abel. Cain grew up to be a farmer and Abel grew up to be a shepherd.

We also learn that the practice of making offerings to the Lord was going on. Abel seemed to get it. He offered up a sacrifice of the lives of some of his lambs. Cain brought some of his produce, but that was not what God was looking for. Instead of getting right with God, Cain got angry at Abel.

Bad news: Cain killed his brother and was sentenced to be a wanderer on the earth.

Cain left his parents and siblings, with his wife to wander. Cain built the first city, naming it after his son Enoch. His descendants became musicians, bronze workers, iron workers, and ranchers. This was all before the flood. (Genesis 4:17-22)

Meanwhile, back to Adam and Eve. They had several children, but were given a special son to replace Abel named Seth. When Seth grew up, married, and had his own son, Enosh, men began to call upon the LORD again (Genesis 4:26) We don't know if Abel's murder and Cain's banishment scared people and they stopped worshipping the LORD for a season, but somehow the earlier practice of making offerings to God took a long pause.

The First Man Could Write

Inspired by God, Adam wrote the account of The Fall, his son's untimely death, his other son's banishment, and the birth of Seth. Seth continued the story. As you read Genesis, remember this is a true story of real, flawed people who stumbled and fumbled in their attempt to serve the True and Living God. It is also the story of a Holy, Loving God who intervenes in the affairs of men, not because we deserve it, but because He loves us.

3 Cain & Abel published by the Providence Lithograph Company between 1896 and 1913

The Holy Bible: Book of Genesis

Genesis is the first book in the Holy Bible. Genesis was written centuries ago and took over 3,000 years to write—no other book took so long to produce! Genesis begins with Adam, the first man, writing about his firsthand experience. He was on the scene when God created Eve, sin came into the world, and one of his sons killed the other one. (Genesis 5:1)

Ruth Beechick explains who wrote Genesis at the end of her novel *Adam and His Kin*. "Dr. Henry M. Morris has suggested a division of the early portions of *Genesis* according to which patriarch wrote each portion (*The Genesis Record*: Baker Book House, 1976). Upon examination, this system seems reasonable. The Hebrew word *toledoth* appears between each division, and it translates into English "generations" or "origins." By extension, the whole statement means, "This is the record of the generations of…" And by inference it could mean, "This is the written record of the generations of the generations of …" For concreteness and clarity, this latter form is used in this book. The key to seeing this pattern is to realize that the toledoths come at the end of a man's writing instead of at the beginning, as the verse divisions, and even chapter divisions, make them appear. One can even see that in every man's case except Terah's the writer who signed off with a toledoth could know the information proceeding the signature, but not that which follows." (*Adam and His Kin* by Ruth Beechick, Arrow Press, Pollack, CA; 1990.)

Looking at Genesis this way makes Moses the compiler of the book. Here are the writers. Remember, though men wrote this book, they were inspired by God. This book is written by the Lord.

Genesis 1 to Genesis 2:4: The Lord Himself (Moses or Adam probably wrote this down though)

Genesis 2:4 to Genesis 5:1: Adam

Genesis 5:2-Genesis 6:9: Noah

Genesis 6:10-Genesis 10:1: The Sons of Noah

Genesis 10:2-Genesis 11:27: Terah

Genesis tells us about Creation, the long, but sinful lives of early mankind, and God's sadness that he ever made mankind. We read about God's redemptive plan to destroy the whole world with a flood, but rescue Noah, a preacher of righteousness, and his family. From Noah's three sons, Ham, Shem, and Japheth, every nation on earth descended.

Though Noah was righteous, many of descendants turned back to sinful living, including the worship of false gods. They built a huge ziggurat, or temple for idols, to make a name for themselves. God scattered them and confused their languages so they could not work together on such wicked projects.

Genesis relates God's choosing of Abraham. Abraham lived in the land of Ur, but left in obedience to God. God promised Abraham his descendants would be as numerous as the stars in the sky, but there was a problem: Sarah could not conceive. Follow the adventures, romance, and drama of the Patriarchs, as the nation of Israel is birthed. This book ends with Joseph's amazing story. He was strategically chosen by God to go on ahead of his family to Egypt.

As you read Genesis, you will meet real people with real problems who encounter a real God who changes everything! I want you to learn more about the people in *Genesis*.

Genesis People Chart

Fill out this chart based on your reading of Genesis.

Chapter in Genesis	Events in Chapter	People in Chapter	Choose one Person, List Character Strengths	Same person, how Character is Affected by Circumstances (can be positive or negative influence)
Genesis chapter one				
Genesis chapter two				
Genesis chapter three				

Chapter in Genesis	Events in Chapter	People in Chapter	Choose one Person, List Character Strengths	Same person, how Character is Affected by Circumstances
Genesis chapter four				
Genesis chapter five				
Genesis chapter six				
Genesis chapter seven				

Chapter in Genesis	Events in Chapter	People in Chapter	Choose one Person, List Character Strengths	Same person, how Character is Affected by Circumstances
Genesis chapter eight				
Genesis chapter nine				
Genesis chapter ten				
Genesis chapter eleven				

Chapter in Genesis	Events in Chapter	People in Chapter	Choose one Person, List Character Strengths	Same person, how Character is Affected by Circumstances
Genesis chapter twelve				
Genesis chapter thirteen				
Genesis chapter fourteen				
Genesis chapter fifteen				

Chapter in Genesis	Events in Chapter	People in Chapter	Choose one Person, List Character Strengths	Same person, how Character is Affected by Circumstances
Genesis chapter sixteen				
Genesis chapter seventeen				
Genesis chapter eighteen				
Genesis chapter nineteen				

Chapter in Genesis	Events in Chapter	People in Chapter	Choose one Person, List Character Strengths	Same person, how Character is Affected by Circumstances
Genesis chapter twenty				
Genesis chapter twenty-one				
Genesis chapter twenty-two				
Genesis chapter twenty-three				

Chapter in Genesis	Events in Chapter	People in Chapter	Choose one Person, List Character Strengths	Same person, how Character is Affected by Circumstances
Genesis chapter twenty-four				
Genesis chapter twenty-five				
Genesis chapter twenty-six				
Genesis chapter twenty-seven				

Chapter in Genesis	Events in Chapter	People in Chapter	Choose one Person, List Character Strengths	Same person, how Character is Affected by Circumstances
Genesis chapter twenty-eight				
Genesis chapter twenty-nine				
Genesis chapter thirty				
Genesis chapter thirty-one				

Chapter in Genesis	Events in Chapter	People in Chapter	Choose one Person, List Character Strengths	Same person, how Character is Affected by Circumstances
Genesis chapter thirty-two				
Genesis chapter thirty-three				
Genesis chapter thirty-four				
Genesis chapter thirty-five				

Chapter in Genesis	Events in Chapter	People in Chapter	Choose one Person, List Character Strengths	Same person, how Character is Affected by Circumstances
Genesis chapter thirty-six				
Genesis chapter thirty-seven				
Genesis chapter thirty-eight				
Genesis chapter thirty-nine				

Chapter in Genesis	Events in Chapter	People in Chapter	Choose one Person, List Character Strengths	Same person, how Character is Affected by Circumstances
Genesis chapter forty				
Genesis chapter forty-one				
Genesis chapter forty-two				
Genesis chapter forty-three				

Chapter in Genesis	Events in Chapter	People in Chapter	Choose one Person, List Character Strengths	Same person, how Character is Affected by Circumstances
Genesis chapter forty-four				
Genesis chapter forty-five				
Genesis chapter forty-six				
Genesis chapter forty-seven				

Chapter in Genesis	Events in Chapter	People in Chapter	Choose one Person, List Character Strengths	Same person, how Character is Affected by Circumstances
Genesis chapter forty-eight				
Genesis chapter forty-nine				
Genesis chapter fifty				

Dress Up & Act it Out!

Choose your favorite character in Genesis.

Research that character so that you know them well. Imagine how they would think, dress, act, and speak.

Dress up as your favorite character and introduce yourself to your family or co-op class.

Be sure to take pictures.

Here is the info to share.

- Your Name
- Where You Lived
- The People in Your Life (Parents, Children, Family, Friends)
- Your Relationship with God

August Week Four Home

☐ Read "Crash Course in Ancient History: Early Civilizations"

Crash Course in Ancient History: Early Civilizations

From Adam to Noah

The following information is taken from Genesis 5.

At the age of 130, Adam became the father of Seth, as well as other sons and daughters. He died at the age of 930.

At the age of 105, Seth became the father of Enosh, as well as other sons and daughters. He died at the age of 912.

At the age of 90, Enosh became the father of Kenen, as well as other sons and daughters. He died at the age of 905.

At the age of 75, Kenen became the father of Mahalalel, as well as other sons and daughters. He died at the age of 910.

At the age of 65, Mahalalel became the father of Jared, as well as other sons and daughters. He died at the age of 895.

At the age of 162, Jared became the father of Enoch, as well as other sons and daughters. He died at the age of 962.

At the age of 65, Enoch became the father of Methuselah, as well as other sons and daughters. He did not die. *"Then Enoch walked with God; and he was not, for God took him"* (Genesis 5:24 NASB).

At the age of 187, Methuselah became the father of Lamech, as well as other sons and daughters. He died at the age of 969.

At the age of 182, Lamech became the father of Noah, as well as other sons and daughters. He died at the age of 777.

God Calls The World to Repentance

The earth was filled with evil everywhere you turned. Violence and sexual sin saddened the Lord's heart. Only one man found favor with God. Noah was a preacher of righteousness. Our Creator assigned Noah a project that would make it possible for mankind to live on.

Noah and his sons built an ark exactly the way God told Noah to build it. Once the ark was completed, they had to gather animals and food for their journey. Imagine how people must have laughed at him. Noah's family was constructing a huge zoo inside a ship. What kind of crazy man would build a boat in the middle of dry land?

Noah preached righteousness as he built the ark with his sons, but no one listened. He warned that it would rain, but you see no one had ever seen rain. They did not know what on earth Noah was saying. Or maybe they just did not want to understand Noah's message and be held accountable for their sins. God gave all of mankind the chance to repent, but in the end, only eight people survived a worldwide flood. Until the day of the first raindrop, people continued on with life as usual.

"For in those days before the flood they were eating and drinking, marrying and giving in marriage, until the day Noah entered the ark" (Matthew 24:38 NASB).

The Flood

When Noah was 600 years old, everything was ready. He gathered the animals, food, and his family and boarded the ark. For seven days, they waited. Then, came the rain. (Noah 7:6-10)

It rained for forty days and forty nights. (Genesis 7:12) For 150 days, the water covered the earth. (Genesis 7:24)

"God caused a wind to pass over the earth, and the water subsided. Also the fountains of the deep and the floodgates of the sky were closed, and the rain from the sky was restrained; and the water receded steadily from the earth, and at the end of 150 days, the water decreased. In the seventh month, on the seventeenth day of the month, the ark rested on the mountains of Ararat. The water decreased steadily until the tenth month; in the tenth month, on the first day of the month, the tops of the mountains became visible" (Genesis 8:1-5 NASB).

4 Noah Thank Offering Rainbow by Joseph Anton Koch

While God was stopping the flood and causing the waters to recede, Noah and his family were eager to exit the ark. First, Noah sent out a raven. Next, Noah sent out a dove, but the dove returned. The second time the dove was sent out, she returned with an olive leaf. The third time Noah sent out the dove, the dove did not return. (Genesis 8)

Finally, God spoke to the family and told them to come out with all the animals. Noah immediately constructed an altar and sacrificed to the Lord. This pleased the Lord. (Genesis 8) God made a covenant with Noah requiring mankind to be fruitful and multiply, punish murder with the life of the murderer, and enjoy freedom to eat animals for food. (Genesis 9) God provided a rainbow as a sign of this covenant. The LORD would never again destroy the entire world with a flood.

As soon as they got settled, Noah planted a vineyard. Read the rest of that story in Genesis chapter nine. Noah lived to be 950 years old and his descendants would repopulate the world.

We can only imagine that there were many changes in the earth before and after the flood. For one thing, there was no rain before the flood and since the flood, we experience precipitation in the form of rain, hail, snow, sleet, and ice storms. There are many theories about life before and after the flood, but suffice to say, there were huge changes and one change was that men and women's lifespans became much shorter.

The Ice Age

As rain fell during the Flood of Noah's day, the fountains of the deep were opened and water gushed forth. Was this accompanied by volcanic activity too? At the very least, this water gushing out was much hotter than the water flowing through the seas. Warm water evaporates more quickly than cooler water. This excessive evaporation caused frequent violent storms because the evaporating water rose high in the sky to form clouds. As the water condensed, it fell as snow. This cycle escalated until the snow piled up into glaciers and polar caps. The Ice Age had begun! With so much water stored as ice, the water level in the oceans went down exposing continental shelves, which created land bridges. When the Ice Age ended, the water level in the oceans went up again and the land bridges disappeared, dividing the continents again.

Tower of Babel & Diversity of Language

For many decades people stayed together, eventually settling on a plain in the land of Shinar. I am sorry to tell you that they build a huge temple to worship demons, or false gods. They worked together to make a name for themselves and build the temple as high into the sky as they could, giving no thought to serving or pleasing God. (Genesis 11)

God, not pleased, came down and confused their language so that their work could not continue. He also scattered them to the ends of the earth. (Genesis 11)

The Book is Passed On

God's Holy Book, The Bible, continued to be written and passed down carefully to the next generation. Years later, Moses would edit it, inspired, of course, by the Lord. The Holy Spirit inspired men who wrote down the words God wanted written down.

The Fertile Crescent

Named after the original rivers that bordered the Garden of Eden, the Tigris and Euphrates Rivers were part of a Fertile Crescent (moon-shaped) area of land that was great for growing crops. Its temperate climate made it ideal for culture to flourish. Mesopotamia, or land between rivers, was the land between the Tigris River and the Euphrates River and extending to the other sides of those rivers. Mesopotamia is considered the "Cradle of Civilization." Three ancient empires were birthed in Mesopotamia: Sumer, Assyria, and Babylon.

Sumer

After the Flood, several ancient Sumerian city-nations sprang up in the area including Eridu, Ur, Lagash, Umma, Sippar, Nippur, Uruk, and Kish. Each city was independent, ruling itself. Temples to worship pagan gods, palaces for rulers, and thousands of homes were built inside the sturdy defensive walls. Outside the walls, farms, irrigation canals, and clusters of homes were home to people who lived outside the city. Like cities today, each city bustled with people selling, buying, and transacting business with one another.

Farmers grew wheat, barley, lentils, rye, cucumbers, lettuce, peas, garlic, carrots, cabbage, beets, radishes, dates, apples, cherries, apricots, plums, grapes, and figs. Oxen helped with the planting while flocks of goats, sheep, and cattle were tended and moved from pasture to pasture. Pigs, cattle, sheep, goats, donkeys, geese, and ducks were domesticated and raised for meat, milk, and to help with the labor.

Ancient Cities in Sumer

When Uruk was excavated, ancient writings from the region (*Epic of Gilgamesh*) were confirmed that one-third of the city was devoted to the temple with its pagan worship, one-third of the city was taken up by the palace and government buildings, and the rest of the city was homes and shops.

There were many different jobs in these ancient cities. Bronze workers, silversmiths, goldsmiths, potters, cloth and basket weavers, glassmakers, shoemakers, painters, and sculptors created beautiful and practical items for families. Carpenters, brick layers, and stone masons built buildings and walls. Fishermen, butchers, bakers, and brewers provided food and drink.

Families were the foundation of Sumerian society. Marriage and child rearing were considered a privilege and blessing. Families took care of each other. Girls stayed under the protection and authority of their parents until they were married, helping mothers care for the homes and families. Women could divorce their husbands if they were beaten, cheated on, or neglected.

Children played with jump ropes and balls. Boys enjoyed slingshots and miniature chariots. Girls played with dolls and miniature furniture.

Most homes had several rooms. Tables were a little lower than tables today, but chairs and stools were similar in height. Bed mattresses were filled with goat hair, wool, or palm fiber. Cushions, mattresses, blankets, and sheets were common. Some people slept on reed mats. Belongings were stored in chests or baskets.

Many women wore make-up including lipstick and eyeliner. Tweezers, mirrors, and combs have all been unearthed in archaeological digs. Also discovered from the Sumerian digs were earrings, necklaces, and hair decorations.

Many people usually bathed in the nearest river or canal, but wealthier families had indoor bathrooms with waste being emptied through clay pipes to cesspools near the house. These were the ancient sewers of Sumer.

Scribes in Sumer

Scribes made their living by writing cuneiform, or wedge-shaped, words on clay tablets. Kings dictated to scribes who were quick at writing things down. Letters, lists, inventories, songs for their gods, histories, fables (stories with a strong theme), laments, and epic poems have been unearthed by archaeologists. Often scribes held high positions in royal and wealthy homes where they managed other employees, as well as slaves. Both men and women worked as scribes.

Celebrating Kings with Epic Poems

Many kings were considered to be the "son of a god". In Ancient Egypt, the Pharaoh was considered to be the "son of Ra, the sun god." As a result of this close connection to the dark spirit world, the Sumerian kings were also the high priests of the nation, celebrating religious festivals and offering sacrifices to their pagan idols. In addition, the king commanded the army, often leading the military into battle.

King Sargon the Great created one of the first empires by conquering Uruk, Ur, Lagash, and other cities all the way to the sea (Persian Gulf).

Epic poems celebrated the exploits of powerful kings and warriors. Not only did these tell heroic adventures, but they explored creation, death, loyalty, love, and the spiritual realm. One of the most famous that we have copies of today is the *Tale of Gilgamesh*. The larger than life hero Gilgamesh experiences one exciting adventure after another searching for the secret of immortality. When he finally finds the secret of immortality, it slips through his fingers.

A delightful way to pass historical events on to the next generation is artwork. The Sumerians created mosaics, or pictures made of tiny tiles fit together. The "Royal Standard of Ur" is a mosaic made of shell, limestone, and blue lapis showing a Sumerian army victory and the celebration that followed. Other mosaics commemorated historical events, especially battle victories.

Sumerian Religion

Sumerians did not worship the True God. Instead, they worshipped a wide variety of pagan idols. Enlil was their most powerful god. Utu was the god of the sun, Nanna the moon goddess, Enki god of the water, and Inanna goddess of love.

As I tell you the story, or Sumerian legend, of Enlil, try to figure out what it remind you of. Enlil was walking in the woods one day and saw a lovely goddess named Ninlil. Even though he wasn't married to her, he pretended that she was his wife. The other gods were furious and banished him from the heavenly city to live in the underworld. The child of Enlil and Ninlil was Nanna, the moon goddess. Both Ninlil and Nanna followed Enlil to the underworld, away from the pure heavenly city. What do you think? Does that remind you of the fall of Lucifer from Heaven? Did the Sumerians worship satan?

Divination, or predicting the future, was an important part of their religion. They used animal behavior, animal organs, the location of heavenly bodies, natural disasters, and daily life events. The "behavior" of their pagan gods often resembled the behavior of biblical demons, rather than angels or God Himself. The gods fought with one another. Sometimes the gods hurt humans and sometimes they protected them.

From Noah to Abraham

The following information is taken from Genesis 5 and Genesis 11. Notice how their lifespans get shorter and shorter.

At the age of 500, Noah became the father of Shem, Ham and Japheth. He died at the age of 950.

At the age of 100, Shem became the father of Arpachshad, as well as other sons and daughters. He died at the age of 600.

At the age of 35, Arpachshad became the father of Shelah, as well as other sons and daughters. He died at the age of 438.

At the age of 30, Shelah became the father of Eber, as well as other sons and daughters. He died at the age of 433.

At the age of 34, Eber became the father of Peleg, as well as other sons and daughters. He died at the age of 464.

At the age of 30, Peleg became the father of Reu, as well as other sons and daughters. He died at the age of 239.

At the age of 32, Reu became the father of Serug, as well as other sons and daughters. He died at the age of 239.

At the age of 30, Serug became the father of Nahor, as well as other sons and daughters. He died at the age of 230.

At the age of 29, Nahor became the father of Terah, as well as other sons and daughters. He died at the age of 158.

At the age of 70, Terah became the father of Abraham, Nahor and Haran, as well as, at the very least, another daughter named Sarai, and possibly other sons and daughters. He died at the age of 205.

God Calls Abram Out of a Sumerian City

5 Abraham & Sarah public domain

Abram lived with his father, Terah, in the Sumerian city-state of Ur. Terah had three sons: Abram, Nahor, and Haran. Haran died in Ur, but left a son named Lot. Both Abram and Nahor got married. Abram married his half-sister Sarai. Nahor married his cousin, Milcah, daughter of Haran. (Genesis 11)

Terah took his sons, their wives, and children out of Ur and headed toward Canaan, but they settled down in Haran. Terah died in Haran. (Genesis 11)

Abram had a relationship with God. He loved and served the LORD to the end of his life. God made a promise to Abram that he would bless him and make him a great nation. He was to leave Haran and set out for the land of Canaan. He took his wife, Sarai, his nephew, Lot, and his entire household which included numerous servants and employees. He also took his herds and flocks. He was a very rich man. He and his family lived in tents.

The Patriarchs

Abraham had many adventures with God including a miracle baby named Isaac. Isaac married his cousin Rebekah and had twin sons, Esau and Jacob. Jacob, chosen by God who changed his name to Israel had twelve sons: Reuben, Simeon, Levi, Judah, Dan, Naphtali, Gad, Asher, Issachar, Zebulun, Joseph, and Benjamin. The descendants of these sons became the twelve tribes of Israel. In addition, Jacob also had a daughter named Dinah.

I encourage you to read about the Patriarchs (Abraham, Isaac, Jacob) and their escapades in Genesis chapters eleven through fifty. It is one exciting adventure after another.

The Book is Passed to Abraham

God's Holy Book, The Bible, continued to be written, passed down carefully to the next generation, and would be later edited by Moses. The Holy Spirit inspired men who wrote down the words God wanted written down.

6 Like his father, Isaac wandered the Promised Land, enjoying God's Favor Providence Lithograph circa 1900 public domain.

September: Ancient World

Foundations of Western Literature

7 The Tower of Babel, Peter Brueghel the Elder 1563

September Week One Class

☐ Discuss Book of Genesis in Book Club

☐ Drama Time: Introduce Your Genesis Character

☐ Mom/Teacher Explain & Discuss with Students Plot, Plot Map, & How to Write an Essay

☐ Mom/Teacher Give Background to Gilgamesh & Explain How to Do Plot Evaluation Paper

Book Club: The Holy Bible, Book of Genesis

Get comfortable. Book club should be fun. Pop some popcorn or bake some cookies and grab a cup of tea, coffee, or hot chocolate. It's time to relax and discuss the first book ever written.

Genesis is the first book in the Holy Bible. It covers a long span of time from Creation through the flood all the way until the Patriarchs. In book club, discuss the people of Genesis.

- Who was your favorite person in the Book of Genesis and why?
- Which person did you admire the most in Genesis?
- Whose bad behavior really surprised you and why?
- Who did you feel sorry for in the Book of Genesis?
- Did *Adam and His Kin* by Ruth Beechick help Genesis come alive for you?

Genesis Character Introductions

Everyone should come to class time dressed as his or her favorite Genesis character. Each person will introduce himself or herself to the rest of the group one at a time.

Here is the info to share.

Your Name

Where You Lived

The People in Your Life (Parents, Children, Family, Friends)

Your Relationship with God

Plot & Plot Map

Plot is the story line of a novel or work of literature. Plot is the events in the story and the order they happen. It is the road map that takes the characters from point A to point B.

A story has **conflict**. The conflict can be conflict between characters, conflict between a character and nature, or internal conflict.

The **exposition**, or introduction of the story, is the beginning of the story where we meet the setting and characters. We learn about the main problem, or conflict, too.

The next part of the story line, or plot, is the **rising action**. A series of events occurs that intensifies until the final climax. The events often become complicated, tense, and exciting.

The conflict will escalate to a crisis point, or **climax** of the story. The turning point in the story, the climax, stirs the emotion and interest of the readers.

The **falling action** is where the story wraps up. Everything is resolved. The story ends.

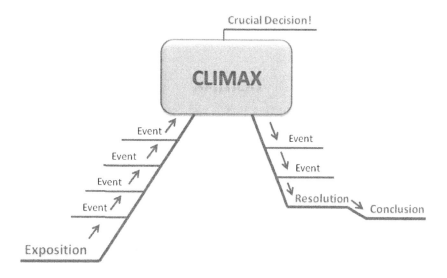

How to Write an Essay

This week you will write an essay.

A good essay makes a strong, clear point about something the writer cares about (introduction), backs it up with evidence (body of the paper), and concludes by reaffirming the point made at the beginning (conclusion).

Topic & Audience & Voice

You might be assigned a topic and audience or choose a topic and audience. The topic is what you will be writing about and the audience is who will read your essay.

Essays can be written in first-person or third-person, but formal essays are written in third-person. Be sure to stay consistent whichever voice you use.

Thesis

A thesis statement is the foundation of a good essay. Mentioned in the introduction, substantiated in the body of the essay, and reaffirmed in the conclusion, a thesis is a strong statement that can be proven or disproven.

How do you arrive at a thesis?

Start with asking a variety of questions about your topic. Ask questions that can be investigated, researched, and pondered. Take some time to investigate the best answer to your question. This might mean researching the facts, exploring others' opinions and the Bible on a moral topic, or just thinking through your own beliefs or personal history to determine what you believe and why. In the end, you should arrive at what you believe to be the best possible answer to your question. This is your thesis!

Now take that answer, your thesis, and try to state it as clearly and briefly as possible in one sentence. That is your thesis statement. Sometimes, it may take two sentences to explain your thesis effectively, and that is okay. Try to get it in one sentence if you can.

After you write your essay, you want to ask if the introduction, body, and conclusion prove the thesis. If it does not, you need to rewrite your essay.

Introduction

Open your paper with a strong opening sentence that is clear and easy to understand. Think about your audience and get your reader's attention by writing about something related to their interests. Introduce your topic in a way that is attention-grabbing.

Here are some different ways to get your reader's attention: historical tidbit, anecdote, example, quote, or strong declaration.

Historical tidbit

The crowd roared with delight as the brand new President Ronald Reagan placed his hand on the Holy Bible and took the oath of office.

Anecdote

Jimmy wiped his sweaty palms on his jeans. He was tired of the painting, but he had a whole wall to go. He wondered why he had volunteered to paint the new church fellowship hall.

Example

Most celebrity marriages end in divorce, but there are some exceptions in Hollywood. Tom Hanks and Rita Wilson have been married for 28 years.

Quote

"Four out of Five dentists recommend Colgate® toothpaste."

Declaration

The cost of higher education has skyrocketed in the last ten years, while the quality of education has decreased, according to government-funded studies. In light of this, there is a push for the government to foot the college bill for all Americans.

The most important part of the introduction is to state the thesis, after you have gotten the reader's attention.

Body

The body of the paper will contain your arguments as you prove your thesis statement. Let your thesis statement guide your paper. Try to keep one point per paragraph. Give examples, illustrations, and evidence from your personal research. Each paragraph in the body of the paper should flow smoothly.

Conclusion

The conclusion is your final attempt to drive your thesis, or point, home. Summarize the thesis statement and main points briefly and then add a twist to make your audience stop and say, "Oh, I never thought of it quite that way!"

Sentences

Essays consist of paragraphs and paragraphs are made up of sentences. Sentences start with a capital letter, end with a punctuation mark, contain a noun and verb, and express a complete thought. Take time to craft each sentence carefully. Use a thesaurus to choose the perfect word. Revise sentences as needed to make them the best they can be.

Make every sentence count. Don't waste time yammering on. State your points clearly using concrete words so you can be concise.

Paragraphs

An excellent paragraph is filled with excellent sentences. Each paragraph should prove the thesis with a specific point that is backed up by examples.

The point of the paragraph should be explained in the topic sentence, often the first sentence. Each sentence should flow smoothly into the next sentence. Use your topic sentence as a guide for the other sentences in the paragraph.

Make sure there are no fragments or run-on sentences in your paragraph and that it flows well when you read the paragraphs aloud.

Each paragraph must flow into the next paragraph too.

When You Finish Your Paper

Read your paper aloud when you finish writing it.

Background for Epic of Gilgamesh

Let's talk a minute about the *Epic of Gilgamesh*.

You have read about Noah and the Flood. Noah had three sons: Shem, Ham, and Japheth. Ham was the father of Cush.

"Now Cush became the father of Nimrod; he became a mighty one on the earth. He was a mighty hunter before the Lord. The beginning of his kingdom was Babel and Erech and Accad and Calneh, in the land of Shinar. From that land he went forth into Assyria, and built Nineveh and Rehoboth-Ir and Calah, and Resen between Nineveh and Calah; that is the great city" (Genesis 10:8-12 NASB).

In another language, the city-state of Erech mentioned in the passage from Genesis is called Uruk. Uruk was one the great city-states of Ancient Mesopotamia. King Gilgamesh may have built this great city. Gilgamesh was a popular leader, mighty warrior, builder, and wise ruler. He was, however, not a Christian and there were many ways in which he behaved badly. The ruins of Uruk are in southern Iraq.

Stories of Gilgamesh were widely known before the earliest versions, inscribed on clay tablets, were found. Tablets with the Epic of Gilgamesh have been discovered on many clay tablets in various languages. This story is not a pure one, so keep that in mind if you choose to read a direct translation because it will contain sexual content. We are going to read *Gilgamesh the Hero* by Geraldine McCaughrean.

The Epic of Gilgamesh was written in Akkadian, the Babylonian language, on twelve tablets. They were popular for centuries in various empires, including the Assyrian Empire. When the Persians conquered the Assyrians, the popularity of *The Epic of Gilgamesh* died out. However, a British archaeologist brought the popular story back in fashion.

Austen Henry Layard excavated 25,000 broken clay tablets from the ruins of Nineveh. Henry Rawlinson deciphered them.

Here are the characters in *The Epic of Gilgamesh*

Gilgamesh

King of Uruk. A strong, brave warrior, Gilgamesh has his own moral code. He is 2/3 god and 1/3 man. He has surrounded the city of Uruk with sturdy walls and stunning ziggurats. He is filled with sorrow when his friend Enkidu dies. He goes on a quest to uncover the mystery of life and death. He was the fifth king of Uruk after the Flood

Enkidu

Friend of Gilgamesh. Hairy, strong, and raised by animals, he is a rough-and-tumble dude. He tries to beat up Gilgamesh, but they end up being best friends. He is punished with death for killing a demon

Shamhat (Hatti in *Gilgamesh the Hero*)

The beautiful woman who lures Enkidu to civilization

Utnapishtim

A king and priest of Shurrupak who survived a great deluge that destroyed almost all life on earth in a great ship, along with his family and one of every living creature. Granted eternal life, along with his wife

Utnapishtim's Wife

Survived the flood with her husband and softens her husband's heart toward Gilgamesh

Urshanabi

Guardian of the "stone things." Pilots a ferryboat across the Waters of Death to Far Away Place where Utnapishtim lives

The Hunter, or Stalker

The hunter who discovers Enkidu at a watering place

Anu

Father of idol/gods, god of the firmament

Aruru

Idol/goddess of creation who fashioned Enkidu from clay and spit

Ea

Idol/god of fresh water transportation, and wisdom. Lives in water below the earth

Humbaba

Ferocious demon who guards Cedar Forest, a place forbidden to mortals. His garments produce fear in people who come against him. He is personification of natural disasters

Scorpion-Man

He and his wife guard the twin-peaked mountain Mashu where the sun god, Shamash, travels through every night

Siduri

Tavern keeper and goddess who comforts and helps Gilgamesh

Tammuz

Called the Shepherd and god of vegetation and fertility

Enlil

Superior deity who hates humankind, god of earth, wind, and fire

Ereshkigal

Queen of the underworld

Ishtar

Called queen of heaven, goddess of war, love, and fertility

Lugulbanda

Third king after the Flood. Hero, protector, and father of Gilgamesh

Ninsun

Mother of Gilgamesh, minor goddess. Married to Gilgamesh's father, Lugulbanda

Shamash

Brother of Ishtar, sun god, patron of Gilgamesh

Gilgamesh the Hero

Epic of Gilgamesh is an epic poem about Gilgamesh, king of Uruk. One of the oldest known works of literature in the world, *Epic of Gilgamesh* was written in ancient Mesopotamia circa 2100 B.C. Lot of other books have been written besides *The Holy Bible* and *Epic of Gilgamesh*, but they have been lost in the rubble of time.

An epic poem is a very, very, very long poem about the exploits of a hero. Epic poems are full of adventure and bravery. You will be focusing on the plot when you read *Epic of Gilgamesh*.

The Plot of *Gilgamesh the Hero*

Remember that the plot is what makes writing a story. A story is a series of events that relate to one another in a pattern, or sequence. (See plot line below) This sequence of events increases in intensity.

A story must have conflict and something that has to be conquered, or overcome, by the hero in the story. In a murder mystery, the detective is the hero and he is in conflict with the murderer. He must discover who the murderer is and see that the killer is brought to justice. In a romance novel, the hero must find and win his true love in spite of every obstacle that stands in the way. In an adventure novel, the hero might be on a quest to find something and must overcome trials and obstacles to finally reach his goal.

It always helps me to understand the plot of a story using a plot line. The story starts with an inciting incident, creating a problem of some sort for the hero. The rest of the story is a series of action, events, and conflicts that increase in size (rising action) until we reach the climax of the story, or the final showdown for the hero.

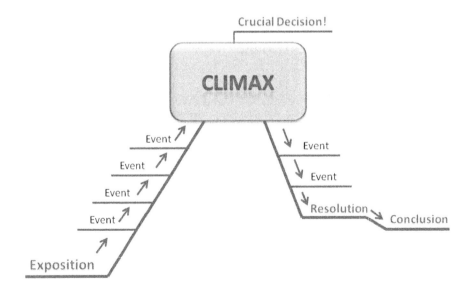

The conflict in the story can be external (wild animals, murderer, tornado, mean person) or internal (hero's thoughts, feelings, or insecurities).

How to Explore Plot in *Gilgamesh the Hero*

It's time to write an essay on the plot of *The Epic of Gilgamesh*. Before we talk about how to write your essay, let's talk about different approaches to investigating the plot. We will look at plot summary and plot interpretation, which begin with comprehending the work of literature you are reading.

Comprehend the Story

First, gain a basic understanding of the story. By comprehending the story, you will be able to write a plot summary.

Plot Summary

A plot summary is a short condensed version of the story. It does not evaluate the plot; it just summarizes it. You might give a brief plot summary as part of an essay or literary analysis.

Interpret the Story

Dig deeper into the details of the story. This will enable you to write a plot interpretation.

Plot Interpretation

The writer interprets the meaning of the literary work, what he believes the author is trying to portray through the plot. You will use plot interpretation when you analyze literature.

A Literary Analysis

In a literary analysis, you examine different elements of the work to help you appreciate and understand the work as a whole. You must start with a narrow focus.

You will need to go beyond superficial reading and delve more deeply. You will need to identify, develop, and support your ideas.

You will need to find evidence to support your ideas, not just explain them. The difference between support and explaining is important. Make sure you understand this. You can use direct quotes from the book to support your ideas, as well as summaries of events, and paraphrases of long quotes.

Secondary sources can be used to support your ideas. These sources could be a book that discuss the work you are analyzing or an article that discusses the theory you are putting forth.

Make sure that you analyze throughout the whole essay, not just in in the conclusion.

Plot Evaluation

In plot evaluation, you evaluate how interesting or how well-developed the plot is. You will use one paragraph, after the introduction, to briefly summarize the entire plot of the story. The next paragraphs will prove your thesis. You will be writing a plot evaluation.

Ask Questions about Plot

No matter what kind of paper you are writing about the plot, you will need to ask questions. Here are questions you can ask at various points in the story. You can use these questions for any novel you read.

Exposition or Beginning

What information does the writer give you at the beginning of the story?

Why was that information important?

Was any of it misleading? Why?

Foreshadowing

How does the author clue the reader into something that will eventually happen? Does this build anticipation or dread?

Rising Action

What event in the rising action drew you into the story more than the others?

How does a specific incident affect the action of the novel and why is it important?

What incidents does the author use to create tension? Are they effective?

Conflict

What types of conflict are present in the story?

How did you identify those conflicts?

Why are these conflicts important to the characters?

Why are these conflicts important to the reader?

Climax

How do events build to the climax and what is the author's intention in using those specific events?

Falling Action

In what way is the action in this part of the story different from the beginning of the story?

Resolution

What emotions does this part of the story arouse in the reader?

What other things could the writer have done?

Analysis

How do two parts of the plot fit together?

How did one event in the plot lead to another event?

Why did the story end the way it did? What led up to this ending?

What could have caused it to end differently?

Keep in mind that we can never know the author's intention perfectly, only what we see them accomplishing.

Taking what you learned, from comprehending and interpreting the story, ask questions that will force you to dig deeper

Questions about *Gilgamesh the Hero*

Here are some questions I asked about the *Epic of Gilgamesh.*

What external conflicts affect Gilgamesh and why?

What internal conflicts make life difficult for Gilgamesh and why?

Why was a friend created for Gilgamesh?

How is suspense built into the story?

Are there any twists and reversals in the story?

Brainstorm and come up with questions together that you can ask as you read *Epic of Gilgamesh*. This will help you to write your paper evaluating the plot of the story. List them here.

_____
_____
_____
_____
_____
_____
_____
_____
_____
_____
_____

Steps for *Epic of Gilgamesh* Plot Evaluation Assignment

Read *Epic of Gilgamesh* with the idea in mind that you are evaluating it. Underline or dog-ear spots that are very interesting to you or raise questions in your mind. The key is as you are reading to ask yourself questions about the plot or aspects of the plot.

Discuss the questions and possible answers in class with family or fellow students in co-op. Analyze several possibilities to take with your paper.

Choose a favorite question that you can answer using evidence and examples from the book.

Go back through the book and find quotes, examples, etc. that provide a possible answer to your questions. Dog-ear, write them down, or circle in book.

Ideas to Evaluate the Plot

Here are some questions you can ask:

- Is the story line exciting or boring?
- Can you, as the reader, predict what will happen next?
- Is the plot believable?
- Is the plot, or story line, too simple?
- Is the plot, or story line, too complex or hard to follow?
- Is the order of events in the story logical?
- Does the ending of the story make you, as the reader, happy? Or if not happy, are you satisfied?
- Does the rising action (events of the story) lead logically to the climax?
- Is there any foreshadowing? Does foreshadowing enhance the story?

Plot Evaluation Paper

You will evaluate how well-crafted the plot is. The first paragraph will be your introduction. You will use the second paragraph to briefly summarize the entire plot of the story. The next paragraphs will prove your thesis.

You could also write your plot evaluation on why you think this story line is a classic and has endured with readers generation after generation. After all, movies are still made today that are adaptations of this story.

Discuss thesis ideas together.

September Week One Home

- [ ] Read *Gilgamesh the Hero* and Answer Book Club Discussion Questions
- [ ] Read "Our Pathway to Literary Analysis"
- [ ] Read *Gilgamesh* & Complete "Coming Up with a Thesis from Questions"
- [ ] Make an Outline for your Plot Evaluation of *Gilgamesh the Hero*

Read Gilgamesh the Hero

I would encourage you to answer these questions about the story as you read. They are the questions you will be discussing in book club.

How did Gilgamesh start his reign as king? What kind of king was he?

_____

_____

_____

What role did Enkidu play in his life? What made him perfect to play this role?

_____

_____

_____

Why does Enkidu die? How does that affect Gilgamesh? What effect does Enkidu's death have on the story?

_____

_____

_____

Why does Gilgamesh go on a journey to find Utnapishtim? Is his journey a success?

_____

_____

_____

What test does Gilgamesh fail? Why does he fail? How does his failure affect the story?

_____

_____

_____

Why does Gilgamesh look for the miraculous plant? How does this affect the story?

_____

_____

_____

What things in this book remind you of things in Genesis?

_____
_____
_____

Why do you think this version is different from the Bible version? Which one is the truth?

_____
_____
_____

Also, keep in mind the questions you will be using to write a paper on the plot of *Epic of Gilgamesh*.

Our Pathway to Literary Analysis

This year we are going to learn to analyze literature step-by-step. In the past, you may have written books reviews or written essays about the plot, theme, characterization, or setting of a work of fiction. This year we will go a little deeper.

We will progress from simple essays to more complicated assignments using analysis. In the beginning of the year, we will write simple essays. At the end of the year, we will research, read, and understand *The Merry Adventures of Robin Hood* so we can write a literary analysis paper.

Literary Analysis Questions

We will be learning to analyze literature all year through discussions and asking questions, as well as in our writing assignments. Our purpose is to learn how to analyze literature. Later on, we will learn how to create an original argument about a literary work, and to learn how to use and cite quotes and examples from a literary work as supporting evidence as an argument.

I will start you off with summary questions and analysis questions. You will brainstorm together in group or family time, coming up with more questions. Later on that week, you will come up with even more questions. Somewhere in all those questions, is one question worth investigating. Once you have a question, you read the book, looking for clues to answer the question. Even though you won't be writing a literary analysis until later in the year, you will begin analysis training now.

Thesis

You can create a thesis from the answer to a chosen question. A thesis is a strategic tool in your hands. It will guide your paper.

Don't create a vague thesis like "Chocolate is an ice cream flavor that kids like." Instead say, "Chocolate is the most popular candy in Easter baskets, Christmas stockings, and St. Valentine's Day gifts." This sets you up with three different paragraphs where you show how chocolate is the most popular of treats. The first paragraph would be chocolate in Easter baskets, the second paragraph about Christmas stockings, and the third paragraph on St. Valentine's Day.

You can write a specific thesis on *The Winged Watchman* by Hilda van Stockum: "Though the Nazis occupied Holland quickly, the Dutch resisted their rule by helping downed Allied pilots escape, sabotaging Nazi equipment, and intercepting telegrams between Nazi officers." This thesis statement is very specific. After introducing your thesis in the first statement, you have a built in guideline for your next few paragraphs. You might need to use more than one paragraph to show how the Dutch helped downed Allied pilots escape (second and third). The fourth paragraph would be on sabotaging equipment, the fifth on intercepting telegrams, and the sixth would be your conclusion. Do you see how helpful a good thesis statement can be?

Introduction

Your introduction will launch your thesis. It should capture your reader's attention and introduce the focus, or subject of your paper. You want to "hook" the reader so that he will keep on reading.

Here are some creative ways to introduce your paper.

Summarize your book briefly with a "what" and "how" statement about the work of fiction you are analyzing.

> In her novel *The Winged Watchman*, Hilda van Stockum takes us back in time to World War II in idyllic Holland where peaceful Dutch country life is turned upside-down by the invading Nazis.

You can start your paper with a quote from the book.

> "Mother was silenced, but she felt sorry for the Schenderhans parents all the same. After the family rosary that night, she added a Hail Mary for them. Mother added so many Hail Marys that Joris sometimes thought he would get holes in his knees. His mother prayed for Queen Wilhelmina in England and the princesses in Canada. She prayed for the Pope and for the Allies, but at first she would not pray for the Germans, though Father said that was wrong."

You could open your paper by explaining the author's purpose and telling your audience how well you think she achieves that purpose.

> In *The Winged Watchman*, Hilda van Stockum set out to show the daily life of a typical family involved in the Dutch Resistance during World War II under Nazi occupation. The reader feels the tension the Dutch people felt as they made moral decisions that were influenced by the evil that surrounded them.

You might begin your paper with a few general statements about life that relate to the focus of your analysis.

> The only thing it takes for evil to triumph is for good men to do nothing. In *The Winged Watchmen*, Hilda van Stockum introduces us to good men who push the tide of evil back with courage and fortitude.

Another way to introduce your analysis paper is to make a general statement about the genre of literature you are reading.

> Good historical fiction makes the setting come alive for the reader. This is certainly true in *The Winged Watchman* by Hilda van Stockum.

Paragraphs

The paragraphs in the body of your paper will be proving your thesis using examples and quotes found in the book. Try to organize each paragraph around a specific idea or point to help your argument flow. Your thesis will guide the body of your paper.

In each paragraph, clearly state the main point you are proving and relate it to the thesis. Support this main point with quotes or details from the work of fiction you are analyzing. Explain how the detail or quote proves your point.

> Mother's strong Catholic faith was tested by the cruel behavior of the Nazis so that it was hard for her to love them. At first, she refused to pray for them, but Father challenged her to pray for them too. Her faith overcame her anger at the Germans.

Conclusions

Your conclusion should restate the thesis showing how the evidence you've used proved it. End in an interesting way by perhaps stating a new question or suggesting the value of understanding the book. Give your reader something to think about long after they finish reading your paper.

> Though the Dutch were conquered quickly by the Nazis, they were never truly conquered because they continued to resist in every way they could, risking their lives. In *The Winged Watchman*, we meet a hidden Jewish child, an "underdiver", a downed RAF pilot, and a brave family who work together to overcome their evil conquerors. In the midst of this, they hold on to their faith, trusting Him even when things go wrong.

Read Gilgamesh the Hero

As you read *Epic of Gilgamesh*, the epic poem about Gilgamesh, king of Uruk and one of the oldest known works of literature in the world, remember that you are going to be writing a Plot Evaluation Essay. Though it was written in ancient Mesopotamia circa 2100 B.C., this story resembles many action movies of today.

Keep the questions you came up with on your own and in group time, when you were brainstorming, in mind as you read.

Coming Up with a Thesis from Questions

Here are some of my questions about *The Epic of Gilgamesh* related to evaluating the plot.

_____
_____
_____
_____
_____
_____
_____
_____

Here are other people's questions about *The Epic of Gilgamesh* related to evaluating the plot.

_____
_____
_____
_____
_____

If you want to come up with a good thesis statement, keep your questions about *The Epic of Gilgamesh* in mind as you read the story. Keep a paper handy to jot down thoughts as you read that answer your questions. Dog ear pages and underline good quotes that you might want to use in your paper. You can also jot down little notes in the margin of the book.

Once you finish the book, sit down, put your feet up, and think about the story in light of your questions. After reading the book, you might have even more questions that you can think about before you come up with a thesis statement.

This thinking time is important and shouldn't be rushed.

Once you decide on your question and how you will answer the question, the answer to your question can be tweaked into a thesis statement. Jot down a clear, concise answer to the question you have chosen to use in your paper. Do you have evidence for the answer you wrote down? Is the evidence strong enough to support a paper?

When you are in this process of putting together a thesis statement, think about how the evidence you have relates to each other. Can you see an argument forming?

This part of the writing a literary evaluation paper might take a long time, but if you work on this part carefully, it will be easy to sit down and write your paper.

My Thesis Statement

_____
_____
_____
_____
_____
_____
_____

Introduction

Your introductory paragraph will present your thesis. This paragraph should capture your audience's attention and introduce the focus, or subject of your paper. You want to "hook" the reader so that he will keep on reading.

Here are some creative ways to introduce your paper.

- You can start your paper with a quote from the book.
- You could open your paper by explaining the author's purpose and telling your audience how well you think she achieves that purpose.
- You might begin your paper with a few general statements about life that relate to the focus of your paper.
- Another way to introduce your analysis paper is to make a general statement about the genre of literature you are reading.

Paragraphs

The paragraphs in the body of your paper will be proving your thesis using the examples and quotes you found in the book. Try to organize each paragraph around a specific idea or point to help your argument flow. Your thesis will guide the body of your paper.

The paragraph following the introductions should be a summary of the plot.

In each paragraph, state the main point you are proving clearly and relate it to the thesis. Support this main point with quotes or details from the work of fiction you are analyzing. Explain how the detail or quote proves your point.

Conclusion

Your conclusion should restate the thesis showing how the evidence you've used proved it. End in an interesting way by perhaps stating a new question or suggesting the value of understanding the book. Give your reader something to think about long after they finish reading your paper.

My Outline for Plot Evaluation of *Gilgamesh the Hero*

You will bring the thesis statement you have created to group time. Create an outline to bring along with your thesis statement. It can be as detailed or sparse as you want it to. An outline is a writing tool.

Here is my Outline

Introduction

_____
_____
_____
_____

First Point

_____
_____
_____
_____

Second Point

_____
_____
_____
_____

Third Point

_____
_____
_____
_____

Fourth Point (you may not have a 4th point!)

_____
_____
_____
_____

Conclusion

_____
_____
_____
_____

September Week Two Class

☐ Book Club! Discuss *Gilgamesh the Hero*

☐ Read & Discuss "Words, Lovely Words"

☐ Read & Discuss "Elements of Literature"

☐ Read Thesis & Outline for Plot Evaluation Paper in Groups/Peer Review

Book Club Discussion on *Gilgamesh the Hero*

Here are some questions to discuss about the *Epic of Gilgamesh*.

- How did Gilgamesh start his reign as king? What kind of king was he?
- What role did Enkidu play in his life? What made him perfect to play this role?
- Why does Enkidu die? How does that affect Gilgamesh? What effect does Enkidu's death have on the story?
- Why does Gilgamesh go on a journey to find Utnapishtim? Is his journey a success?
- What test does Gilgamesh fail? Why does he fail? How does his failure affect the story?
- Why does Gilgamesh look for the miraculous plant? How does this affect the story?
- What things in this book remind you of things in Genesis?
- Why do you think this version is different from the Bible version? Which one is the truth?
- Also, keep in mind the questions you will be using to write a paper on the plot of *Epic of Gilgamesh*.

Words, Lovely Words!

Words are the building blocks of writing. World choice can make the difference between boredom and interest for the reader.

Using a Thesaurus

A Thesaurus is a writer's best friend. If you can't find the right word while you are working on a paper, pull out a thesaurus or use the one on your computer.

When you finish a paper, you can use the thesaurus to replace words you have repeated too often or words that sound boring. If you read the paper aloud you will hear mistakes that you can correct, but you will also notice if you use a word too often.

Words that Make a Paper BORING!

Some words find their way into our papers that cause our readers to yawn. Try to avoid these words:

Then	Just	Went
Very	So	Bad
Really	That	Good
Like	A Lot	Great
About	Nice	
Got	Well	
Said		

Replacement Words

Here are some words you can use to replace boring words.

Instead of **bad**: Awful, Terrible, Horrible, Dreadful, Outrageous, Shameful, Despicable, Disgraceful

Instead of **good**: Superior, Fantastic, Incredible, Excellent, Amazing, Remarkable, Wonderful, Marvelous

Instead of **good (virtuous)**: Honorable, Pure, Upright, Wholesome, Innocent, Trustworthy, Principled

Instead of **good (kind)**: Kindhearted, Courteous, Benevolent, Amicable, Compassionate, Gracious

Instead of **great**: Admirable, Astounding, Grand, Impressive, Spectacular, Commendable, Superior

Instead of **happy**: Contented, Satisfied, Blissful, Joyful, Delighted, Ecstatic, Thrilled, Glad, Pleased

Instead of **large**: Colossal, Enormous, Gigantic, Huge, Massive, Substantial, Significant, Tremendous

Instead of **nice**: Enjoyable, Pleasing, Cordial, Admirable, Considerate, Pleasurable, Congenial

Instead of **sad**: Miserable, Gloomy, Dejected, Depressed, Disheartened, Blue, Wretched, Heartbroken

Instead of **said**: Admitted, Advised, Agreed, Bragged, Joked, Gushed, Exclaimed, Grunted, Snorted, Sputtered, Squealed, Wondered Aloud, Roared, Scolded, Whispered, Stammered, Groaned, Gasped, Cried, Confessed, Shouted, Wailed, Sobbed, Squeaked, Griped, Growled, Hissed, Shrieked, Taunted, Yelled, Commented, Observed, Promised, Stated, Suggested, Sneered, Grumbled, Clucked, Explained, Vowed

Instead of **small**: Diminutive, Miniature, Minute, Petite, Teeny, Tiny, Wee, Slight

Instead of **went**: Inched, Scurried, Shuffled, Shimmied, Slinked, Marched, Meandered, Slithered, Crawled, Climbed, Bolted, Bounded, Bounced, Lunged, Leapt, Jumped, Jogged, Approached, Clambered, Departed, Rambled, Toddled, Strolled, Stomped, Traipsed, Tramped, Raced, Rambled, Sashayed, Waddled, Zoomed, Hiked, Walked, Hustled, Scrambled, Sauntered, Whisked, Glided,

Rushed, Sailed, Rocketed, Wandered

We like to use the word "**very**" in our writing, but try to find a better word depending on the situation.

Instead of saying **very ugly**, say **hideous**.

Instead of saying **very angry**, say **furious**.
Instead of saying **very wet**, say **soaked**.
Instead of saying **very beautiful**, say **exquisite**.
Instead of saying **very bad**, say **atrocious**.
Instead of saying **very roomy**, say **spacious**.
Instead of saying **very large**, say **colossal**.
Instead of saying **very hungry**, say **ravenous**.

Come back to these pages as often as you need to for ideas. And don't forget to use your thesaurus.

Elements of Literature

When you are listening to a song that you like, you might enjoy the catchy beat, the great melody, the singer's voice, or the beautiful words. We don't usually think about the different the elements of a song. We just consider the song as a whole. When you find a movie irresistible, it might be because you appreciate the acting, the soundtrack, the director, or the writing of the screenplay. I don't even think in terms of the elements of a movie when I like it. If reading is one of your delights, there are books you love and others that are less appealing. You might think of the characters as friends, find the story line boring, or wish you could see the setting in real life. We are going to talk about books this year: how much we enjoy them and why we enjoy them.

Let's start with some tools to help us discuss the elements of literature. You may have already learned about the elements of literature, but let's review in case you've forgotten anything.

Literature, separated from other forms of reading material and considered an art, evokes an emotional response from its reader. It is not created simply to inform, instruct, or entertain, literature attempts to make a statement about life, truth, beauty, or purpose in a way that affects the reader at the deepest level. That is why a book or poem would be referred to as a "work of literature" or a "piece of poetry."

Classic literature has stood the test of time, remaining popular with readers many years after it was written. Classics are well-written with universal appeal. They cross barriers of background, nationality, economic level, and race to be reread over and over again. Classics are often reread over and over again. This year we are reading some timeless classics from thousands of years ago

So, what are the ingredients of a literary work?

Setting

Setting is the time and location where the story takes place. A historical fiction novel might be set in Victorian England in the town of Bath in the year 1870. A murder mystery might be set in Orlando in the year 2007 during the month of September. Setting also includes the smaller details such as the kitchen, a cabin in the mountains, or a walk along the beach. A good story will take you to the setting, filling your imagination with vivid details. Describing setting in art terminology would make it the canvas of a painting. Setting also includes how time moves forward.

Plot

Plot is the story line, or chain of events from beginning to end. The plot includes one or more **conflicts**, or problems, which come to a **climax**, and then, afterward, a **resolution** of some kind. [Because literature is an art, plot would be the "line" in art or the "melody" in music.]

Characterization

Characters are the people in the story. The reader meets the characters in a book through their speech, actions, appearance, opinion of other people in the book, and the comments the narrator makes about them. This process of introducing the characters to the audience is called **characterization**. In a well-written literary work, they will come alive through their physical appearance, words, and actions. The reader will not be told how to view them, but will be free to form his/her opinions.

Major characters play a large role in the story. The one you root for throughout the book is the **protagonist**, who is directly involved in the conflict in the plot. Most often, the protagonist is the "good guy." The **antagonist** is the person, animal, force of nature, or problem the protagonist faces. In *The Old Man in the Sea*, the antagonist is the sea itself.

Theme

The **theme** of a book is the main idea about life expressed. Novels often convey a message to their readers. These messages can be positive and encouraging; a "reality check" straight between the eyes; or negative and bleak. Literature will often try to make a significant and universal declaration about God, the human nature, human experience, or society as a whole. Common themes in literature might be "Good friends make hard times bearable;" "You can't beat fate;" or "In the long run, parents know best."

Sometimes the **theme** is directly stated by the author; other times it is simply implied. The theme is the underlying message of the book which elicits an emotional response from the reader. My favorite themes in literature are "Love triumphing over hate," "Good beating evil," and "Wisdom overcoming ignorance."

Point of View

The **point of view** in a novel is the narrative voice the author uses to tell the story. How does he do this? If the author takes on the voice of a character in the story, that is **first-person point of view**. ("I hurried down the flight of stairs.") If he is an objective voice in the story, we refer to the narrator as using **third-person point of view**. "She hurried down the flight of stairs." There is omniscient third-person point of view where the narrative voice is all-knowing, even able to read all character's thoughts and the future, and there is limited third-person point of view, where the reader feels that the narrator is uncovering the events along with the reader.

Sherlock Holmes books are written in first-person by a character in the novel, Dr. Watson. First-person narration can give you an affinity with the narrator and helps you feel part of the drama in the story. It is, however, limiting to the author because you can only reveal the plot to the degree your narrating character is involved. On the other hand, an omniscient third-person narrator can "know too much" and take the mystery out of the story. Point of view definitely affects the reader's experience of the literary work.

Worldview

The author's **worldview** is her personal belief system. This is evident in the theme of the book and the portrayal of characters. "Good" characters often agree with the author's worldview and "bad" characters often disagree. Worldview is a belief system about God, religion, politics, economics, education, science, society, family, and relationships. Each person has a unique worldview. Two people might agree on politics and religion, but disagree on education and relationships. An author will try to reveal, defend, or uphold her worldview in any piece of artwork, including literature. To discern her worldview, you must usually read several of the author's works and biographical information. If an author is alive, you can speak to her.

Read Thesis & Outline in Groups

You will read your thesis statement and your outline aloud to a partner or to a small group. This is very important and will help avoid pitfalls when you write your paper this week. Your listener might be a parent or sibling or fellow students in a co-op class.

Make sure your thesis statement is provable. Make sure that your outline follows the thesis statement. Remember the second paragraph is a summary of the plot.

Here is some helpful advice that I received about my thesis statement and outline:

September Week Two Home

☐ Read *The Art of War* and Complete Book Review

☐ Write *Gilgamesh the Hero* Plot Evaluation Essay

☐ Read "Crash Course in Ancient History: Egypt to Early Greece"

The Art of War Book Review

Read *The Art of War* this week. It is a short book. Fill out the book review below after you read it. Prepare to answer the following questions in book club this coming week.

Author: _____ **Year Written:** _____

This book is about:

_____
_____
_____
_____

My favorite part of *The Art of War*:

_____
_____
_____
_____

Aspects of this book that contradict Scripture:

_____
_____
_____
_____

The Art of War was written over 2,500 years ago in ancient China. What principles still work today and why do they still work?

_____
_____
_____
_____

Life is different now than it was in Ancient China. What things today make the author's advice impractical?

_____
_____

How is Ancient Chinese culture different from Western culture? What things in the book are awkward for us because we are living in Western culture?

_____
_____
_____
_____

Are there any principles in the book that contradict biblical principles? What are they and what biblical principles do they contradict?

_____
_____
_____
_____

Is there anything you can learn about spiritual warfare in this book? Compare these things to Ephesians 6.

_____
_____
_____
_____

Do people follow these principles in the business world? Which principles? How do they put them into practice?

_____
_____
_____
_____

Why I think people still read this book today:

_____
_____
_____
_____

Write Gilgamesh the Hero Plot Evaluation Essay

This week you will take all the input you received from Mom, teacher, siblings, or other people you read your thesis statement and outline to, as you write your essay. Make it the best it can be. Go back to Week One Home if you forgot the directions.

Crash Course in Ancient History: Egypt to Early Greece

We are going on a crash course of Ancient History from the beginnings of Egypt right up to the Greeks.

Beginnings of Egypt

Ancient Egypt grew up along the Nile River in northeast Africa. Upper Egypt and Lower Egypt were two different kingdoms that were eventually united by Pharaoh Menes.

From the beginning, the Nile River was important to the Egyptians. Its predictable flooding allowed the people to take advantage of the fertile farmland around the river. They used the river to irrigate land outside of the flood zone, as well as their water highway for transportation. Boats were used to get from place to place and to ship food and building materials.

The Egyptians were amazing builders. Rock quarries yielded massive stones. Surveyors and architects worked hard to choose locations and construct huge projects such as pyramids, temples, and other buildings. Their architecture had its own unique style that other cultures copied. Of course, they became skilled boat builders too with their life centering on the Nile River.

The Egyptians practiced medicine and used mathematics. They blew glass, wrote books, built planked boats, and designed agricultural production techniques to cultivate healthier crops and increase production.

Their dress and artwork was rich with color, jewels, and gold. The ornate combs, bracelets, and necklaces unearthed in archaeological digs reveal the wealth of the Egyptians. Cosmetics were popular, especially eye liner. Statues, figurines, vases, cups, pottery, and religious amulets were beautifully decorated. Gold, lapis, and ivory were used abundantly in Egypt to create opulent jewelry and elaborate works of art.

Egyptian Writing

Hieroglyphs, the Egyptian system of writing, were made accessible to modern scholars with the discovery of the Rosetta Stone in 1799. The rock had the same message from King Ptolemy V in Ancient Egyptian hieroglyphs, Demotic script, and Ancient Greek. This allowed us to translate hieroglyphs and discover remarkable information about Ancient Egypt.

Hieroglyphics contain picture symbols that stood for whole words or sounds, depending on the symbol. The Egyptians used decorative writing for religious purposes.

Pharaohs, Mummies, & Pyramids

Most people divide the history of Ancient Egypt into three periods: Old Kingdom, Middle Kingdom, and the New Kingdom. These kingdoms were strong and prosperous, but between each one was a period of near-collapse called the Intermediate periods.

The Giza Pyramids and the Great Sphinx of Giza were constructed during the Old Kingdom years. The Giza Pyramid was over 400 feet tall and was one of the Seven Wonders of the Ancient World.

There were over 100 pyramids. The earlier pyramids had steps, or ledges, up the sides, but later pyramids have sloping, flat sides. The base of the pyramid is always a perfect square and the building material was most often limestone.

Inside the pyramids is a pharaoh's burial chamber filled with all kinds of treasures. The walls were often painted with beautiful pictures. I am sorry to tell you that the Egyptians believed they could use these things in the afterlife.

While Joshua was leading the people of Israel in the Promised Land, King Tut was reigning in Egypt. King Tut became Pharaoh at the age of seven years old. His father had changed the religious system of the country to worship only one God. Was that the true God? King Tut, under the influence of his advisors, changed the religious system back to the worship of idols. King Tut was an older teenager when he died and seems to have died from a wound to his leg. From studying his mummy, they found a broken leg with a bad infection.

Let's fast forward thousands of years. Howard Carter, an English artist who was homeschooled, went to Egypt in 1891 when he was only seventeen years old. Howard was seeking adventure so he applied for a job as an assistant to an archaeologist going to Egypt. Carter's job was to copy drawings and inscriptions from artifacts to study later. He loved learning about Egypt and soon became an expert. Eventually, he bought and sold antiques too, while continuing to work as an excavator and illustrator. He decided to hunt for the famous King Tut's tomb. With money from a rich man who believed in his project, he hired fifty men to help him. Howard eventually found a long stairway leading down to a secret door. Howard wanted to open the secret access, but instead he sent for his benefactor, Lord Carnarvon to travel to Egypt enter and examine the hidden space together.

Lord Carnarvon and Howard Carter were amazed when they opened the door. The room was filled with glittery treasures: jeweled chests, vases, chariots, and furniture made of gold. The coffin itself was made of gold. King Tut's face was covered with a gold mask. Inside the tomb, there were statues, gold jewelry, chariots, boats, chairs, and paintings. And, of course, the mummy of King Tut.

Mummies were the Egyptian's method of trying to preserve bodies as long as possible. This elaborate process of embalming included removing water and some organs out of the body. The heart was left inside the body and the brain, thought to be useless, was thrown out. The body was covered with a salty substance called natron for forty days to help the body dry out. After it was dry, lotions were used to preserve the outer shell. The body was packed and then wrapped with strips of cloth. After the mummification process was completed, the body was covered with a sheet and put in a sarcophagus, or stone coffin.

In spite of all their advanced technology, the Egypt was subjugated by the Assyrian Empire for a season and 100 years later, was occupied by the Persian Empire. In 332, Alexander the Great conquered Egypt. Egypt also became part of the Roman Empire. So, her glory days ended, but her mysterious lure to people around the world continued throughout history. People in all times and from all places, love to go to Egypt to see the legendary pyramids and other famous sites.

Egyptian Culture

Here are some fun facts about Egyptian culture.

- Egyptians lived in sun baked mud homes. The inside walls were painted with beautiful colors or charming scenery. They slept on the roof in the summer and bathed in the Nile River.
- Both men and women wore make-up as a religious practice, believing it had healing powers. Egyptian inventors were constantly improving make-up.

- Egyptians used calendars, musical instruments, plows for farming, and medicine. They even used toothpaste. They used moldy bread for infections.
- Egyptians wrote with hieroglyphics on papyrus, a kind of paper. They used ink.

I am sorry to tell you that Egyptians did not worship the true God. They worshipped idols. Cats were considered sacred in Ancient Egypt.

Incubation of the Nation of Israel

8 *Joseph is Sold into Slavery by His Brothers by Providence Lithograph Company circa 1900 public domain.*

Joseph, the favorite son of Jacob was intensely disliked by his brothers. They were jealous of his father's affection. One day, they sold him into slavery and Joseph ended up in Egypt. God's favor was upon him and he ended up interpreting a dream for Pharaoh which landed him a prestigious job as second-in-command to Pharaoh himself.

Meanwhile, famine came to Canaan where his father and brothers were living. Their search for food led them to Egypt where they were reunited with their long-lost brother/son Joseph. Joseph urged them to stay in Egypt and they did.

In time, other pharaohs forgot about Joseph and came to despise these shepherds living in the best part of Egypt. They enslaved the Israelites who worked to build pyramids and other national projects. Life became harder and harder. Soon the Israelites cried out to God to rescue them.

By this time the nation of Israel had grown from one large family to 600,000 men plus women and children. The people were healthy and hearty, though they were becoming weary and eager to be free from slavery.

Exodus

God heard the prayers of his people and raised up a deliverer for them. His name was Moses, a humble man who loved the Lord with all his heart.

He went to Pharaoh and asked if his people could be given freedom to go worship God in the desert. Pharaoh refused. From that point on, there was a showdown: Pharaoh and his magicians versus God and His people. After a serious of plagues, the final one was the death of all the firstborn sons in Egypt. The only way to keep death from hitting your household was to kill a lamb, eat it, and wipe the blood on the doorpost of the house. The angel of death passed through Egypt, but did not touch any of the Israelite's homes because of the blood of the lambs. Since the angel of death passed over, the feast celebrated in remembrance of this is called Passover. Passover is still celebrated by Jews today throughout the world.

After this last plague, the Pharaoh relented and allowed the people to flee. A huge group of Israelites hit the road with all their possession bound for the Promised Land with God leading the way. Originally promised to Abraham, this land was flowing with milk and honey. Pharaoh changed his mind and set off after Moses and the Jews. Arriving at a desperate place, the Israelites found themselves between Pharaoh's army and the Red Sea. Miraculously, God parted the Red Sea so that the Israelites could pass over and once they reached the other side, the waters rolled back and drowned Pharaoh's army.

The nation of Israel began a journey to their Promised Land, receiving the Ten Commandments and building a Tabernacle for worship on the way. Unfortunately, their sin postponed their initial arrival time and they had to wander in the desert for 40 years.

Read Exodus, Numbers, Leviticus, and Deuteronomy to learn more about their exciting adventures.

Moses Writes it All Down

God's Holy Book, *The Bible*, continued to be written, passed down carefully to the next generation, until it passed into the hands of Moses. The Holy Spirit inspired Moses who wrote down the words God wanted written down about Israel's adventures in Egypt, their miraculous escape, and the journey to the Promised Land.

Joshua is the Hero and the Writer

Joshua took the helm after Moses died, leading the people to cross the Jordan River into the Promised Land. With a few defeats because of their sin and many victories, they conquered the heathen people to take the land. The Israelites settled down to enjoy their new freedom. Joshua wrote everything down. Read Joshua to learn more about these exciting adventures.

9 Joshua Renews the Covenant with Israel by Providence Lithograph Company circa 1900 public domain

Israel's Saga Continues

After Joshua died, judges ruled the nation of Israel. I am sorry to tell you that the people did what was right in their own eyes instead of obeying the Lord. God would give them over to oppressors to punish their sin until they cried out to the LORD for a deliverer. God would use a hero to rescue them, but soon the Israelites were back in their sin. You can read Judges for the whole story.

The final judge was Samuel, a righteous man without righteous sons to follow in his footsteps. The people began to cry out for a human king even though the Lord was their king. God, saddened by their rejection of him, gave them their first king, Saul. Saul was eventually rejected by God who raised up a king after his own heart, David. David was a mighty warrior who extended the kingdom's boundaries and ruled in righteousness. During his son Solomon's reign, Israel was at the height of her glory with a huge territory, wealth beyond measure, and a wise king who wrote the book of Proverbs. After Solomon's death, the kingdom was split between two kings. One ruled ten tribes from Samaria and was known as Israel. The other king ruled over Judah and Benjamin from Jerusalem and was called Judah. You can read I Samuel, II Samuel, I Kings, II Kings, I Chronicles, and II Chronicles for the full story.

The Old Testament

Book after book in the Old Testament tells the story of the nation of Israel. Their history, poems, songs, and prophetic words were carefully recorded, inspired by the Lord, and preserved for us to read today.

Early Greece

Ancient Greece was not one nation, but several independent city-states that shared a religion of worshipping idol/gods. Each city was a self-ruling nation. The Greeks flourished in the warm climate and fertile land.

The Trojan War

The Trojan War took place in the twelfth or thirteenth century while the Greek city-states existed, but the Greek culture was in its infancy. Our understanding of the Trojan War comes from two works by Homer, a Greek writer, and one epic poem by Virgil, a Roman writer. Truth was mixed in with mythology. Their idol/gods and idol/goddesses were involved in the battles and underlying goals of the war.

When Paris, a prince of Troy, kidnapped Helen, the Queen of Sparta, the Greek city-states came together to rescue Queen Helen from Troy.

September Week Three Class

☐ Book Club! Discuss *The Art of War*

☐ Mom/Teacher Explain Setting & Background for *The Iliad* & Archilles Heel

☐ Discuss & Come Up with Questions to Analyze Setting in *The Iliad*

☐ Read Plot Evaluation Papers Aloud & Complete Peer Review

Book Club Discussion on *The Art of War*

Here are some questions to discuss about *The Art of War* by Sun Tzu.

- *The Art of War* was written over 2,500 years ago in ancient China. What principles still work today and why do they still work?
- Life is different than it was in Ancient China. What things today make the author's advice impractical?
- How is Ancient Chinese culture different from Western culture? What things in the book are awkward for us because we are living in Western culture?
- Are there any principles in the book that contradict biblical principles? What are they and what biblical principles do they contradict?
- Is there anything you can learn about spiritual warfare in this book? Compare these things to Ephesians chapter six.
- Do people follow these principles in the business world? Which principles? How do they put them into practice?
- Why do you think people still read this book today?

The All-Important Question!

Questions guide us in our reading and help us to learn new things. Asking questions and discussing these questions, with their answers, together is great training in literary analysis. When we get to the point where we are writing a literary analysis, we will be ready.

Each week we will ask many questions about the books we are reading. We will also come up with our own questions. Asking the right questions will be a skill worth having as your grow intellectually and educationally.

Setting

Setting often plays a big role in how an audience responds to the story. **Setting** is the time and location where the story takes place. It also includes how time moves forward. A historical fiction novel might be set in the Middle Ages inside a monastery, taking place over ten years. A murder mystery might be set in

Ontario, Canada in the year 2016 during a five-day snowstorm. Setting also includes the smaller details such as the kitchen, a cabin in the mountains, or a walk along the beach. A good story will take you to the setting, filling your imagination with vivid details. Describing setting in art terminology would make it the canvas of a painting.

Background on *The Iliad*

The Iliad is a famous Greek classic set in the same time as *The Odyssey*. If you want to learn more about the history and religion of Ancient Greece, this is the place to start. *The Iliad* is an epic poem (that means it is super, super, super long).

Homer, a blind poet, lived on the Greek island of Chios in the Mediterranean. Homer wrote many books, but is best remembered today for *The Odyssey* and *The Iliad*.

Read and enjoyed for centuries, *The Iliad* is a suspenseful adventure story filled with romance, fighting, battles, trickery, idol/gods who behave like rebellious teenagers, bravery, and flashes of honor. This is one complicated tale.

The Iliad, like most epic poems, is a long, involved adventure tale with a hero. The perfect hero is strong, handsome, a skilled warrior, and an honorable man who is willing to give his life for a noble cause. Achilles and Hector are the main heroes in *The Iliad*.

Though written in the 700s B.C., the story is actually set in the 1200s B.C. For many years, people thought that this story was a myth and that Troy was a made-up city-state. However, in 1870 Heinrich Schliemann, digging for archaeologist Frank Calvert, found the original site of Troy at Hisarlik, a tell in Turkey. *The Iliad* is set inside and outside the walled city of Troy. This area is part of modern-day Turkey today.

Since the purpose of reading *The Iliad* is to study the story, characters, and setting, rather than ancient Greek poetry, it is fine to read *The Iliad for Boys & Girls* by A.J. Church. It is easier to understand and follow the story than the poem itself. Even better, it is well-written and leaves the sexual content and more graphic violence out. Yes, I'm sorry to tell you that Ancient Greek Literature isn't wholesome.

From *The Iliad* to Modern Culture: Achilles Heel

Achilles, the bravest hero in *The Iliad* was the son of Peleus and the idol/goddess Thetis of Greek mythology. After his birth, his mother dipped him in a magic river to make him immortal. As she immersed him, she held him by the heel so the heel never got wet. That was his weak spot. His ankle stayed mortal.

In modern times, it is a weakness or point of vulnerability, in spite of overall strength. This could be a flaw, negative character trait, susceptibility to temptation, imperfection, or problems that often lead to downfall. Can you think of characters who seem almost perfect, but have one weakness?

The Story Before the Iliad Begins

Peleus, king of Phythia, and Thetis, a sea goddess, got married and had a son, Achilles. Peleus and Thetis celebrated with a great feast that included men, women, idol/gods, and idol/goddesses. Athena, Hera, and Aphrodite, three goddesses, were at the feast enjoying themselves when an apple rolled up to the goddesses. The golden apple, tossed by the idol/goddess Eris who was angry at being excluded, was inscribed "To the fairest." Zeus was asked to choose which of the goddesses was the most beautiful, a task he quickly delegated to Paris, a prince of Troy. Each goddess offered bribes to Paris to get him to choose her as the fairest of them all. Aphrodite offered Paris the lovely Queen Helen of Sparta. It didn't matter that she was married to the king of Sparta, Menalaos. Aphrodite was actually killing two birds with one stone. Angry at the royal house of Sparta because they forgot to sacrifice to her, she doomed all the daughters to be known as adulteresses. Prince Paris of Troy awarded Aphrodite the golden apple and visited Spartan King Menalaos as a friend, but eloped with his wife Helen.

Meanwhile, Athena and Hera were furious at not being chosen, and decided to destroy Troy. Yes, these idol/gods and goddesses sound nothing like our amazing God Most High, Creator of the all things. They lied, cheated, threw temper tantrums, fought on behalf of certain men, and fought against other men. Though bigger and more powerful than men and women, they were not very godly and loving.

The Iliad tells the story of the Greek battle to rescue Helen, a Spartan queen, from her captivity in Troy.

Questions for Setting Analysis of *The Iliad*

It's time for everyone to brainstorm together. Come up with some questions about *The Iliad*. This week we will ask questions about the setting in *The Iliad*.

Here are some to ask about the setting of *The Iliad*. Discuss these ideas and your own ideas with your family or co-op members.

What effect does the setting have on the characters in *The Iliad*?

Does the setting increase your knowledge of the Trojan War?

What do you learn about Greek customs and ideas from *The Iliad*?

Does it make a difference to you, as the reader, that Troy was a real, rather than mythical city?

Where do the gods live? How is that different from where the humans live?

How do the world of the gods and the world of the humans intersect? How does this add to the story?

_____

_____

_____

_____

_____

_____

Analyzing the Setting in *The Iliad*

The Iliad is an epic poem about a quarrel between King Agamemnon and Achilles, a great warrior that lead to weeks of battles and events. The setting is the ten-year siege of Troy during the Trojan War in Ancient Greece.

An epic poem is an extremely long poem about the exploits of a hero. Epic poems are full of adventure and bravery. You will be focusing on the setting when you read *The Iliad*.

The setting is the historical moment in time and place, or geographical location, where a story takes place. It might be very specific (Philadelphia July 4, 1776) or general (beach cottage on a sunny day).

The setting influences the story. Sometimes the setting just provides a backdrop for the plot and characters, but other times it provides the mood or emotional impact of the story. *The Hound of the Baskervilles* is set in the Scottish moors, a perfect location for a scary tale by Sir Arthur Conan Doyle.

The setting of *The Iliad*, Troy is now Hisarlik, a city in Turkey. Troy was a thriving nation until the Trojan War.

Directions for *The Iliad* Setting Analysis Assignment

Read *The Iliad* with the idea in mind that you are analyzing it. Underline or dog-ear spots that are very interesting to you or raise questions in your mind. The key is as you are reading to ask yourself questions about the plot or aspects of the plot.

We will discuss *The Iliad* next week and as a group, we will brainstorm other settings for the story and how those new settings would impact the story.

Read Plot Evaluation Essays in Groups

You will read all your papers aloud to a partner or to a small group. This practice will help you to keep your audience in mind as you write. Your listener might be a parent or sibling or fellow students in a co-op class.

Give one another input about your plot evaluation essays through a peer review.

Peer Review for Plot Evaluation Essay

		Yes or No	Comments
Audience	Paper is interesting & enjoyable to read		
Thesis	Thesis is clearly stated and **evaluative** in nature		
Introductions	Introduction captures my attention and contains Thesis Statement		
Paragraphs	Each paragraph supports the thesis statement. Second paragraph summarizes the story **briefly**. Every other paragraph is clear and easy-to-understand, makes a strong point and supports it with examples & illustrations		
Flow of Paper	Paragraphs and the sentences within those paragraphs flow into one another		
Grammar	Spelling/Grammar		

September Week Three & Four Home

☐ Read *The Iliad for Boys & Girls* and Answer Book Club Discussion Questions

☐ Rewrite Your Plot Evaluation Paper on *Gilgamesh the Hero*

Read *The Iliad for Boys & Girls*

People have enjoyed *The Iliad* for centuries. I would encourage you to answer these questions about the story as you read. They are the questions you will be discussing in book club.

How did it benefit the Trojans to fight on their own turf?

_____

_____

_____

_____

What was the most exciting battle scene in the book? Did it end the way you wanted it to?

_____

_____

_____

Describe the rivalries between the idol/gods. How do these rivalries lead to events involving the Greeks and the Trojans?

_____

_____

_____

_____

Which idol/gods fought for the Greeks?

_____

_____

_____

_____

Which idol/gods fought for the Trojans?

_____

_____

_____

In what way are the Greeks' values different from the Trojans' values? How does this affect the story?

_____

_____

_____
_____

Describe scenes where our heroes behave badly. Does this bad behavior affect the readers' view of them?

_____
_____
_____
_____

Describe scenes where our heroes are noble and brave. Does this affect who the readers root for?

_____
_____
_____
_____

When and why did Troy fall?

_____
_____
_____
_____

Can you think of any story lines in books or movies that remind you of _The Iliad_?

_____
_____
_____
_____

It's time to come up with some of your own questions about the setting of _The Iliad_.

Here are some of my questions about _The Iliad_.

_____
_____
_____
_____

Here are other people's questions about _The Iliad_.

_____
_____
_____
_____

Rewrite Your Plot Evaluation Paper

With the input you received in group time, rewrite your plot evaluation paper on _Gilgamesh the Hero_, making corrections and adding any needed changes.

Grading Rubric for Plot Evaluation Paper

With the input you received in group time, rewrite your plot evaluation paper, making corrections and adding any needed changes.

		Comments	Possible Points	Points
Audience	Paper is interesting & enjoyable to read		10/10	/10
Thesis	Thesis is clearly stated and **evaluative** in nature		20/20	/20
Introductions	Introduction captures my attention and contains Thesis Statement		10/10	/10
Paragraphs	Each paragraph supports the thesis statement. Second paragraph summarizes the story **briefly**. Every other paragraph is clear and easy-to-understand, makes a strong point and supports it with examples & illustrations		30/30	/30
Flow of Paper	Paragraphs and the sentences within those paragraphs flow into one another		20/20	/20
Grammar	Spelling/Grammar		10/10	/10
Grade			100/100	/100

October: Greek Literature

Foundations of Western Literature

10 Homer, a painting by Raphael

October Week One Class

- ☐ Book Club Discussion! *The Iliad*
- ☐ Read Papers Aloud in Groups & Turn into Mom/Teacher
- ☐ Read and Discuss "Background on *The Odyssey*"
- ☐ Go Over Questions to Ask about Characters in *The Odyssey*
- ☐ Go Over Directions for "My Character in *The Odyssey*"

Book Club Discussion on *The Iliad*

Here are some questions to discuss about *The Iliad*.

- How did it benefit the Trojans to fight on their own turf?
- What was the most exciting battle scene in the book? Did it end the way you wanted it to?
- Describe the rivalries between the idol/gods. How do these rivalries lead to events involving the Greeks and the Trojans?
- Which idol/gods fought for the Greeks?
- Which idol/gods fought for the Trojans?
- In what way are the Greeks' values different from the Trojans' values? How does this affect the story?
- Describe scenes where our heroes behave badly. Does this bad behavior affect the readers' view of them?
- Describe scenes where our heroes are noble and brave. Does this affect who the readers root for?
- When and why did Troy fall?
- Can you think of any story lines in books or movies that remind you of *The Iliad*?

Read *Gilgamesh the Hero* Re-written Plot Evaluation Essays in Groups

You will read all your papers aloud to a partner or to a small group. This is very important and will help you to keep your audience in mind as you write. Your listener might be a parent or sibling or fellow students in a co-op class. Jot down suggestions from your listeners.

Background of *The Odyssey*

The Odyssey is another Greek epic poem written by Homer involving the end of the Trojan War and Odysseus', or Ulysses, long journey home. Odysseus is the Greek name and Ulysses is the Roman translation of that name. Since we are not studying Ancient Greek poetry, but rather the story itself, I recommend *The Odyssey for Boys and Girls* by A.J. Church because it is well-written, wholesome, and an accurate retelling, just leaving out the sexual content.

The story begins ten years after the Trojan War has ended. Ulysses is still not home and his wife, Penelope, and son, Telemachus, are living in their palace on the island of Ithica. They are sharing their palace with over 100 "suitors," or men who wish to marry Penelope. The suitors are eating them out of house and home.

With the help of the idol/goddess Athena, Telemachus travels to the Greek city-state of Pylos on the Greek mainland where he seeks help from King Nestor. From there, he travels to Sparta where he visits with the newly reunited King Menelaus and Queen Helen (the cause of the Trojan War). Telemachus learns that his father is a captive of Calypso.

At this point, the tale picks up with Calypso setting Ulysses free on a raft on the open sea. You will have to read the rest of the story to find out what happens.

The word "odyssey" has come to mean an "epic voyage."

Characterization

Before we start reading *The Odyssey*, let's talk a little about characterization. Writers reveal their characters through their actions, speech, and interactions with other characters. We can also get to know a character in a story by reading what other characters in the story say about him, or her, and by how they interact with him, or her.

When we like characters, we can root for them to win or overcome. When we like a book, it is often because we like the characters in the book, or at least the hero.

Here are some of the most important characters in *The Odyssey*.

Ulysses

Ulysses is the hero of Homer's Odyssey and king of Ithaca. He is trying to get home to his beautiful wife and son in Ithaca

Telemachus

Royal prince waiting at home for his father, Ulysses, while trying to rescue his beautiful mother, Penelope, from the rude suitors in Ithaca. Eventually, he goes searching for his father

Penelope

Beautiful wife of Ulysses who refuses to marry any of her suitors, believing that Ulysses is still alive

Athena

Idol/goddess of wisdom, daughter of Zeus who helps Ulysses on his journey

Zeus

Head idol/god in Greek mythology

Poseidon

Idol/god of the sea who causes harm to Ulysses

Antinous

A suitor of Penelope, living in the castle of Ulysses, wasting her money and resources

Eurymachus

Another suitor

Amphinomus

Another suitor

Eumaeus

A shepherd and employee of Ulysses who helps his boss

Cyclops

One-eyed giants who eat people

Circe

A witch, or sorceress, who harms Ulysses' men and later helps them

Calypso

Idol/goddess who keeps Ulysses on her beautiful island for seven years

Laertes

Father of Ulysses and former king of Ithaca

Nestor

King of Pylos who shows hospitality to Telemachus on his quest to find Ulysses

Menelaus

King of Sparta, brother of Agamemnon, husband of Helen

Agamemnon

Former king of Mycenae, killed in Trojan War

Helen

Wife of Menelaus, queen of Sparta, and cause of the Trojan War

Nausicaa

Daughter of King Alcinous who rescues Ulysses

Alcinous

King of Phaeacians, who offer hospitality to Ulysses

Achilles

Half man and half idol/god. He can only be hurt in his heel

Questions for Character Paper about *The Odyssey*

It's time for everyone to brainstorm together. What are some questions that we can ask about *The Odyssey*, focusing on characterization? Here are some from your book club discussion questions. Can you think of more?

What do we learn about Ulysses through his encounter with the Cyclops?

Why did Penelope hold on to hope that Ulysses was alive after twenty years of waiting for his return?

What does Ulysses learn about Penelope's suiters from disguising himself as a beggar?

_____
_____
_____
_____
_____
_____
_____
_____
_____
_____

Directions for "My Character in *The Odyssey*"

The Odyssey gives us characters worth caring for and rooting for as the events of the story unfold. There might be some characters you laugh at, while you feel sorry for others. You might even dislike, or hate, some characters in the story. Literature arouses our emotions. But, why do we have feelings for the characters?

Homer introduces his characters to us through the things they say and do, as well as what the characters say about one another.

Choose one character in *The Odyssey* and describe this character, how the author has introduced him or her to you, and how you feel about him or her.

Describe the character's major trait or traits. Is he noble and brave or foolish and fearful? Is she beautiful and kind or cruel and selfish? Does he or she worship the True God or sacrifice to idol/gods and idol/goddesses? How does this affect his or her character?

Think of and look for positive character traits such as hardworking, confident, courageous, careful, just, peaceful, sincere, truthful, generous, and reasonable. Think of and look for negative traits such as careless, hot-headed, deceitful, lazy, underhanded, or reckless. What about physical appearance? That is often important in how we feel about a character. Is your character like a real person with positive traits and flaws or a heroic ideal?

When you write your character, use examples from *The Odyssey* as evidence that your character is exactly as you are describing.

Here is some evidence to look for in *The Odyssey*:

- What your character says (dialogue)
- What your character does (behavior, actions)
- What other characters say about them
- What Homer says about them as the narrator of the story (A.J. Church is just retelling what Homer has already said)

You can write this essay three different ways.

1. Choose one central character trait (generosity, kindness, bravery) that is tested by a difficulty or set of trials, but still shines through.
2. Choose to focus on how your character changes. Again focus on only one or two aspects of that change. For example, is your character fearful at the beginning, but learns to be brave. Or, conversely, is your character reckless at the beginning and learns prudence throughout the story.
3. Choose a few events in the story that highlight a consistent trait in your character. You might use three battle scenes to show how your character is brave, but prudent.

As you write your story, be sure to use examples from the book with quotes or paraphrases.

October Week One Home

☐ Read The Odyssey

☐ While you read *The Odyssey,* answer the Book Club Questions

Reading *The Odyssey*

Read *The Odyssey.* I would encourage you to answer these questions about the story as you read. They are the questions you will be discussing in book club.

What do we learn about Ulysses through his encounter with the Cyclops?

_____

_____

_____

_____

Why did Penelope hold on to hope that Ulysses was alive after twenty years of waiting for his return? What does this show us about Penelope?

_____

_____

_____

_____

Ulysses rarely shows fear. Is he afraid and hiding it? Or is he very brave?

_____

_____

_____

_____

What do you like about Ulysses? What do you dislike about him? What about him makes you want him to get home to his family?

_____

_____

_____

_____

For any character: what do you like about him/her? What do you dislike? How does he/she change in the story, if at all?

_____

_____

_____

_____

What does Ulysses learn about Penelope's suiters from disguising himself as a beggar? How does this affect the story and the readers' feelings toward Ulysses?

_____
_____
_____
_____

Why does Ulysses kill Antinous first? What does this reveal about Ulysses?

_____
_____
_____
_____

Do Ulysses and Penelope have a healthy relationship? How can you tell?

_____
_____
_____
_____

October Week Two Class

☐ Read & Discus "Writing Review: Sentences Make a Difference"

☐ Classroom Project: David & Goliath in Literature"

Writing Review: Sentences Make a Difference

Your job as a writer is pass on interesting information to your reader in an engaging way.

Sentence Structure

Sentences are the building blocks of paragraphs. If you can write a good sentence expressing interesting ideas or information, you can write a first-rate paragraph.

A sentence has five ingredients: it begins with a capital letter, ends with a punctuation mark (period, exclamation point, or question mark), contains a noun (subject), a verb, and contains a complete thought. I know this is basic, but it helps to remember the basics.

Read the following and decide if they are sentences. (You might want to write them on a white board.)

- Tony ran.
- Stella offered me her sandwich
- How fast will they?
- Susie and Bert wandered aimlessly among the rose garden with a pail of sandwiches.
- Will Fred go to the big game tomorrow?
- God will come through for you!
- Because she loves flowers.
- The Lord is good and His mercy is everlasting.
- Which helps to keep them cool in the heat.

Change the incomplete sentences to real sentences.

Write a complete sentence here:

_____

_____

Fixing Sentences to Make them More Effective

You can combine ideas together in one sentence. Here are two different thoughts. In vain, the suitors are urging Penelope to marry again. Penelope still believes that Ulysses will come home.

You can show a cause and effect relationship between the two sentences by using **as**, **because**, or **since**.

Because Penelope still believes that Ulysses will come home, the suitors are urging Penelope in vain to marry again.

You can combine the sentences using an adjective clause.

In vain, the suitors are urging Penelope, who still believes Ulysses will come home, to marry again.

Here is one more way to combine the sentences.

Even though the suitors are urging Penelope to marry again, she still believes that Ulysses will come home.

Take turns at the white board, coming up with different sentences to come the following ideas. See how many different sentences you can come up with that sound good.

1. The sirens make a beautiful melody that captivates the listener. Ulysses tells his men to be careful of the sirens.
2. Telemachus misses his father very much and wants to search for him. Telemachus is tired of the way the suitors treat his mother.
3. Ulysses disguises himself as a beggar and visits the royal palace. Ulysses doesn't reveal himself to his wife when he first gets home.
4. The Greek idol/gods and idol/goddesses behave like immature teenagers. The idol/gods and idol/goddesses fight against each other and competed to see who is the best.

Write the best sentence from each of the sentences you come up with below.

Classroom Project: David & Goliath in Literature

We love to read the story of David and Goliath. David, a young shepherd boy with only a sling and a stone goes after a huge giant who is unstoppable, unbeatable, and unwavering in his mockery of the Lord Most High. David, who loves the Lord, fights to defend His honor, and kills the giant of a man. You can see this theme throughout Western Literature.

Read the story aloud. Summarize it. Now, brainstorm as many examples as you can of "David & Goliath" in literature and movies. David is the underdog sure to be defeated, but he wins anyway.

Here are some examples to get you started:

- *Facing the Giants* (Sherwood Films)
- *Star Wars* (Luke Skywalker vs. Darth Vader)
- *The Three Little Pigs* (Pigs vs. the Wolf)
- *The Lord of the Rings* (Frodo Baggins)
- *Oliver Twist*
- *Cinderella*
- *Rudy*
- *Rocky*
- *Cinderella Man*
- *Remember the Titans*
- *Hoosiers*
- *Miracle*
- *Cool Runnings*
- *The Hunger Games: Mockingjay I*
- *Braveheart*
- *The Rookie*

October Week Two Home

☐ Read "Crash Course in Ancient History: Assyria to Greece"

☐ Finish Reading *The Odyssey*

☐ Complete Outline for your "My Character in *The Odyssey*" Essay

☐ Write "My Character in *The Odyssey*" Essay

Crash Course in Ancient History: Assyria to Greece

Let's continue our crash course of Ancient History from the Assyria to the Greeks.

Assyria

Time moved on and other kingdoms arose. Assyria and Babylon often vied for supremacy in the Fertile Crescent. Here is a map of various kingdoms in the Fertile Crescent, as well as Egypt.

The city-state of Assur and Nineveh existed back in Sumerian times, ending up in Sargon the Great's kingdom, the Akkadian Empire. Assyria gets its name from the city-state of Assur. Under the leadership of Sargon the Great and his successors, the area that become Assyria thrived, prospered, and enjoyed rigorous trade with other parts of the kingdom, as well as other empires and city-states. After the Akkadian Empire fell, Assyrians enjoyed self-rule once again.

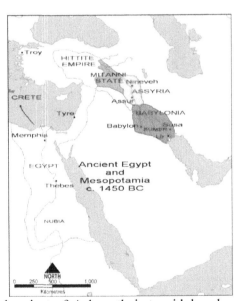

Sometimes Assyria quietly ruled herself. For centuries, however, a power struggle existed between Assyria and Babylon. Sometimes Assyria found herself ruling Babylon while other times under Babylon's dominion.

The king of Assyria was the leader of the army as well as the high priest of Ashur, their top idol-god. Known for their well-bred and trained horses, the Assyrians' fertile land left them with lots of time to invest in horse ranching. Books on horse breeding and training have been unearthed in archaeological digs. The Assyrians exported horses, lumber, and metal ore.

Assyria became a military powerhouse with all men obligated to serve in the military. One ruler of Assyria, King Arvad, managed to conquer the Phoenician city-states of Tyre, Sidon, Simyra, Beirut, and others. The Assyrians were ruthless killers in battle. Many times, people would commit suicide rather than fall into Assyrian hands as prisoners of war. This ruthlessness spread into their society where laws were harsh, women had few rights, and people were raised to see might as right.

Israel & Assyria

After King Solomon's reign ended with his death, the kingdom of Israel was divided. Judah and Benjamin, called Judah, and the other tribes, referred to as Israel, lived on as separate nations.

We meet an Assyrian king in II Kings 15.

"In the thirty-ninth year of Azariah king of Judah, Menahem son of Gadi became king over Israel and reigned ten years in Samaria. He did evil in the sight of the LORD; he did not depart all his days from the sins of Jeroboam the son of Nebat, which he made Israel sin. Pul, king of Assyria, came against the land, and Menahem gave Pul a thousand talents of silver so that his hand might be with him to strengthen the kingdom under his rule. Then Menahem exacted the money from Israel, even from all the mighty men of wealth, from each man fifty shekels of silver to pay the king of Assyria. So the king of Assyria returned and did not remain in the land" (II Kings 15: 17-20 NASB).

And later in the chapter, we meet another Assyrian king.

"In the days of Pekah king of Israel, Tiglath-pileser king of Assyria came and captured Ijon and Abel-beth-maacah and Janoah and Kedesh and Hazor and Gilead and Galilee, all the land of Naphtali; and he carried them captive to Israel" (II Kings 15: 29 NASB).

In Israel, none of the kings served the LORD. Eventually, God used the Assyrians to judge the nation of Israel. Assyrians captured the nation and removed the Jews from their land and transplanted people from other nations to live in Samaria, the capital of Israel.

"In the ninth year of Hoshea, the king of Assyria captured Samaria and carried Israel away into exile to Assyria, and settled them in Halah and Habor, on the river of Gozan, and in the cities of the Medes. Now this came about because the sons of Israel sinned against the LORD their God, who had brought them up from the land of Egypt from under the hand of Pharaoh, king of Egypt, and they had feared other gods and walked in the customs of the nations whom the LORD had driven out before the sons of Israel, and in the customs of the kings of Israel which they had introduced. The sons of Israel did things secretly which were not right against the LORD their God. Moreover, they built for themselves high places in all their towns from watchtower to fortified city. They set for themselves sacred pillars and Asherim on every high hill and under every green tree, and there they burned incense on all the high places as the nations did which the LORD had carried away to exile before them; and they did evil things provoking the LORD. They served idols" (II Kings 17: 6-12 NASB).

"The sons of Israel walked in all the sins of Jeroboam which he did; they did not depart from the them until the LORD removed Israel from His sight, as He spoke though all His servants and prophets. So Israel was carried away into exile from their own land to Assyria until this day. The king of Assyria brought men from Babylon and from Cuthah and from Avva and from Hamath and Sepharvaim, and settled them in the cities of Samaria in place of the sons of Israel. So they possessed Samaria and lived in its cities. At the beginning of their living there, they did not fear the LORD; therefore the LORD sent lions among them which killed some of them. So they spoke to the king of Assyria, saying, 'The nations whom you have carried away into exile in the cities of Samaria do not know the custom of the god of the land; so he has sent lions among them, and behold, they kill them because they do not know the custom of the god of the land. Then the king of Assyria commanded, saying, 'Take there one of the priests whom you carried into exile and let him go and live there; and let him teach them the custom of the god of the land. So one of the priests whom they had carried away into exile from Samaria came and lived at Bethel, and taught them how to fear the LORD. But every nation still made gods of its own and put them in the houses of the high place which the people of Samaria had made, every nation in their cities in which they lived" (II Kings 17: 22-29 NASB).

This group of people became the Samaritans of Jesus' day.

Judah & Assyria

11 Triumph of King Hezekiah over Assyria Painting public domain

In Judah, there were good kings and bad kings. Some kings served the Lord and others did not. Ahaz did not serve the Lord. King Ahaz of Judah even sacrificed one of his sons to an idol/god. When the kings of Aram and Israel attacked Judah, King Ahaz sent to Assyria for help.

Not only did King Ahaz of Judah not cry out to the Lord and seek help from a pagan ruler, he actually gave treasures from the temple to King Tiglath-pileser as a gift. This greatly angered the LORD. (II Kings 16:7-18) But Assyria didn't stop trying to conquer Jerusalem.

"Now in the fourteenth year of King Hezekiah, Sennacherib king of Assyria came up against all the fortified cities of Judah and seized them. Then Hezekiah king of Judah sent to the king of Assyria at Lachish, saying 'I have done wrong. Withdraw from me; whatever you impose on me I will bear.'" (II Kings 18: 13-14 NASB).

So Hezekiah took gold and silver from God's temple to pacify Sennacherib, but that wasn't enough for the Assyrian king. He sent his army to Jerusalem anyway and the Assyrian leaders called out to Hezekiah, the leaders of Jerusalem, and all the people in Jerusalem to surrender so that they would be treated well. The Assyrian leaders also mocked God's ability to save them and called Hezekiah a liar. Hezekiah told the people to ignore the Assyrian threats and the Jews obeyed.

Hezekiah was scared, but the prophet *"Isaiah said to them, 'Thus you shall say to your master, "Thus says the LORD, 'Do not be afraid because of the words that you have heard, with which the servants of the king of Assyria have blasphemed Me. Behold I will put a spirit in him so that he will hear a rumor and return to his own land. And I will make him fall by the sword in his own land.'"'"* (II Kings 19:6-7 NASB).

Hezekiah prayed to the Lord about this terrible situation and God heard his prayer. Isaiah gave another prophetic word to stir up their faith and let them know that he would take care of their problem. God defended Judah against the Assyrians.

"Then it happened that night that the angel of the LORD went out and struck 185,000 in the camp of the Assyrians; and when men rose early in the morning, behold, all of them were dead. So Sennacherib king of Assyria departed and returned home and lived at Nineveh. It came about as he was worshipping in the house of Nisroch his god, that Adrammelech and Sharezer killed him with the sword; and they escaped into the land of Ararat. And Esarhaddon his son became king in his place" (II Kings 19: 35-37 NASB).

Cities that surrendered to Assyria without a fight were absorbed into the empire. I am sorry to tell you that cities that tried to defend themselves were destroyed. Each Assyrian soldier had a lance, a sling, and a bow.

Their armor was a pointed helmet and a long leather robe. Soldiers had assistants who carried their shields for them. War was glorified in Assyrian culture.

Assyrian Culture

Looking back at the Assyrians, we have to be repulsed by their cruelty, brutality, and worship of idol/gods, but we can also be impressed by their culture. Just as people collect books today, wealthy Assyrians collected large collections of tablets (their books). King Ashurbanipal, who ruled the Assyrian Empire from Nineveh, was a former scribe. He collected 20,000 tablets that we know of. That is one big book collection!

Gilgamesh was considered to be the direct ancestor of King Sargon who was the father of King Sennacherib. One of the favorite pastimes of Assyrian kings was hunting lions.

Assyrian men and women dressed more modestly than their Egyptian and Babylonian neighbors with long robes that covered their entire torso. Clothing was made of brightly colored linen or cotton. Men were very proud of their long beards and mustaches that curled down from their faces. In murals, it looks like Assyrian men wore mullets, a popular haircut in American in the 1980s.

Assyrian sculptors created many statues across the empire. I saw several in the British museum. Another Assyrian art form I really enjoyed was reliefs, or raised carved scenes on a flat surface. Many battles and historical events were memorialized in reliefs.

Assyrians had locks and keys to protect their property from intruders and thieves. Inside their locked homes, walls were painted white with a red band near the floor across the walls. Brightly colored rugs adorned the floors. Their homes were built around a central courtyard and they spent most of their time outside in the courtyard.

Assyrian Religion

"Bull men" (huge carved stone bulls with human heads, beards, hats, five legs, and wings) guarded ancient Assyrian palace entrances. These "bull men" were believed by the Assyrians to be friendly little demons that protected the kings.

The Assyrian religion was dark and scary. Ashur, the chief god was originally the sun god and he demanded a steady diet of executed prisoners of war. Demons who wanted to harm mankind dominated their belief system. Their ghoulish worship rituals are very similar to the Aztec religion. Assyrians believed that they were surrounded all the time by thousands of demons. They tried to appease them so they would not be harmed. If a demon entered someone's body, it was believed to cause disease or death. They practiced a ritual with sheep livers was believed to help them foretell the future.

Babylon

Babylon was a small city-state that was part of the ancient Akkadian Empire. Centuries later, the now independent city-state of Babylon remembered their prestige during the reign of Hammurabi who created a Babylonian Empire that existed only during his lifetime. After this, Babylon found itself part of the Assyrian, Kassite, and Elamite dominions at one time or another. They were very proud of their heritage under Hammurabi and grew nostalgic for the old ways of centuries earlier. They even had their own archaeology digs to discover old sites important to their history as Babylonians. The practice of appointing a royal princess to serve as a priestess of the moon-god Sin was reinstituted.

The Assyrians and Babylonians engaged in a power struggle for centuries, but the tide eventually turned in favor of the Babylonians. Joining the Medes, Persians, and other peoples, they sacked Nineveh in 612 B.C.

A thriving empire, the center of every city in Babylon was a temple where idol-gods were worshipped. Each city had local autonomy with laws, courts, and decision-making assemblies. Irrigation systems were build to create large farms and ranches.

Babylonian artists created beautiful murals in royal palaces throughout the Babylonian Empire. In these realistic murals, beings from the spirit world are portrayed as influencing kings and government leaders in a variety of situations. Murals were painted on dry walls. As time went on, frescos began to appear. Frescoes were painted on wet plaster walls before the plaster dried. The paint and plaster dried together, causing the paint to last longer.

Some of the most famous creations of Babylon are the Hanging Gardens and the Ishtar Gate.

Babylonian Captivity

12 Hanging Gardens of Babylon public domain

Nebuchadnezzar II was a great builder. He rebuilt all of Babylon's major cities on a much more lavish scale. His own city, Babylon, was surrounded by a moat and a double circuit of walls. The Euphrates River flowed through the center of the city with a beautiful stone bridge crossing it. In the very center of Babylon was a ziggurat, or temple where their idol-gods were worshipped. The city was considered impenetrable. But God is bigger than any walls or moats.

Nebuchadnezzar II forced tribute from Syria, Phoenicia, Damascus, Tyre, and Sidon. He also attacked and conquered Jerusalem, deposing King Jehoiachin and occupying the city. While Babylon was busy fighting the Egyptians, Jewish King Zedekiah revolted, but after an 18 month long siege, Jerusalem was captured in 587 B.C. and thousands of Jews were deported to Babylon, including Daniel, Shadrach, Meshach, and Abednego. This is called the Babylonian Captivity, a punishment for the sins that the nation of Judah committed against the LORD. Read Daniel to learn more about the adventures of some heroic, godly young men who were taken to Babylon during the Babylonian Captivity.

One night, years later, Belshazzar, the current ruler of Babylon was enjoying a drunken feast with his friends. He called for the Jewish temple gold and silver vessels to be brought out. He and his friends drank from them, while worshipping their pagan-gods to mock the God of Israel.

"Suddenly the fingers of a man's hand emerged and began writing opposite the lampstand on the plaster of the wall of the king's palace, and the king saw the back of the hand that did the writing. Then the king's face grew pale and his thoughts alarmed him, and his hip joints went slack and his knees began knocking together" (Daniel 5: 5-6 NASB).

The king, scared to death, asked for all his diviners and magicians to interpret the words written on the walls, but no one could. Finally his queen reminded him of Daniel. Daniel was brought in and offered riches and gifts if he could interpret the writing on the wall. He told the king to keep his gifts, but did interpret the writing, after first reminding the king of his ancestor's experience with the God of Israel.

"Now this is the inscription that was written out: MENE, MENE, TEKEL, UPHARSIN. This is the interpretation of the message. MENE—God has numbered your kingdom and put an end to it. TEKEL—you have been weighed on the scales and found deficient. PERES—your kingdom has been divided and given over to the Medes and Persians. Then Belshazzar gave orders, and they clothed Daniel with purple and put a necklace of gold around his neck, and issued a proclamation concerning his that he now had authority as the third ruler in the kingdom. That same night Belshazzar, the Chaldean king was slain. So Darius the Mede received the kingdom at about the age of sixty-two" (Daniel 5:25-31 NASB).

You see, Cyrus the Great invaded Babylonia that very night. His engineers diverted the Euphrates River and the Mede-Persian Army entered the city under the walls through an empty moat. So much for a city that can mock the LORD.

Cyrus the Great allowed the Jews to go back to Jerusalem, but that's another story.

Babylonian Religion

Babylonians did not worship the True God. Instead, they worshipped a wide variety of pagan idols very similar to the Sumerian pantheon. A pantheon is a collection of gods and goddesses worshipped by a people group. Marduk (Sumerian Enlil) was their most powerful god. Shamash (Sumerian Utu) was the god of the sun, Sin (Sumerian Nanna) the moon goddess, Ea (Sumerian Enki) god of the water, and Ishtar (Sumerian Inanna) goddess of love.

Greek City-States

13 Greek Statue in British Museum

East of Babylon, Greece was, and still is, a beautiful land made up of two peninsulas and thousands of islands in the Aegean and Ionian Seas. With a warm climate and great soil for growing crops, God blessed them with a long growing season. Greece was not one big country like we think of today. Greece was made up of many city-states that ruled and defended themselves. Each city-state had its own flavor. For example, Spartans lived simple lives, glorified war, and focused completely on raising soldiers to fight victoriously, while Athenians promoted beauty, grace, and philosophizing. All the Greeks did share a common culture, language, and religion. They worshipped many idol-gods who behaved badly.

Very competitive, the Greeks city-states often fought with one another. However once a year, all the Greeks agreed to refrain from fighting long enough to compete with one another in the Olympic Games.

When Persia decided to conquer Greece one city at a time, the city-states came together under the leadership of Athenian generals to protect their freedom. Once they were safe from Persian bullying, Athens, one of the larger Greek city-states, entered her golden years. Art, architecture, music, drama, and writing flourished. It was important to say beautiful things, appreciate beautiful things, and be as beautiful inside and outside as possible. Their sculptures were lifelike.

While Daniel was serving the Lord during the Babylonian Captivity, Aesop was writing his fables that are still enjoyed today.

While Ezra was serving the captives who returned to Jerusalem, Socrates was teaching his disciples Greek philosophy.

Plato was teaching his own disciples in Athens while Malachi was prophesying the Word of the Lord.

The Greek historian, Herodotus, wrote popular histories and is considered the father of history.

One of the things we can thank the Greeks for is their architectural columns

Greek Columns

Greek architecture brought us the column. Greek buildings had large decorative columns at the front of their buildings and in their courtyards. There were three types of columns: Doric, Ionic, and Corinthian.

These columns were all over Greece and were adopted by the Romans. Centuries later, in the Renaissance, Greek columns became popular again. Our capitol and Supreme Court building have beautiful Greek columns.

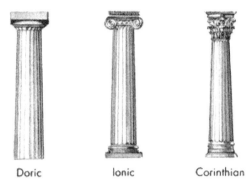

Doric   Ionic   Corinthian

Athens

Athens was named after Athena, the goddess of wisdom and war. In the center of the city, inside the Acropolis, a shrine was built for her. This shrine, the Parthenon was a place for worship and to store gold.

The Acropolis was built on a hill with large thick walls and was used as a fortress when the city was attacked. Beside the Parthenon, the Acropolis was home to several outdoor theatres where plays were performed.

The Agora was the center of business and government with an open area for meetings surrounded by temples to various gods. Elders in the city would come together to discuss issues and make decisions in the Agora. Citizens in Athens could vote for their leaders and vote on laws. When people participate in the choosing and running their government, we call it democracy, or rule by the people.

Greek Clothing

Greek clothing was made of wool (from sheep) and linen (from flax). Some wealthy Greeks had clothing made of imported silk from China. They wore long tunics, usually white, with a long sash. The men's tunic was shorter than the women's tunic. They also wore leather sandals.

Men and women wore rings, necklaces, earrings, and pins. Women wore makeup to make their skins pale, as well as lipstick. Men and women oiled and perfumed their hair.

Greek Language

The Greek language spread throughout Eastern Europe, Northern Africa, and Europe and was spoken in Eastern Europe for hundreds of years. Many of our words have Greek roots. We still use Greek letters in math, science, and engineering equations. College Fraternities and Sororities use Greek letters in their names.

Most importantly, the New Testament was written in Ancient Greek. Pastors and Bible scholars have studied Ancient Greek for centuries so they can study the Bible in its original language.

Dining in Greece

Men and women often ate separately. The Greeks ate three meals a day and drank water or wine. Breakfast was a light meal of bread or porridge. Lunch was another light meal with bread, cheese, and figs. Dinner was the big meal and it was a feast with a variety of food including meat, fish, bread, eggs, vegetables, and cheese. Bread was used to soak up soup or sauce, or sometimes as a napkin. At dinner banquets, they laid on their sides to eat.

Media & Persia

14 Cyrus II by Jean Fouquet public domain

The Medes, a combination of tribes united under King Deioces, lived in present-day Iran and included the city of Laodicia. The Magi were a special caste of Medes that ministered to the spiritual needs of their people. This role was hereditary and passed from father to son. The wise men who visited baby Jesus were Magi.

The Medes spent time under Assyria's rule, conquered the Persians, and were eventually brought into the Persian Empire by Cyrus the Great. Not much is known about the Medes and mention of them is usually as part of the Persians.

Persians were nomads who lived in the area of present-day Iran. Eventually they found themselves under the rule of the Medes. Cyrus the Great led a revolt against Media and went on to conquer Lydia and Babylon. Cyrus the Great is considered the founder of the first Persian Empire. He was a famous builder and able administrator. His kingdom was the largest of all the ancient empires. At one point it spanned from the Balkan Mountains to the Indus Valley (under Darius the Great). He built roads, had a mail system, declared an official language, and set up a strong administration where he gave his conquered peoples autonomy to make decisions, practice their own religion, and enjoy relative freedom. They were able to retain their own culture and laws.

Persian Culture

Here are some interesting things about Persian culture.

Truth was important to the Persians and liars might be executed.

Persians drank wine liberally.

They loved desserts and celebrated birthdays by consuming lots of sweet treats.

Persians enjoyed the foods of all the people they conquered, giving them a diverse diet.

The original Persians and Medes were ranchers with cattle and horses.

Persian rugs were beautifully ornate and are still popular today.

The Persians used the Aramaic language for writing using the Phoenic ian alphabet, and writing on papyrus.

The Persians did everything in grand style. They constructed beautiful buildings, gardens, and artwork. Murals, Frescoes, statues, pottery, and jewelry were crafted from the finest materials and decorated with gold, silver, ebony, and precious stones. Darius the Great collected artists from all over his vast empire, enjoying a wide variety of artistic style and expression.

Queen Esther Saves the Day

15 Persian Soldier Relief in British Museum

King Xerxes, a Persian king, threw a party for all his officials in his kingdom for 180 days. For the most part, he wanted to show off all his wealth and glory while feasting and drinking with abandon. When this was over, he held a party for seven days for all the people in Susa from the greatest to the least. Lots of drinking took place. Meanwhile, his wife, Queen Vashti gave a party for the ladies. On the seventh day, the extremely intoxicated king sent for his wife to show off her beauty. She refused to come to be gawked at, so he decided to find another queen. He already had many wives.

After a long series of beauty treatments, a lovely Jewish girl named Esther was chosen from among all the virgins in the land. King Xerxes made her his queen.

In time, a leader in the kingdom named Haman developed a dastardly plan to destroy all the Jews in the Persian Empire. After fasting and prayer, Esther pleaded to the king for her life and the life of her people. God used her to protect His people.

Of course, there is much more to this exciting adventure and you can read all about it in the book of Esther.

Finish Reading The Odyssey

Finish reading *The Odyssey*. Continue to answer the book club questions about the story as you read. They are the questions you will be discussing in book club.

Write "My Character in *The Odyssey*"

This week you will write an essay about a character from *The Odyssey*. The directions for this paper are in October week one if you need to reread them to refresh your memory.

Choose one character in *The Odyssey* to describe.

Here are some questions to keep in mind:

- How did the author introduce him or her to you?
- What are some major character traits that stand out in the story?
- Does he or she worship the True God or sacrifice to idol/gods and idol/goddesses? How does this affect his or her character?
- What about physical appearance? That is often important in how we feel about a character.
- Is your character like a real person with positive traits and flaws or a heroic ideal?

When you write your "My Character in the Odyssey" paper, use examples from *The Odyssey* as evidence that your character is exactly as you are describing.

As a reminder, here is some evidence to look for in *The Odyssey*:

- What your character says (dialogue)
- What your character does (behavior, actions)
- What other characters say about them
- What Homer says about them as the narrator of the story

As a reminder, you can write this essay three different ways.

1. Choose one central character trait (generosity, kindness, bravery or foolish, weak) that is tested by a difficulty or set of trials, but still shines through.
2. Choose to focus on how your character changes. Again focus on only one or two aspects of that change. For example, is your character fearful at the beginning, but learns to be brave. Or, conversely, is your character reckless at the beginning and learns prudence throughout the story.
3. Choose a few events in the story that highlight a consistent trait in your character. You might use three battle scenes to show how your character is brave, but prudent.

As you write your story, be sure to use examples from the book with quotes or paraphrases.

My Thesis Statement

_____

_____

_____

Introduction

Your introduction will basically be introducing your thesis about your character. Your introduction should capture your reader's attention and introduce the focus, or subject of your paper. You want to "hook" the reader so that he will keep on reading.

Here are some creative ways to introduce your paper.

- You can start your paper with a quote from the book.
- You might begin your paper with a few general statements about people that relate to the character you have chosen.

Paragraphs

The paragraphs in the body of your paper will be proving your thesis using the examples and quotes you found in the book relating to your character. Try to organize each paragraph around a specific idea or point to help your argument flow. Your thesis will guide the body of your paper.

In each paragraph, state the main point you are proving clearly and relate it to the thesis. Support this main point with quotes or details from *The Odyssey*. Explain how the detail or quote proves your point.

Conclusion

Your conclusion should restate the thesis showing how the evidence you've used proved your thesis about your character. End in an interesting way by perhaps stating a new question or suggesting the value of understanding the book. Give your reader something to think about long after they finish reading your paper.

My Essay Outline

Introduction

My Hook

_____
_____
_____

My Thesis Statement

_____
_____
_____

First Paragraph/First Point from My Thesis Statement

_____
_____
_____

Example

_____

_____

_____

Example

_____

_____

_____

Illustration

_____

_____

_____

Second Paragraph/Second Point from My Thesis Statement

_____

_____

_____

Example

_____

_____

_____

Example

_____

_____

_____

Illustration

_____

_____

_____

Third Paragraph/Third Point from My Thesis Statement

_____
_____
_____

Example

_____
_____
_____

Example

_____
_____
_____

Illustration

_____
_____
_____

Fourth Point (you may not have a 4th point!)

_____
_____
_____

Examples

_____
_____
_____

Illustration

_____
_____
_____

Fifth Point (you may not have a 5th point!)

_____
_____
_____

Example

_____
_____
_____

Example

_____
_____
_____

Illustration

_____
_____
_____

Conclusion

Restate My Thesis Statement

_____
_____
_____

Call Reader to Action

_____
_____
_____

Grading Rubric for Character Paper

With the input you received in group time, rewrite your plot evaluation paper, making corrections and adding any needed changes.

		Comments	Possible Points	Points
Audience	Chose one of 3 ways to write essay? Which way?		15/15	/15
Thesis	Thesis is clearly stated and **answers a question about a character?**		20/20	/20
Introductions	Introduction captures my attention and contains Thesis Statement		10/10	/10
Paragraphs	Each paragraph supports the thesis statement and uses evidence from the book. Each paragraph is clear and easy-to-understand, makes a strong point and supports it with examples & illustrations		35/35	/35
Flow of Paper	Paragraphs and the sentences within those paragraphs flow into one another		10/10	/10
Grammar	Spelling/Grammar		10/10	/10
Grade			100/100	/100

October Week Three Class

☐ Book Club Discussion on *The Odyssey* (Answer Book Club Discussion Questions)

☐ Read "My Character in *The Odyssey*" in groups and do Peer Reviews

☐ Read & Discuss Theme: Between a Rock & A Hard Place from *The Odyssey*

☐ Read & Discuss "Writing Review: Let the Paper Flow "

☐ Read & Discuss Theme & *Aesop's Fables* & How to Analyze Theme & Questions about Theme

Book Club Discussion on *The Odyssey*

Here are some questions to discuss about *The Odyssey*.

- What do we learn about Ulysses through his encounter with the Cyclops?
- Why did Penelope hold on to hope that Ulysses was alive after twenty years of waiting for his return? What does this show us about Penelope?
- Ulysses rarely shows fear. Is he afraid and hiding it? Or is he very brave?
- What do you like about Ulysses? What do you dislike about him? What about him makes you want him to get home to his family?
- For any character: what do you like about him/her? What do you dislike? How does he/she change in the story, if at all?
- What does Ulysses learn about Penelope's suiters from disguising himself as a beggar? How does this affect the story and the readers' feelings toward Ulysses?
- Why does Ulysses kill Antinous first? What does this reveal about Ulysses?
- Do Ulysses and Penelope have a healthy relationship? How can you tell?

Read "My Character in *The Odyssey*" in Groups

Read papers aloud to one another in groups. Fill out a Peer Review Sheet for at least one paper.

Peer Review: My Character in the Odyssey

Let a peer review your essay as you read it aloud or as they read it on their own. You can use this information to rewrite your essay.

		Yes or No	Comments
Audience	Did Student chose one of 3 ways to write essay? Which way?		
Thesis	Thesis is clearly stated and **answers a question about a character?**		
Introductions	Introduction captures my attention and contains Thesis Statement		
Paragraphs	Each paragraph supports the thesis statement and uses evidence from the book. Each paragraph is clear and easy-to-understand, makes a strong point and supports it with examples & illustrations		
Flow of Paper	Paragraphs and the sentences within those paragraphs flow nicely		
Grammar	Spelling/Grammar		

Theme: Between a Rock and a Hard Place

"I'm between a rock and a hard place," your older brother admits at the family dinner table.

What does your brother mean and where does that phrase come from?

In *The Odyssesy,* Ulysses has to cross the Strait of Messina between the island of Sicily and the Italian peninsula. On the Italian side was a six-headed sea monster (Scylla) and on the other side was a whirlpool (Charybodis). If Ulysses avoided Carybodis, the whirlpool, he would pass too close to the Scylla, the sea monster. Ulysses opted to pass close to Scylla, the sea monster, knowing he would lose a few men versus losing his whole ship in the whirlpool.

Having to navigate between two horrible hazards found its way into many cultures that followed the Greeks. In English, we say "between a rock and a hard place" to mean that someone had to choose between two equally bad situations. Over the years, the image of this dilemma found its way into many political cartoons, making it clear that no matter which route they chose, there would be terrible consequences.

Writing Review: Let the Paper Flow!

Your job as a writer is pass on interesting information to your reader in an engaging way. I am going to give you some helpful tips to make your paper interesting and fun to read.

Sentence Structure

Sentences are the building blocks of paragraphs. Sentences should be able to stand alone to deliver information. If you struggle with writing sentences, try reading your writing aloud to a parent or sibling. Can they follow you? Are they confused? Ask them to be honest and evaluate your writing.

Rewrite your sentences in one paragraph and read it aloud again.

Use active verbs and concrete nouns.

Which sentence sounds better.

- A body part was washed by Sally.
- Sally washed her hair.

Get rid of extra words.

Which sentences sounds better?

- Sally is taking medication prescribed by her doctor
- Sally takes prescription medicine.

Let the Thesis Guide the Paper and the Paragraphs

Your thesis is a handy-dandy writing tool that you can use every time you write an essay. Let it guide your paper. Here is an example.

Thesis statement: Living debt free requires delayed gratification, prioritizing needs, and a saving plan.

Your introduction could explain the benefits of living debt-free, as well as sharing your thesis statement.

Your second paragraph might define delayed gratification and explain how to exercise it in the area of finance, giving examples.

Your third paragraph would talk about prioritizing needs, giving examples.

Your fourth paragraph might define a saving plan, giving examples and inspiring readers to make one. You might add a fifth paragraph that explains step-by-step how to make a saving plan.

The final paragraph should summarize your thesis and main points, while inspiring your readers to make changes in their spending habits.

Topic Sentences

Each paragraph should have a topic sentence that summarizes the main points in a paragraph. It is often the first sentence.

Supporting Topic Sentences

If my topic sentence is "Dragons appear in the legends and folk tales of several countries in each continent except Antarctica," then the next sentences would give examples of the legends and folk tales, as well as their countries of origin.

Aesop's Fables

Aristotle speaks of Aesop in his writings as a slave from Thrace, on the Black Sea. He was born around 630 B.C. The famous Greek historian Herodotus informs us that Aesop was a Greek slave who won his freedom because he was such a great storyteller.

Beyond this, it is hard to say with certainty anything else about him. Stories about Aesop include him stealing figs, mingling with kings, and adopting a young boy.

Fables are short stories with a strong moral lesson. Often read aloud to children, they teach lessons that bring lifelong blessing if put into practice.

Theme

Theme can be subtle or obvious in a novel or short story. In Aesop's fables, the theme is often disclosed boldly in the last line of the story.

The theme is the message or moral of the story. Two different writers could write articles on a prisoner on death row, sharing the same details. One writer's theme might be that capital punishment is a good punishment for violent murderers, while the other author might be completely against capital punishment. They would have the same facts, but a different theme. How would they promote their message? It is all in what you share and what you don't share, how you share facts, and how you describe the people in your article or story.

In a story, authors will often reward what they consider good and punish what they consider evil to communicate their message. The character who agrees with the author's point of view on a particular subject is often more likeable and the one that readers identify with and root for. Sometimes the main character will "come to see the light" in a story. "The light" would be the author's message.

Authors will also show good consequences for behavior that agrees with the author's theme and bad consequences for behavior that goes against his message.

Questions about Aesop's Fables

It's time to brainstorm together and come up with questions about *Aesop's Fables* related to theme.

_____

_____

_____

_____

_____

_____

_____

_____

_____

How to Analyze Theme

You are going to write a short paper on the theme of a fable. You won't have any problem finding the theme because Mr. Aesop blurts it out. However, I want you to write a paper about how he illustrates the theme in his story. You will write an analysis paper on one of Aesop's fables and how he demonstrates his message in the story.

October Week Three & Four Home

☐ Read *Aesop's Fables* and Answer Book Club Discussion Questions

☐ Come Up with Questions about *Aesop's Fables*

☐ Plan "Aesop's Theme Analysis Paper"

☐ Write "Aesop's Theme Analysis Paper"

Read *Aesop's Fables*

I would encourage you to answer these questions about the story as you read. They are the questions you will be discussing in book club.

What was your favorite fable and why?

_____

_____

_____

What was your least favorite fable and why?

_____

_____

_____

Which story did you think illustrated its moral the best?

_____

_____

_____

Which moral do you think is most important for people to learn?

_____

_____

_____

Which story do you think children would like best and why?

_____

_____

_____

Do you think fables are a good way to teach morals? Why or why not?

_____

_____

_____

Choose one fable. Summarize it and share the moral lesson.

_____
_____
_____

Questions about *Aesop's Fables*

Here are some of my questions about my chose fable from *Aesop's Fables*.

_____
_____
_____
_____
_____
_____

Here are other people's questions about *The Iliad*.

_____
_____
_____
_____
_____
_____

How is Aesop's Fable Theme Illustrated? Paper

Remember to choose a favorite fable from the book you read. The theme will be easy to discover because Mr. Aesop blurts it out. Write a paper about how he illustrates the theme.

My Thesis Statement

_____
_____
_____

Introduction

Your introduction will basically be introducing your thesis. Your introduction should capture your reader's attention and introduce the focus, or subject of your paper. You want to "hook" the reader so that he will keep on reading.

Here are some creative ways to introduce your paper.

- Summarize your book briefly with a "what" and "how" statement about your chosen fable.
- You can start your essay with a quote from the fable.
- You could open your essay by explaining Aesop's purpose and telling your audience how well you think he achieves that purpose.
- You might begin your essay with a few general statements about life that relate to the focus of your fable or the theme of the fable.
- Another way to introduce your essay is to make a general statement about the genre of literature (fables, folk tales) you are reading. "Fables make you stop and think."

Paragraphs

The paragraphs in the body of your paper will be proving your thesis using the examples and quotes you found in your favorite fable. Try to organize each paragraph around a specific idea or point to help your argument flow. Your thesis will guide the body of your paper.

In each paragraph, state the main point you are proving clearly and relate it to the thesis. Support this main point with quotes or details from the fable. Explain how the detail or quote proves your point.

Conclusion

Your conclusion should restate the thesis showing how the evidence you've used proved it. End in an interesting way by perhaps stating a new question or suggesting the value of understanding the book. Give your reader something to think about long after they finish reading your paper.

My Essay Outline

Introduction

My Hook

_____
_____
_____

My Thesis Statement

_____
_____
_____

First Paragraph/First Point from My Thesis Statement

_____
_____
_____

Example

_____
_____
_____

Example

_____
_____
_____

Illustration

_____
_____
_____

Second Paragraph/Second Point from My Thesis Statement

_____
_____
_____

Example

_____
_____
_____

Example

_____
_____
_____

Illustration

_____
_____
_____

Third Paragraph/Third Point from My Thesis Statement

_____
_____
_____

Example

_____
_____
_____

Example

_____
_____
_____

Illustration

_____
_____
_____

Fourth Point (you may not have a 4th point!)

_____
_____
_____

Examples

_____
_____
_____

Illustration

_____
_____
_____

Conclusion

Restate My Thesis Statement

_____
_____
_____

Call Reader to Action

_____
_____
_____

November: Greeks & Romans

Foundations of Western Literature

16 Aeneus' Flight from Troy, a painting by Federico Barocci

November Week One Class

☐ Book Club Discussion on *Aesop's Fables* (Answer Book Club Discussion Questions)

☐ Read "How is Aesop's Fable Theme Illustrated?" paper in groups & do Peer Reviews

☐ Read & Discuss "Background to *The AEneid* by Virgil"

☐ Read & Discuss "Background on *Rhetoric* by Aristotle"

Book Club Discussion on *Aesop's Fables*

Here are some questions to discuss about *Aesop's Fables*.

- What was your favorite fable and why?
- What was your least favorite fable and why?
- Which story did you think illustrated its moral the best?
- Which moral do you think is most important for people to learn?
- Which story do you think children would like best and why?
- Do you think fables are a good way to teach morals? Why or why not?

Read "How is Aesop's Fable Theme Illustrated?" Paper in Groups

You will read all your papers aloud to a partner or to a small group. This is very important and will help you to keep your audience in mind as you write. Your listener(s) might be a parent or sibling or fellow students in a co-op class.

Peer Review: "How is Aesop's Fable Theme Illustrated?" Paper

		Yes or No	Comments
Audience	This paper is about one fable.		
Thesis	Thesis is clearly stated about how Aesop illustrates his theme?		
Introductions	Introduction captures my attention and contains Thesis Statement		
Paragraphs	Each paragraph supports the thesis statement. Each paragraph is clear and easy-to-understand, makes a strong point and supports it with examples & illustrations from the fable chosen.		
Flow of Paper	Paragraphs and the sentences within those paragraphs flow into one another		
Grammar	Spelling/Grammar		

Background on *The Aeneid* by Virgil

The Aeneid is an epic poem written by Virgil, a Latin author, about twenty or thirty years before Jesus was born. It tells the story of AEneas, a Trojan survivor, who leads a group of Trojans to Italy to lay the foundation for Rome. AEneas, a moral Trojan in Homer's *Iliad* becomes the central character in Virgil's tale. Because we are studying the story, characters, and setting, rather than Ancient Greek poetry, you can read *The Aeneid for Children* if you prefer, a version the leaves out the sexual content of the original story.

The story begins with the Trojan Horse and sack of Troy, ending ten years of war between the Greeks and the Trojans. The displaced Trojans try to build a new city nearby, but the "gods" will that the Trojan survivors, led by AEneas, are to be part of the founding of the great nation of Rome. The story is a saga, an adventure tale of humans, "gods", and "goddesses" who battle it out in various locations around the Mediterranean Sea.

The Aeneid is an interesting story because it finds its back-story in the famous and popular epic poems of Homer. Though the Romans were mighty militarily, they were impressed by Greek culture. The Romans imitated their art, architecture, and literature. The Greek tales of the idol/gods and idol/goddesses were retold using Roman names.

But Virgil stands toe to toe with the Homer and other amazing Greek writers. He does for Rome what Homer did for Greece with his adventure tale, a literary masterpiece.

Characters In The Aeneid

Here are some of the characters in the Aeneid

AEneas

AEneas, a Trojan warrior who survives the destruction of Troy by the Greeks, leads Trojan survivors to settle in Italy where they lay the foundation of the Roman Empire. Before embarking on his adventure to the new land, he rescues his son and elderly father, but his wife is lost. Heartbroken, he searches for her desperately, but she "appears" to him as a ghost and encourages him to move on and fulfill his destiny. You see, somehow, AEneas, like many of the Greek heroes, is the offspring of a mortal, Anchises, and a goddess, Venus, the goddess of love and beauty

Dido

Queen Dido is the founder and ruler of Carthage on the coast of North Africa. Originally from Tyre, she is forced to flee when her husband is murdered by her brother. Dido falls in love with AEneas when his ship is blown off course during a storm and he washs ashore in Dido's realm

Turnus

Turnus, suitor of a Latin princess who is rejected by the King in favor of AEneas, does not respond well to the change in his fate. Choosing AEneas over Turnus unleashes a chain of events which culminates in a showdown between Turnus and AEneas

Ascanius

Ascanius is the son of AEneas and his first wife. He is brave and loyal to his father

Anchises

Anchises, AEneas's father, dies during the journey from Troy to Italy. After death, his "spirit" appears to Aeneas to show him the glory of Rome that awaits his descendants

Creusa

Creusa, AEneas's first wife, is killed as the family is fleeing Troy. She "appears" as a "spirit" telling AEneas that he will get a new wife in Italy

Latinus

King Latinus rules the Latins who live near the Tiber River. He welcomes AEneas into his kingdom and wants him to marry his daughter

Lavinia

Lavinia, daughter of King Latinus, was supposed to marry Turnus, but AEneas arrives on the scene, causing conflict between the two men and ultimately starting a war.

Pagan Deities in The Aeneid

Here are some of the pagan "gods" and "goddesses" in the Aeneid

Jupiter

Jupiter, son of Saturn, is the king of the idol/gods. When there is a disagreement between idol/gods and idol/goddesses, Jupiter's will prevails. He is identified with fate. In the Aeneid, Jupiter is controlled and levelheaded

Juno

Juno, sister and wife of Jupiter and daughter of Saturn, sets herself against AEneas in this story. As patron-goddess of Carthage, she knows that AEneas's Roman descendants will destroy Carthage, a Phoenician city-state

Saturn

Saturn, the father of the gods, was known as Chronos in Greek mythology. He was king of Olympus until his son Jupiter overthrew him

Venus

Venus, the goddess of love and mother of AEneas, is known as Aphrodite to the Greeks. She helps her son whenever Juno stirs up trouble for him

Neptune

Neptune, god of the sea, is known as Poseidon in Greek mythology

Mercury

Mercury, messenger god, was known as Hermes in Greek mythology. Other gods sent him to deliver messages to AEneas

Aeolus

Aeolus, the wind god, helped Juno cause trouble for AEeneas by creating bad weather

Cupid

Cupid, the god of desire and son of Venus, was known as Eros in Greek mythology. Cupid caused Dido to fall in love with AEneas

Allecto

Allecto, a Furie, was sent by Juno to get the Latin people angry enough at AEneas to declare war on the Trojans

Vulcan

Vulcan, god of fire and husband of Venus, is known as Hephaestus to the Greeks. Vulcan crafted a superior set of weapons for AEneas

Tiberinus

Tiberinus, river god of Tiber River, suggests to AEneas that he travel upriver to make allies of the Arcadians

Minerva

Minerva, the goddess who helped the Greeks conquer Troy, is known as Pallas Athena in Greek. She hates the Greeks because Trojan hero Paris calls Venus the most beautiful among the goddesses

Apollo

Apollo, god of the sun and son of Jupiter, helps the Trojans in their voyage when they stop at Delos, where Apollos was born

Background on *Rhetoric* by Aristotle

Aristotle, student of Plato, son of the Macedonian king's physician, and tutor of Alexander the Great, was a prolific writer, scientist, and philosopher. Part of Plato's Academy in Athens for almost twenty years, Aristotle wrote about animals, music, languages, government, politics, logic, ethics, physics, biology, and rhetoric. He wrote hundreds of books and influenced thinking in the Middle Ages. Thomas Aquinas was famous for trying to synchronize Scripture with Aristotle's teachings. In fact, it was some of Aristotle's teachings that kept science from progressing. Galileo's theories contradicted Aristotle's ideas, not the Bible's.

Soon, after his teacher Plato died, he was asked by the King of Macedon to tutor his son, Alexander. He was also appointed the head of the royal academy of Macedon. Aristotle also tutored Ptolemy and Cassander, who both became future kings. He encouraged Alexander to extend his kingdom to the east.

Aristotle studied formal logic. He wrote on rhetoric. His viewpoint is that rhetoric is the art of observing in any given situation, the "available means of persuasion." Aristotle believed that speakers should develop sound, convincing arguments. He believed there were three important elements to consider in delivering a strong, persuasive argument: yourself the speaker, the listener, and the subject.

Anytime you are trying to influence another person with your communication, it is rhetoric. You might be writing an ad, trying to get your parents to buy you a car, trying to get your sister to watch a movie you like, or trying to convince a young woman to not abort her baby. All of these situations require the use of rhetoric. Lawyers use rhetoric in the courtroom and children use rhetoric on the ball field.

Words you need to know to understand Aristotle's essay:

Syllogism
A logical argument that applies deductive reasoning to arrive at a conclusion based on two or more propositions

Logos
The actual content of a speech (or conversation from one speaker) and how it is organized. Is the argument clear, logical, and easy to understand?

Ethos
Elements of the speech reflecting character and perspective of speaker. Is speaker trustworthy and credible?

Pathos
The elements of a speech that refer to the audience's perspective and have the potential to influence the audience through their emotions, senses, or reasoning. Is the audience able to identify with the speaker?

Telos
The speaker's attitude or purpose in making the speech

Kairos
The parts of the speech that acknowledge and draw support from the setting, time, and place where the speech takes places

November Week One Home

- Read Crash Course in Ancient History: Rome
- Read *The AEneid for Boys & Girls* & Answer Book Club Discussion Questions
- Read *Rhetoric* by Aristotle"
- Complete "*Rhetoric* by Aristotle Assignment"
- Rewrite "How is Aesop's Fable Theme Illustrated?" Paper

Crash Course in Ancient History: Rome

Alexander the Great

17 Alexander the Great with his Horse by John Abbot public domain.

Alexander the Great was the king of Macedonia, a Greek city-state that began to conquer other Greek city-states. Alexander was a mighty soldier and amazing military commander. Ruling all of Greece was not enough for Alexander. He wanted to conquer the entire world. Growing up, Alexander loved to read Homer. Homer's tales of the Iliad and the Odyssey may have inspired Alexander to be a great military hero.

First, Alexander conquered all of Asia Minor (currently Turkey). Next, he defeated the Persian to conquer Syria, and moved on to Tyre. Alexander the Great went on to conquer Egypt, Babylonia, and the entire Persian Empire.

At this point, Alexander the Great had the largest empire in history. Before he could rule his vast empire, he died in 323 B.C. His empire was divided up between four of his generals.

He was tutored by Aristotle, a disciple of Socrates. Alexander was steeped in Greek culture, language, and philosophy. Everywhere he went, he spread Greek culture and language.

Now let's talk about Rome.

The Roman Republic

18 Ruins of the Coloseum in Rome, Italy March 2018

The king of Rome was overthrown in 509 B.C. and was replaced with a republican form of government.

Ancient Rome was a Republic from 509 B.C. to 45 B.C., ruled by elected senators who served for a limited amount of time. They had a constitution, a balance of power, and written laws. Though slaves had no rights, freemen could vote and have a say in their government.

The highest position in government was the consul. To limit the power of the consul, two consuls served at the same time.

During the Roman Republic centuries, Rome faced destruction when Hannibal invaded with his Carthage army by crossing the Alps on elephants. (The Second Punic War)

The Roman Empire

The Republic came to an abrupt end when Julius Caesar took over the Senate and made himself dictator for life, but was assassinated a year later. In 27 B.C. Caesar Augustus became the first Roman emperor. The Roman Republic was over and the mighty empire began to extend its kingdom.

Roman Engineering & Building

The Romans were amazing engineers and builders. They built thousands of miles of road, including 29 highways that connected important cities to Rome. That's why we still have the saying, "All roads lead to Rome." The roads were built with a hump causing water to flow to the edges.

Via is the Latin word for road. So, a road might be named Via Corinth, or Corinth Road.

The Romans constructed hundreds of bridges, built of stone and concrete, throughout the Roman Empire, many of which are still standing today. Arches made the bridges strong.

The Romans used domes and arches to create high ceilings with wide-open spaces.

People lived in Villas, or fancy houses with many rooms and courtyards. The greatest building project of the Romans was the Colosseum, a huge outdoor stadium that seated 50,000 people who came to watch gladiator games, mock battles, and plays.

Aqueducts were long channels built to carry water into cities for drinking water, baths, and sewers. Roman plumbing was very advanced.

Roman Numerals

We still use Roman numerals today, especially when writing outlines. Here is a list of numbers 1-10, Roman numeral style: I, II, III, IV, V, VI, VI, VII, VIII, IX, X

Here are some of the other important numbers

I = 1

V = 5

X = 10

L = 50

C = 100

D = 500

M = 1,000

Latin

The Latin language was the official language of the Roman Republic and Roman Empire. Because Latin remained an important intellectual language for centuries, many great works were written in Latin. Latin also developed into the Romance languages such as Spanish, French, Portuguese, and Italian.

Many words in English have Latin roots.

Roman Writers

We have access to many Ancient Roman works. **Virgil**, a poet, wrote *The Aeneid, The Eclogues*, and *The Georgics*. **Lucius Annaeus Seneca** wrote plays, essays, and letters. **Livy**, or Titus Livius, a Roman historian, wrote *History of Rome*. **Publius Cornelius Tacitus**, senator and historian, wrote *The Anals* and *The Histories*. **Pliny the Younger**, playwright and poet, is remembered for his letters which give us a glimpse of Roman life. **Petronius**, a courtier of Nero, wrote *Satyricon*, a novel, and other literature. **Marcus Aurelius**, Roman Emperor and Stoic, wrote *Meditations*, a favorite of the future Frederick the Great. **Titus Maccius Plautus**, a playwright, wrote comedies still enjoyed today.

Read *The Aeneid for Boys & Girls* by A.J. Church (Virgil)

I would encourage you to answer these questions about the story as you read. They are the questions you will be discussing in book club.

What virtues did the Romans esteem? How are they demonstrated in AEneas?

_____

_____

_____

Describe the idol/gods and idol/goddesses in this story. Is there anything admirable about them? What do they add to the story?

_____

_____

_____

What idol/goddess is upset with AEneas in the beginning of the book?

_____

_____

_____

Why does Laocoon fear the Greeks, even when they are bringing gifts?

_____

_____

_____

What did Laocoon suspect about the Trojan Horse? How do his suspicions affect how the reader views Laocoon?

_____

_____

_____

Who appears to AEneas in a vision warning him to flee the city?

_____

_____

_____

What does Juno propose to Venus relating to AEneas's future? How does this affect events in the story?

_____

_____

_____

What are Turnus and AEneas fighting over?

_____
_____
_____

In what ways does *The Aeneid* remind you of the *The Odyssey* and *The Iliad*?

_____
_____
_____

Rewrite How is Aesop's Fable Theme Illustrated? Paper

With the information from your peer review, rewrite your paper.

Optional: Play Logic Games

God is the Author of logic, but Aristotle popularized logic with the Greeks. Logic games are fun to play and give your brain a workout. Thanks, Aristotle.

Chess is a logic game. Look for logic games online to play or play chess.

Rhetoric by Aristotle Assignment

First, you will need to read Aristotle's essay. Then you will examine three advertisements on Youtube or television in light of Aristotle's thoughts on rhetoric. One needs to be a political commercial.

Fill in the chart based on the commercials. Be prepared to play your commercials in class, if needed.

Name of Commercial:	#1:	#2:	#3:
Speaker: Who is the Speaker?			
Argument: What is the argument?			
Audience: Who is the audience the ad is intending to reach?			
Logos: What is the message? Is the argument clear, logical, and easy to understand?			
Ethos: Is the speaker trustworthy and credible? Why or why not?			
Pathos: Is the audience able to identify with the speaker? Why or why not?			
Telos: What is the speaker's purpose?			
Kairos: How does the setting influence the argument?			

Grading Rubric: How is Aesop's Fable Theme Illustrated? Paper

With the input you received in group time, rewrite your plot evaluation paper, making corrections and adding any needed changes.

		Comments	Possible Points	Points
Audience	This paper is about one fable.		10/10	/10
Thesis	Thesis is clearly stated about how Aesop illustrates his theme?		20/20	/20
Introductions	Introduction captures my attention and contains Thesis Statement		10/10	/10
Paragraphs	Each paragraph supports the thesis statement. Each paragraph is clear and easy-to-understand, makes a strong point and supports it with examples & illustrations from the fable chosen.		30/30	/30
Flow of Paper	Paragraphs and the sentences within those paragraphs flow into one another		20/20	/20
Grammar	Spelling/Grammar		10/10	/10
Grade			100/100	/100

November Week Two Class

☐ Read & Discuss "Aristotle & Logic"

☐ Read "*Rhetoric* by Aristotle Assignment" Aloud & Correct Answers

☐ Read & Discuss "From *The AEneid* to Modern Culture " &s "Possible Questions on *The AEneid* "

☐ Turn in How Theme is Illustrated in Aesop's Fable Paper

☐ Optional: Play Logic Games

Aristotle & Logic

Aristotle, student of Plato and tutor of Alexander the Great, is called the Father of Formal Logic. Aristotle's logic revolved around the deduction (syllogism). Aristotle recognized deductive reasoning and inductive reasoning, but favored deductive reasoning. Conclusions follow deductive reasoning.

Aristotle saw scientific and mathematical knowledge as the goal of using logic. He advocated proofs, believing that science and mathematics were very logical.

Syllogism was his favorite form of logic. In a syllogism, the premise and conclusion fit together in such as way that if the premise is accepted as true, the conclusion is true as well. Here is his famous example.

Premises that are true:

All men are mortal

Socrates is a man

Conclusion:

Socrates is mortal.

Categorical statements were important to Aristotle too. He like to divide things into categories. Universal statements are statements about an entire category.

All drums are loud.

Particular statements give examples about at least one member of a category.

Some monkeys run fast.

You can look for a quick course in formal logic on YouTube.

Read Aristotle Assignment in Groups

Read your charts aloud to one another. You may want to play the ads too and see if everyone else agrees with your conclusions.

From *The AEneid* to Modern Culture

Trojan Horse

The Trojan Horse appears in Virgil's *AEneid*.

The Greeks pretended to abandon Troy, but left a large wooden horse outside the city with Greek soldiers inside. The Trojans took it inside their city and at night, the soldiers got out of the horse and opened the city gate. The Greek soldiers streamed in and trounced the Trojans.

In modern times, a Trojan horse would be any person, thing, or event, which seems beneficial, but is intended to bring harm.

In the computer world, a Trojan Horse is a computer program installed illegally in another software program to cause harm.

"Beware of Greeks Bearing Gifts"

"Beware of Greeks Bearing Gifts" is another phrase related to the Trojan Horse from *The Aeneid*. In other words, don't trust your enemies.

Possible Questions on *The AEneid*

Here are some questions you can ask when you read *The AEneid* by Homer. Discuss these questions and how you would take them and research/read the book to come to your own conclusions. You will not write a paper on the AEneid, but I want you to explore the possibilities of an analysis paper and see what you come up with.

Here are some questions you could ask about *The AEneid*:

- Why did the Trojans believe Simon the Greek instead of their priest Laocoon? Do we buy Simon's tale or know better? Why?
- What kind of role do secrets and deception play in the Trojan War (on both sides)? What do you think this reveals? What impression do we get from this of the Greeks?
- AEneas's mother is the goddess Venus. What role do the idol/gods play in this tale? Why is that important?
- The idol/gods destroyed Troy and selected AEneas and his family to escape. Why? What does it do to the plot and purpose of the tale that AEneas's wife is lost?

- How are the idol/gods characterized in this book? Why are their frequent sacrifices?
- How was Helenus already established when AEneas's crew reaches it? How did his treaty with her serve the writer's purpose?
- How and why is Rome "the first city in the world"?
- Why is Carthage in Africa part of this story?
- Why does everyone memorialize Troy and its loss?
- Page 39. Compare this work's view of Troy with the Bible's portrayal.
- Page 41. All the idol/gods seem bent on the founding of Rome as of chief good, except for Juno. Why? How does this serve the author's purpose?
- When Dido had come through and accomplished so much, why did she kill herself over AEneas's departure? What purpose in the narrative does this serve?
- Why does everywhere they go have a tie to Troy? Why was AEneas's father buried in Sicily?
- Page 45-46. Why are games, competition, their way of memorializing loved heroes? Competition and victory seem to mean so much more than compassion, mercy, and justice. What values of this culture does the chapter on games reveal?
- Why do the idol/gods lead the way in wrongdoing?
- Purpose of the Narrative: Why do the weak and fainthearted stay behind and only the strong and brave go? What does this say about Rome?
- Who was Brutus and why is a hero "freeing a city from tyrants"?
- Page 53. "It is the work of your children's children to rule the world." What does this mean?
- Page 54-55. What does it mean that the prophecy about eating their tables in hunger was fulfilled in a positive way?
- Page 56-58. Why would it be significant that non "Romans"—Latinus—are having prophecies about AEneas and Rome's greatness?
- What is the effect on the narrative's meaning and purpose that the cause of division between AEneas and Latinus is Juno's work? Blameshifting?
- Why is the river Tiber important symbolically?
- Why did help come from the Greeks? Does this suggest or imply anything?
- What purpose does the story of Hercules and Cacus serve, embedded as it is in the larger narrative?

Here are some conclusions, questions, and plans to research that we came up with together:

_____
_____
_____
_____
_____
_____
_____
_____
_____

Optional: Play Logic Games

God is the Author of logic, but Aristotle popularized logic with the Greeks. Logic games are fun to play and give your brain a workout. Thanks, Aristotle.

Chess is a logic game. Look for logic games online to play.

November Week Two Home

☐ Read "Crash Course in Ancient History: Jesus"

☐ Finish Reading *The AEneid for Boys & Girls* by A.J. Church (Virgil)

Crash Course in Ancient History: Jesus

Jesus Christ, the Messiah, the Anointed One

"In the beginning was the Word, and the Word was with God, and the Word was God. He was in the beginning with God. All things came into being through Him, and apart from Him nothing came into being that has come into being. In Him was life, and the life was the Light of men. The Light shines in the darkness, and the darkness did not comprehend it" (John 1:1-5 NASB).

From the beginning, before the earth was created, Jesus was God and was with God. Right after Rome became an empire, a miracle happened in one of the Roman provinces, in Bethlehem, near Jerusalem. It was the greatest event in history.

Jesus' Birth

Jesus Christ was born in Bethlehem over 2,000 years ago to a virgin named Mary. His real father was God Himself. What?! Yes, it's true. Jesus Christ is fully human and fully God. It is so hard to wrap your mind around it, isn't it? You see, Jesus is the Messiah that was promised to the Jewish people. He is God in the flesh, the hope of all mankind.

Jesus' birth was announced by an angel named Gabriel to a young virgin named Mary, who was engaged to a righteous man named Joseph. Mary was a little dazed, but grateful for God's choosing her to be the mother of the long-awaited Messiah. When Joseph found out Mary was pregnant, he wanted to divorce

19 Nativity of Jesus Christ by Govaert Flinck public domain.

her quietly, but God appeared to him in a dream so he took Mary as his wife. They traveled together to pay taxes in Bethlehem where Jesus was born in a stable because the city hotels were all full since everyone from the line of David was returning to Bethlehem to pay taxes.

Jesus' Life

20 Jesus at the Home of Mary & Martha by Harold Copping. public domain.

Jesus grew up as an obedient son to his parents, who were the perfect parents for the Son of God. He learned the trade of carpentry from His father. Jesus was able to provide for His brothers and sisters financially as a carpenter after Joseph died until His ministry began.

Jesus was led by His Father to be baptized by His cousin, John the Baptist. As He was coming out of the water, the Holy Spirit descended on Him in the form of a dove. God the Father spoke words of affirmation over His Son Jesus, "This is my beloved Son. In Him I am well-pleased."

Immediately following His baptism, the Holy Spirit led Jesus out to the desert to fast for forty days and forty nights. After these forty days, Satan tempted Him. But Jesus refuted each temptation with Scripture.

One of Jesus' first miracles was at a wedding in Cana where He turned water into wine when the host ran out of wine before the party was over. But, most of Jesus' early ministry was preaching and teaching in the synagogues across Israel. Wherever He went, Jesus taught people about the Lord and how to live a righteous life. He spoke with love and authority.

Jesus also told many stories to help people understand what He was teaching. He made complex truths simple. He told jokes in the midst of His sermons and was a favorite of the children.

Miracles happened wherever Jesus went. People came to him with deformities, blindness, deafness, leprosy, and seizures. Jesus healed them all. What excitement surrounded His every move! Some of the people who had been healed followed Him as He traveled around Israel preaching the Good News of the Kingdom of God.

Demonized men and women were delivered from their bondage when Jesus and His disciples cast out demons. Yes, Jesus had disciples, or students, who traveled with Him. They learned from Him, watched Him, and were sent out by Him on trial runs to preach repentance and the Kingdom of God.

Jesus had many close friends, including Mary, Martha, and Lazarus. Near the end of His life, Jesus' friend Lazarus died from a sickness. When Jesus finally arrived at his house, He raised Lazarus from the dead! Wow! How exciting it was for His friends!

Many more miracles took place. Jesus walked on water. He fed huge crowds of people. He stilled storms. Most of all, Jesus healed broken hearts and broken lives. Wherever He went, there was transformation. Jesus turned the nation of Israel upside-down. However, things took a turn after three years of ministry.

Jesus' Death & Resurrection

21 Jesus Resurrection Tapestry in Vatican Gallery March 2018.

Jesus celebrated the Passover with His disciples. He washed their feet and told them to celebrate Communion in the future to remember His death and resurrection.

After dinner and a time of worship, Jesus and His disciples went to the Garden of Gethsemane. He prayed for every one of His believers, present and future. He prayed for you and me! Then, He cried out to God in agony about His upcoming Heavenly Assignment. You see, Jesus had come to earth on a Mission. His mission was a rescue operation. He would take the weight of the world's sin on Himself and die on the cross to redeem mankind.

The events that followed were full of terror and torture. Jesus was arrested, endured a trial that was a mockery, and was sentenced to death. He had to carry his own cross to the place of crucifixion after being beaten with whips.

On the cross, He forgave His murderers, asked John to take care of His mother, and declared, "It is finished!" He paid the price of the world's sin. He was the Perfect Sacrifice, the Lamb that was slain. His followers took the body, prepared it for burial, and buried Jesus in a large tomb. Roman guards were stationed at the tomb to stop anything weird from happening. But, God was not finished yet!

Early Sunday morning, the stone was rolled away, and Jesus came out of the tomb! Jesus had risen from the dead! Jesus conquered death and sin for you and me! After His resurrection, Jesus spent several weeks with His disciples, getting them ready for His final departure. He ascended right up into the sky to Heaven and was gone! But, very soon, God poured out His Holy Spirit on the 120 believers who were praying and fasting in the Upper Room in Jerusalem. Then the work of His Glorious Church began and continues to this day. Jesus was with His disciples through the Holy Spirit. His work continued on by the power of the Holy Spirit.

Jesus, our King

Jesus is our King. The Bible calls Him the King of Kings. Jesus does all things well including running the universe and running our lives. Jesus is worshipped by angels, nature, and people He has rescued sinners and turned them into saints. His Kingdom is eternal. It will last forever. A million years from now we will still be worshipping our King Jesus!

Jesus, the Law Giver and Fulfiller

Jesus Fulfilled the Law. He is our Righteousness. What does that mean? Jesus obeyed every single command in Scripture perfectly. He never slacked off. He never compromised. In this way, He was able to be the Perfect Sacrifice. By meeting the righteous requirements of the law, Jesus fulfilled the Law.

When Jesus taught about the Law, he took it to a higher plane. He revealed true virtue, rather than just legalistic adherence to a bunch of rules. Jesus taught us that God is looking at our hearts. When Jesus changes our hearts, we will want to do what is right, fulfilling the Old Testament promise that God would write His Word on our hearts.

Jesus, our Judge

One day every knee will bow and every tongue confess that Jesus is Lord to the glory of God the Father we are told in Philippians chapter two in *The Holy Bible*. Everyone will acknowledge that Jesus is Lord, that no one is higher.

Jesus will also judge the living and the dead. Every person will stand before Jesus as his, or her, judge.

Jesus Loves You!

You, dear friend, were the joy set before Jesus when He endured the cross. He died so that your sins could be forgiven and wiped away if you repent and believe. Jesus had an unique heavenly assignment for you. He stands at the door and knocks. Don't miss out knowing the One who loves you best! Jesus is the Alpha and Omega, the Bright Morning Star, the Everlasting Father, Mighty God, our Good Shepherd, and the Risen Lamb. Get to know Him and you will experience the true joy in life!

"Behold, I stand at the door and knock; if anyone hears My voice and opens the door, I will come in to him and will dine with him and he with Me," Revelation 3:20 NASB).

Jesus' Twelve Apostles

Jesus chose twelve men that he worked with very closely, preparing them to take His Good News to the ends of the earth: Andrew, Nathaniel, John, James brother of John, James, Judas, Thaddeus, Matthew, Simon Peter, Philip, Simon the Zealot, and Thomas. Except for Judas who betrayed Jesus and committed suicide, the disciples received the Great Commission in Galilee and watched Jesus ascend into Heaven. They waited in Jerusalem for the promised Holy Spirit and spent their lives sharing the Gospel.

Jesus' brother James became a leader in the church. Paul, a former persecutor of Christians, was radically converted and traveled the rest of his life to preach the Good News. The Gospel spread around Asia, into Africa, and all the way to Europe. Local churches were established everywhere that people got saved.

According to tradition, this is how the other eleven apostle died. James was the first apostle martyred. The other James was sawn in pieces. Andrew was crucified and Peter was crucified upside-down. Thaddeus was killed with arrows. Simon was martyred. Thomas was killed with a spear. Nathanael was flayed alive with knives. Philip was hung. Matthew was martyred in Ethiopia. John was the only one who died of natural causes.

Matthew, Mark, Luke, & John Write about Jesus

After 400 years of silence, God was writing His Book again. This time He inspired four very different men (a young fisherman, an older fisherman, a doctor who traveled with Paul, and a young man who traveled with Barnabus and was close to the Apostle Peter. They wrote about the birth, life, death, and resurrection of Jesus. The Gospels are filled with miracles, teaching, parables, and adventures.

John & Polycarp

For over thirty years, Apostle John ministered in Ephesus. Afterward, he was exiled to Patmos. He discipled Polycarp, who accepted Christ as a young child, and ordained him as Bishop of Smyrna. For 86 years, Polycarp served the Lord until he was arrested and threatened with death unless he renounced Christ. He refused to dishonor Christ and was burned to death. Polycarp was a teacher of Truth and helped to lay the foundation of the early Church.

Apostolic Fathers

Along with Polycarp, Clement of Rome and Ignatius of Antioch are considered Apostolic Fathers of the Church. Bishop of Rome, Clement is considered the first Pope by the Roman Catholic Church. He was consecrated as the fourth Bishop of Rome. Ignatius accepted Christ as a young boy and, along with Polycarp, was a disciple of John. Tradition says that he was one of the children that Jesus blessed. Ignatius was martyred by wild beasts. All three of the Apostolic Fathers wrote many letters to the churches, in the tradition of Paul, John, and Peter.

Eusebius

Eusebius, Bishop of Caesarea (260-340) and Father of Church History, wrote a chronological account of church history from the first century to the fourth century. He shares information about church leaders, battling heresies, Jewish history, martyrdoms, and treatment of the Church by the world. His book is divided up by according to the reigns of different emperors, except for the first section on Jesus Christ.

Finish Reading *The Aeneid for Boys & Girls* by A.J. Church (Virgil)

Finish reading *The Aeneid* by Virgil.

November Week Three Class

☐ Book Club Discussion on *The AEneid* using Book Club Discussion Questions

☐ Read & Discuss "Background on the Gospel of Matthew"

☐ Read & Discuss "Prodigal Son Theme in Literature"

☐ Brainstorm Thesis Ideas

Book Club Discussion on *The Aeneid*

Here are some questions to discuss about *The AEneid*.

- What virtues did the Romans esteem? How are these virtues demonstrated in AEneas?
- Describe the idol/gods and idol/goddesses in this story. Is there anything admirable about them? What do they add to the story?
- What idol/goddess is upset with AEneas in the beginning of the book?
- Why does Laocoon fear the Greeks, even when they are bringing gifts?
- What did Laocoon suspect about the Trojan Horse? How do his suspicions affect how the reader views Laocoon?
- Who appears to AEneas in a vision warning him to flee the city?
- What does Juno propose to Venus relating to AEneas's future? How does this affect events in the story?
- What are Turnus and AEneas fighting over?
- In what ways does *The Aeneid* remind you of the *The Odyssey* and *The Iliad*?

Background on Gospel of Mathew

The first book in the New Testament was written by Matthew, a former tax collector whose life was transformed by Jesus Christ. Matthew followed Jesus and was an eyewitness to the events in the *Gospel According To Matthew*.

Christians over the centuries have enjoyed reading this Gospel, making it a favorite and often quoted book. Containing the Beatitudes, the Sermon on the Mount, and the Great Commission, the verses in Matthew have helped to lay the foundation of the thriving Church of Jesus Christ.

This Gospel is written to a strongly Hebrew audience. In light of this, Matthew stresses that Jesus is the Christ, or Anointed One. He also begins the Gospel with a carefully documented genealogy, Like Luke, Matthew talks about the birth of Jesus, calling of the first disciples, ministry, miracles, parables, death, resurrection, and ascension.

FOUNDATIONS OF WESTERN LITERATURE

Prodigal Son Story

In the story Jesus told of the Prodigal Son, the focus is on the love of the Father for his foolish, rebellious child. A young man asks for his inheritance and spends it all on sinful living ending up in a pigpen eating pig slop. When the man comes to his senses, he decides to go back to the Father, repent, and ask to be treated as a servant. The father, who sees him from a long way off, throws off his dignity, and runs to his son, taking him in his arms, forgiving him, and throwing him a party.

Prodigal Son Theme in Literature

The Prodigal Son theme is a popular one in modern literature. What is the theme of Jesus' parable of the Prodigal Son? Everyone share what they think it is.

Here are some books with a Prodigal Son theme.

Heidi Grows Up by Charles Tritten

Great Expectations by Charles Dickens

David Copperfield by Charles Dickens

The Lion, the Witch, and the Wardrobe by C.S. Lewis

The Robe by Lloyd C. Douglas

The Ultimate Gift

Iron Man

The Prodigal (Billy Graham Ministries 1983 movie)

Madagascar: Escape 2 Africa

The Lion King

Wayward: The Prodigal Son

A Christmas Carol

Brainstorm Thesis Ideas

Think of some ideas for a thesis for the "God's Love in the Prodigal Son" essay. Write the ideas you like here.

_____

_____

_____

_____

_____

_____

November Week Three & Four Home

☐ Write Thesis Statement & Outline for "How God's Love is Portrayed in Prodigal Son"

☐ Write "How God's Love is Portrayed in Prodigal Son"

☐ Read Gospel of Matthew chapters 1-20 and Fill Out Chart

How God's Love is Portrayed in Prodigal Son Paper

Many people in our culture are used to the Prodigal Son theme in books and movies, but because it is often tweaked and twisted, most men and women do not understand God's love.

You will write an essay on how God's love is portrayed through the Parable of the Prodigal Son. Maybe when you are done with your essay, you can pass it on to someone who struggles to understand and receive God's love.

My Thesis Statement

_____

_____

_____

_____

My Essay Outline

Introduction

My Hook

_____

_____

_____

My Thesis Statement

_____

_____

_____

First Paragraph/First Point from My Thesis Statement

_____

_____

_____

Example

_____

_____

_____

Example

_____

_____

_____

Illustration

_____

_____

_____

Second Paragraph/Second Point from My Thesis Statement

_____

_____

_____

Example

_____

_____

_____

Example

_____

_____

_____

Illustration

_____

_____

_____

Third Paragraph/Third Point from My Thesis Statement

_____

_____

_____

Example

_____

_____

_____

Example

_____

_____

_____

Illustration

_____

_____

_____

Fourth Point (you may not have a 4th point!)

_____

_____

_____

Examples & Illustrations

_____

_____

_____

Conclusion

Restate My Thesis Statement

_____

_____

_____

Call Reader to Action

_____

_____

_____

Read Gospel of Matthew

You will read the *Gospel of Matthew* chapters one through twenty. Please fill out the chart after you read each chapter.

You will look for messages in each chapter. You only have to share one message per chapter and how that message was communicated. For example, you might share Jesus calming the storm as the story, miracle, or event with the message being that God controls nature.

Chapter in Matthew	Event, Miracle, Story, or Teaching	Message
Matthew 1		
Matthew 2		
Matthew 3		
Matthew 4		
Matthew 5		
Matthew 6		

Chapter in Matthew	Event, Miracle, Story, or Teaching	Message
Matthew 7		
Matthew 8		
Matthew 9		
Matthew 10		
Matthew 11		
Matthew 12		
Matthew 13		

Chapter in Matthew	Event, Miracle, Story, or Teaching	Message
Matthew 14		
Matthew 15		
Matthew 16		
Matthew 17		
Matthew 18		
Matthew 19		
Matthew 20		

December: Symbols & Images

Foundations of Western Literature

22 Jesus Calls His Disciples

December Week One Class

☐ Book Club Discussion on *The Gospel of Matthew* with Book Club Discussion Questions

☐ Read & Discuss "Gospel Themes in Literature"

☐ Read & Discuss "Symbolism & Imagery in Literature"

☐ Read & Discuss "Background to Sower & the Seed" & "Sower & the Seed Project"

☐ Read Prodigal Son Papers in Groups & Complete Peer Reviews

Book Club Discussion on *The Gospel of Matthew* chapters 1-20

Here are some questions to discuss about *The Gospel of Matthew*.

- Share a parable, summarize it, and explain the message.
- Share one miracle, summarize how it happened, and explain the message.
- Share one situation, conversation, or event, summarize what occurred, and explain the message.

Gospel Themes in Literature

Last week we saw how the story of the Prodigal Son has found its way into Western Literature. You will see many other Gospel themes in modern literature. One of the most common is giving one's life in place of another, to rescue them from death. Charles Dickins uses this theme beautifully in *A Tale of Two Cities*.

The "Christ figure" in literature is a hero who displays kindness, forgiveness, justice, or mercy. He may be guided by his father. Ultimately, he will give his life for a cause larger than himself. The "Christ figure" may experience a resurrection or he may just be a martyr.

Just because a movie uses the Christ figure doesn't mean it is a Christian movie or gives a true representation of Christ.

Here are some books and movies that have a "Christ figure"

Chronicles of Narnia by C.S. Lewis (Aslan)

Tale of Two Cities by Charles Dickens (Sydney Carton)

Uncle Tom's Cabin by Harriet Beecher Stowe (Uncle Tom)

The Lord of the Rings by J.R.R. Tolkien (Aragon, Gandalf, and Frodo in different ways)

The Matrix Trilogy (Neo)

Superman, the Movie and *Superman Returns* (Superman)

The Terminator (John Connor)

Star Trek II: The Wrath of Khan (Spock)

Robo Cop (Alex J. Murphy)

Symbolism & Imagery in Literature

Sometimes writers use symbols in their writing. A red rose might symbolize love or a snake symbolize evil. You might be reading a story about a girl who is walking home from school when a snake slithers across her path. The author is using the snake as a symbol of evil to foreshadow something terrible happening to the girl.

Common Symbols in literature:

Snake = evil or temptation

Dove = purity, peace

Light = truth, holiness

Darkness = sin, lies

Red Rose = love

Imagery

Imagery is the use of vivid and descriptive language to create a picture in the reader's mind. Rain coming down in sheets, bacon popping and crackling in the frying pan, and the smiling brook tripping over stones on its way to the sea are all phrases that provoke an image in your mind.

Imagery can be created with similes, metaphors, and hyperbole.

A simile compares two things using the words 'like' or 'as'.

> My love is like a red, red rose.

> The snow is like a blanket of white.

> She is as innocent as a dove.

A metaphor compares two things without the use of 'like' or 'as'.

> My love is a red, red rose.

> The snow was a blanket of white.

> She is an innocent dove.

Now, of course, love isn't a red rose, snow isn't a blanket, and a lady isn't a dove, but each of these comparisons creates an image in your mind that enhances your understanding of what the author is trying to communicate.

Hyperbole is obvious exaggeration. My suitcase weighs a ton. She's as fat as a whale. This cold is killing me.

Symbolism, imagery, and hyperbole are all used in Scripture.

Symbols in Scripture

Here are some symbols used in Scripture.

Rainbow = God's Covenant (Genesis 9:13, Ezekiel 1:28, Revelation 4:3)

Fire = Holy Spirit (Acts 2:3)

Signet Ring = Authority (Esther 8:10, Haggai 2:23)

Capstone = Pre-eminence (Psalm 118:22, Matthew 21:42, Mark 12:10-11, Luke 20: 17)

Serpent = Satan (Genesis 3:1, Numbers 21:6, Isaiah 14:29, Revelation 12:9, Revelation 20: 1-3)

Lamb = Jesus Christ's Sacrifice (Revelation 5:6)

Dove = Holy Spirit (Matthew 3:16, Mark 1:10, Luke 3:22)

Baptism = Salvation in Jesus Christ (Acts 22:16, Romans 6:33-4, I Peter 3:21)

Cedars of Lebanon = Strength, Stature, or Pride (Judges 9:15, II Kings 19:23, Psalm 29:5, Psalm 72:16, Psalm 104:16, Song of Solomon 5:15, Isaiah 2:13, Isaiah 37:24, Zechariah 11:1)

Sheep = Followers of God (Psalm 23:1, Psalm 95:7, Isaiah 53:6-7, Jeremiah 23:1, Ezekiel 34:11, Matthew 9:36, John 10:11)

Jesus used lots of symbolism in his teaching. He referred to Himself as a Shepherd, Sower, Bridegroom, Door, Cornerstone, Vine, Light, Bread, and Living Water.

Hyperbole in Scripture

Here are some passages that use hyperbole to make a point.

"You blind guides! You strain out a gnat and swallow a camel" (Matthew 23:24)

"If your right eye makes you stumble, tear it out and throw it from you" (Matthew 5:29 NASB).

Background on "The Sower and His Seed"

You will read one of the parables that Jesus told to the crowds and explained privately to His disciples. "The Sower and His Seed" is rich in symbolism and imagery.

The people that Jesus was teaching were familiar with sowing seed, farming, and gardening. They understood that you need the right kind of soil to get a crop.

As a group, decide what the following symbols represent in the story. Write everything on the white board.

- Sower
- Seed
- Beside the Road (Pathway)
- Rocky Places
- Thorns
- Good Soil
- Crop

"The Sower and His Seed" Project

This story is very familiar to Christians. Now, we have uncovered all the symbolism. Our assignment this week is going to tell the same story with the same message/theme using different symbols. Brainstorm together some ideas to replace the symbols.

Here are some ideas to get you started.

- Boats (row boat, paddleboat, sailboat, cruise ship)
- Transportation (motorcycle, convertible, minivan, truck)
- Cell Phone Coverage
- Cell Phone Plans
- Football Teams
- Olympic Competitions
- Animals
- Batteries
- Homes

Choose one of these ideas or come up with your own to write your brand new version of "The Sower and the Seed."

Read Prodigal Son Essays in Groups

You will read all your papers aloud to a partner or to a small group. This will help you to keep your audience in mind as you write. Your listener might be a parent or sibling or fellow students in a co-op class.

Fill out Peer Review for an essay and have someone fill out one for you.

Peer Review: "How God's Love is Portrayed in The Prodigal Son" Paper

		Yes or No	Comments
Audience	Paper explains God's love in an interesting & enjoyable way		
Thesis	Thesis is clearly stated and **mentions the Prodigal Son**		
Introductions	Introduction captures my attention and contains Thesis Statement		
Paragraphs	Each paragraph supports the thesis statement. Each paragraph is clear and easy-to-understand, makes a strong point and supports it with examples & illustrations from "The Prodigal Son""		
Flow of Paper	Paragraphs and the sentences within those paragraphs flow into one another		
Grammar	Spelling/Grammar		

December Week One Home

☐ Rewrite Prodigal Son Paper

☐ Write Up Sower & His Seed Project

☐ Read Gospel of Matthew & Fill Out Chart

Rewrite "How God's Love is Portrayed In The Prodigal Son" Paper

With the information from your peer review, rewrite your paper.

Write Up "The Sower and His Seed" Project

We have uncovered all the symbolism and brainstormed some replacement symbols. Choose one of these ideas or choose a new one and write a brand new version of "The Sower and the Seed."

Write down your news symbols below.

Sower _____

Seed _____

Beside the Road (Pathway) _____

Rocky Places _____

Thorns _____

Good Soil _____

Crop _____

My idea for the story is _____
_____
_____
_____

Read *Gospel of Matthew*

You will read the *Gospel of Matthew* chapters twenty-one through twenty-eight. Please fill out the chart after you read each chapter.

Chapter in Matthew	Event, Miracle, Story, or Teaching	Message
Matthew 21		
Matthew 22		
Matthew 23		
Matthew 24		
Matthew 25		
Matthew 26		

Chapter in Matthew	Event, Miracle, Story, or Teaching	Message
Matthew 27		
Matthew 28		

Grading Rubric for "How God's Love is Portrayed in The Prodigal Son" Paper

With the input you received in group time, rewrite your plot evaluation paper, making corrections and adding any needed changes.

		Comments	Possible Points	Points
Audience	Paper explains God's love in an interesting & enjoyable way		10/10	/10
Thesis	Thesis is clearly stated and **mentions the Prodigal Son**		20/20	/20
Introductions	Introduction captures my attention and contains Thesis Statement		10/10	/10
Paragraphs	Each paragraph supports the thesis statement. Each paragraph is clear and easy-to-understand, makes a strong point and supports it with examples & illustrations from "The Prodigal Son""		30/30	/30
Flow of Paper	Paragraphs and the sentences within those paragraphs flow into one another		20/20	/20
Grammar	Spelling/Grammar		10/10	/10
Grade			100/100	100/100

December Week Two Class

☐ Book Club Discussion on *The Gospel of Matthew* using Discuss Questions

☐ Discuss Your New Symbols for "Sower and the Seed Project" in Groups

☐ Discuss Story Ideas for Your "Sower and the Seed Project"/Give & Get Feedback.

☐ Turn in "How God's Love is Portrayed in the Prodigal Son"

Book Club Discussion on *The Gospel of Matthew*

Here are some questions to discuss about *The Gospel of Matthew*.

- Share a parable, summarize it, and explain the message.
- Share one miracle, summarize how it happened, and explain the message.
- Share one situation, conversation, or event, summarize what occurred, and explain the message.

Read "Sower and His Seed" Project in Groups

You will read your new symbols aloud to a partner or to a small group. This will help you to keep your audience in mind as you plan your story. Your listener might be a parent or sibling or fellow students in a co-op class.

Share your story ideas, too. Give and get feedback from one another. This will make your writing easier this coming week.

December Week Two Home

☐ Write "Sower and His Seed" Project Story

☐ Start Reading *Pllutarch's Lives*

Write "Sower & His Seed" Project Story

You have your symbols to replace those symbols in The Sower and His Seed parable. You will retell the Sower and His Seed with your new symbols and story ideas. Have fun!

Grading Rubric for "Sower & His Seed" Paper

With the input you received in group time, rewrite your plot evaluation paper, making corrections and adding any needed changes.

		Comments	Possible Points	Points
Audience	Story is interesting & enjoyable to read		15/15	/15
Thesis	The Story follows along the same plot line as "The Sower and His Seed"		30/30	/30
Paragraphs	The symbols are clear and easy to see. You can match each symbol to the seed, the sower, the pathway, etc. The message of the story lines up with the message of Jesus' Parable "The Sower and His Seed"		30/30	/30
Flow of Paper	Paragraphs and the sentences within those paragraphs flow into one another		20/20	/20
Grammar	Spelling/Grammar		15/15	/15
Grade			100/100	100/100

December Week Three Class

☐ Read & Discuss "Background on *Plutarch's Lives*"

☐ Discuss Parallel Lives & Why the Combinations were Chosen of Greek & Roman

☐ Brainstorm some Parallel Lives, Lives that Fit Together because of Character

☐ Come Up with Questions to Ask Yourself as You Read *Plutarch's Lives*

☐ Turn in "Sower and His Seed" Paper

Background on *Plutarch's Lives*

The son of Aristobulus, a writer and philosopher, Plutarch was a disciple of Ammonius. He studied mathematics and physics under Ammonius at the Academy of Athens. Born a few years after Christ's death and resurrection, in A.D. 46 in Chaeronea, Greece, he was a historian and biographer. His most famous work in our time is *Lives*, a compilation of biographies arranged in pairs.

Born into a wealthy family, he married Timoxena, had several children, and enjoyed a comfortable life. Plutarch lived a life of public service. He served in his city as a chief magistrate, occasionally took on the role of ambassador visiting foreign cities, ran a school of philosophy in his home town that had relational ties to the Academy of Athens, and served as a priest of Apollo at the Oracle of Delphi. By this time, Rome was an empire and he eventually became a Roman citizen.

Plutarch, estimated to have written between 200 and 300 books, was quite popular with readers. His home was bustling with visitors. Many of his books inspired moral living with titles such as *The Art of Listening*, *Checking Anger*, and *Advice to the Bride and Groom*.

Lives was written to honor his own Greek culture, as well as the Roman culture of the Empire he was a part of. Each Greek biography was paired with a Roman biography. Plutarch highlighted both virtues and vices, focusing more on noble character, or lack of it, than on historical events.

Here are the biography pairs.

Greek	Roman
Alcibiades	Coriolanus
Alexander	Caesar
Aratus & Artaxerxes	Galba & Otho
Aristides	Cato the Elder
Nicias	Crassus
Demetriius	Antony
Demosthenes	Cicero

Dio	Brutus
Pericles	Fabius Maximus
Cimon	Lucullus
Lysander	Sulla
Lycurgus	Numa
Pelopidas	Marcellus
Philopoemen	Flamininus
Phocion	Cato the Younger
Agesilaus	Pompey
Solon	Publicola
Pyrrhus	Marius
Theseus	Romulus
Eumenes	Sertorius
Agis	Tiberius Gracchus
Cleomenes	Gaius Gracchus
Timoleon	Paullus
Themistocles	Camillus

Parallel Lives Brainstorming

I wonder what Plutarch was thinking when he chose the people he did to write biographies on. He was not trying to write a history, he was making a moral statement with each biography. He focused on their virtues and vices, sharing anecdotes and incidents revealing his subjects' character. He even compared the physical appearance of his subjects to their virtues and vices.

Discuss lives that go together because of talents.

For example, Jenny Rose sings beautifully just like Kari Jobe. Or my Laura is creative on her computer just like Bill Gates. Or Hosanna can paint just like Thomas Kinkade.

List some combinations you come up with in your group:

_____   _____

_____   _____

_____   _____

Questions for Plutarch's Lives

It's time for everyone to brainstorm together. What questions could you ask about each pair of Plutarch's biographies? Here are some questions you will answer in book club. Can you think of other questions?

Why do you think Plutarch chose these two people to pair up?

What is similar about these two men?

What differences can you point out about the men?

Did any of these men improve a Greek city-state? If so, how?

Did any of these men improve Rome? If so, how?

Here are some more questions we came up with:

_____
_____
_____
_____
_____
_____
_____
_____

December Week Three & Four Home

Read *Plutarch's Lives* and Answer Book Club Discussion Questions as you Read

Read "How to Write Parallel Lives Biographies"

Brainstorm and Answer Questions from "How to Write Parallel Lives Biographies"

Start Writing Parallel Lives Biographies

Read *Plutarch's Lives* by Plutarch

I would encourage you to answer these questions about the story as you read. They are the questions you will be discussing in book club. Choose a pair of biographies from *Lives*.

Why do you think Plutarch chose these two people to pair up?

_____
_____
_____
_____
_____

What is similar about these two men?

_____
_____
_____
_____
_____

What differences can you point out about the men?

_____
_____
_____
_____
_____

Did any of these men improve a Greek city-state? If so, how?

_____
_____
_____
_____
_____

Did any of these men improve Rome? If so, how?

_____
_____
_____
_____
_____

How to Write Parallel Lives Biographies

First, you will need to read at least half of *Plutarch's Lives* before you start your own Parallel Lives. Choose a person you know personally and a famous person you do not know that has virtues similar to your friend/acquaintance. Let's not focus on vices—it's so negative.

You will need to narrow down the biography to focus on the virtues you want to highlights. Share life events and anecdotes that highlight these virtues.

You can start working on your Parallel Lives biographies now.

My famous person is _____

Here are some things I already know about this person

_____
_____
_____
_____
_____
_____
_____

Here are some things I would like to find out about this person:

_____
_____
_____
_____
_____
_____
_____

Here are some stories I can use in my paper::

_____
_____
_____
_____
_____
_____
_____

The person I know is _____

Here are some things I already know about this person

_____
_____
_____
_____
_____
_____
_____

Here are some things I would like to find out about this person:

_____
_____
_____
_____
_____
_____
_____
_____

The character traits (virtues) I would like to focus on are:

_____
_____
_____
_____
_____
_____
_____
_____
_____

Here are some stories I can use in my paper::

_____
_____
_____
_____
_____
_____
_____
_____
_____
_____
_____
_____
_____

January: Parallel Lives

Foundations of Western Literature

23 A Portrait of the Evangelist, a Radoslav's Gospel Miniatures

January Week One Class

☐ Read & Discuss "Narrowing Down the Focus of a Biography"

☐ Read & Discuss "Pay Attention to Sources"

☐ Brainstorm Parallel Lives Combinations

Narrowing Down the Focus of a Biography

How can you capture the essence and all the information about a person in a short book, or biography? It seems impossible.

Most biographies don't try to share everything. They focus on a certain aspect of the person's life or character. I read a biography on Winston Churchill that focused on his leadership abilities. The parts of his life that illustrated the author's beliefs about Churchill's leadership were included. If the focus of the biography was his relationships, the book would have been written differently.

What are you focusing on in your biography?

Think about the virtue you chose. You want to focus on things that exemplify that virtue. Don't try to cover more than you need to. Highlight the most important things. And remember, the two biographies need to parallel one another.

Plutarch's Biographies

Plutarch was very purposeful in his writing. He did not share all that he knew about the person's lives. He shared what was important to prove his point. Remember he focused on the virtues and vices.

Reminder about Parallel Lives Biographies

We have been working on our Parallel Lives assignment. Take time to share concerns, problems, and successes you are having on the assignment. This might be the first time you have written a biography, so be sure to get and give input.

Brainstorm in Groups

Share your ideas for the parallel assignment with your family and friends.

Parallel Lives Brainstorming

We have already talked about Plutarch and how he wrote his biographies in combinations, or parallels. He is not here to tell us exactly why he chose the combinations he did, but we can make logical assumptions as we read and study his work. Remember, he was not trying to write a history, he was making a moral statement with each biography. He focused on their virtues and vices, sharing anecdotes and incidents revealing his subjects' character. He even compared the physical appearance of his subjects to their virtues and vices.

Last class we brainstormed about combinations based on talents. How about this week we brainstorm combinations based on character traits, virtues or vices.

Discuss lives that go together because of a character trait.

For example, my Aunt Mimi is funny just like Robin Williams. Or my friend Sam likes everything to be in its proper place just like Detective Monk. Or my daughter Julianna is generous just like John Rockefeller.

List some combinations you come up with in your group:

_____	_____
_____	_____
_____	_____
_____	_____
_____	_____

You should have already started your Parallel Lives biographies, but this should help you to tweak and finish your biographies with the right focus. Don't forget to include lots of stories.

Pay Attention to Sources

Finding Sources for Your Paper

When you are writing about people you know personally, you have your own opinion and experience with the person, but you will want to expand your research to include more sources of information. If I were writing about one of my daughters, I would use my own observations, but I would also interview my daughter, her siblings, father, co-workers, and friends. This would give me a more balanced view to write about.

Since your biography should "show" more than "tell", sources will be an important way to gather stories and illustrations that "show" the character trait in your parallel biography assignment.

When you write about people you don't know, you will need sources.

Primary Sources are the best way to find out about the person you are writing about. Primary sources can be autobiographies, autobiographical articles, interviews. If you are using someone famous as the person you don't know, it will probably next to impossible to interview them, so instead, watch interviews of them on TV or read interviews in magazines and books.

Secondary Sources are another option. You can talk to someone who knows them or read a book written by someone who knows them.

Quoting Sources

You will want to give credit to your sources in your paper.

If you are using an exact quote, you will need to use quotation marks, as well as a footnote or parenthetical reference. If it is a paraphrase or just an idea that you found and expanded upon you will just need a footnote or parenthetical reference, or in-text.

 You can use footnotes (easy to do on Word® from Microsoft® or you can credit your sources using parenthetical reference, or in-text, inside parenthesis right before the period at the end of your sentence.

A footnote looks like this:

Her brother tripped and fell on a beam. Clara took care of him for several months. This led to her becoming a nurse. [1] You can see what would appear at the bottom of your page, along with all your other footnotes.

A parenthetical reference looks like this:

Her brother tripped and fell on a beam. Clara took care of him for several months. This led to her becoming a nurse (Angel 53). Information on the book would appear at the end of your paper in a bibliography, or Works Cited page.

Bibliography, or Works Cited

At the end of your paper, you will need to have a bibliography, or works cited page. This page needs to be in alphabetical order, based on the authors last name.

Here are the ingredients of a Bibliography, or Works Cited page

- Alphabetical
- Authors Listed Last, First (first in entry)
- Title in Italics (second in entry)
- Publication Info: City, State, Publisher, Year Published, Print or Web (third in entry)
- Online information need to include Database (or Website Title) and Date Accessed

[1] Angel, Merci *Clara Barton, Angel of Mercy*, New York, NY, Christian Publishing; 2015; print, page 53.

January Week One Home

☐ Finish Reading Parallel Lives

☐ Write Your Parallel Lives Biographies

Finish Reading Plutarch's Lives by Plutarch

I would encourage you to answer these questions about the story as you read. They are the questions you will be discussing in book club. Write the answers in December's space.

Choose one set of biographies from Plutarch's *Lives*.

- Why do you think Plutarch chose these two people to pair up?
- What is similar about these two men?
- What differences can you point out about the men?
- Did any of these men improve a Greek city-state? If so, how?
- Did any of these men improve Rome? If so, how?

You will need to finish reading the book this week.

Write Parallel Lives Biographies

Complete your Parallel Lives Biographies.

January Week Two Class

- ☐ Book Club Discussion: *Plutarch's Lives*
- ☐ Read & Discuss "Grammar Review" and Fill Out Glad Libs
- ☐ Read & Edit Parallel Lives in Groups
- ☐ Read & Discuss "Background on Book of Acts"

Book Club Discussion on *Plutarch's Lives*

Here are some questions to discuss about *Plutarch's Lives*.

- Why do you think Plutarch chose these two people to pair up?
- What is similar about these two men?
- What differences can you point out about the men?
- Did any of these men improve a Greek city-state? If so, how?
- Did any of these men improve Rome? If so, how?

Grammar Review

Let's go over some grammar basics. If you would like to watch some Grammar Rock videos, you can find them on YouTube. There are eight parts of speech: nouns, pronouns, verbs, adjectives, adverbs, prepositions, conjunctions, and interjections.

Nouns are persons, places, things, ideas, or concepts. (Mom, love, Betty, Florida, park, mall, Disney World)

Pronouns take the place of nouns. (he, she, our, his, her, it, me, you)

Verbs express actions or a state of being. (find, run, swim, eat, jump, is, seems, looks)

Adjectives describe nouns and pronouns. They answer the questions how much, how many, what color. (red, little, happy, tired, seven)

Adverbs describe verbs, adjectives, and other adverbs. Words that end in "ly" are almost always adverbs. They answer the questions how, when, where, how much, and how often. (slowly, quickly, lively, boldly, cheerfully)

Prepositions are used to modify space and time (in, on, of, under, over, to, out, through)

Conjunctions (for, and, nor, but, or, yet, so) combine thoughts and **Interjections** are used to express strong emotion (wow, gee, whoa, how, bravo)

Let's play some Grammar Glad Games in Class to review parts of speech.

Chocolate Chip Cookies Grammar Glad Lib

Chocolate chip cookies were invented by a _____ who owned an
(Noun)

_____, called the _____ _____ _____. She _____
(Noun)   (Proper Noun) (Building Noun) (Building Noun) (Verb Past Tense)

a restaurant that _____ home-style cooking. She served ice cream
(Verb Past Tense)

with _____ nut cookies, but she _____ to be creative,
(Adjective)   (Verb Past Tense)

so she _____ the nuts with _____ _____. Her
(Verb Past Tense)   (Adjective)   (Noun)

customers _____ the brand new cookies and _____ them
(Verb Past Tense)   (Verb Past Tense)

_____. _____ children still _____ chocolate chip
(Adverb)   (Adjective)   (verb)

cookies, so moms still _____ _____ Toll House
(Adverb)   (Verb)

_____ to make their children _____.
(Noun)   (Adjective)

Read & Edit Parallel Lives in Groups

You will read all your papers aloud to a partner or to a small group. This is very important and will help you to keep your audience in mind as you write. Your listener might be a parent or sibling or fellow students in a co-op class. Here are some tips on helping each other edit your Parallel Lives assignments.

- Who are the two lives your friend has chosen?
- What is the parallel between them?
- How are they alike?
- How are they different?
- Are there lots of stories and illustrations?
- Is the paper enjoyable, easy to understand, and interesting? Explain.

Fill out this short chart for each parallel lives paper you read or listen to.

Author's name: _____

Who are the two lives your friend has chosen?

_____   _____

Are there lots of stories to "show" you the people? _____

What is the parallel between them?

_____
_____

How are they alike?

_____
_____
_____

How are they different?

_____
_____
_____

Is the paper enjoyable, easy to understand, and interesting? Explain.

_____
_____
_____
_____

How can the author show more than tell? _____
_____
_____
_____

Author's name: _____

Who are the two lives your friend has chosen?

_____   _____

Are there lots of stories to "show" you the people? _____

What is the parallel between them?

_____

_____

How are they alike?

_____

_____

_____

How are they different?

_____

_____

_____

Is the paper enjoyable, easy to understand, and interesting? Explain.

_____

_____

_____

_____

How can the author show more than tell? _____

_____

_____

_____

Author's name: _____

Who are the two lives your friend has chosen?

_____   _____

Are there lots of stories to "show" you the people? _____

What is the parallel between them?

_____
_____

How are they alike?

_____
_____
_____

How are they different?

_____
_____
_____

Is the paper enjoyable, easy to understand, and interesting? Explain.

_____
_____
_____
_____

How can the author show more than tell? _____
_____
_____
_____

Background on The Book of Acts

The Book of Acts begins with Jesus promising to send the Holy Spirit to his disciples if they will wait in Jerusalem. Written by Luke who also wrote the Gospel of Luke, this book is one adventure after another as the disciples face trials, persecution, and death in their quest to proclaim the Good News to Israel and the entire Roman Empire.

Like all Scripture, this book is written by God Himself, though he uses Luke as His scribe. Luke was inspired by the Holy Spirit as he wrote these words. God guided him as he wrote chapter after chapter of this true adventure story.

Luke traveled with Paul on some of his missionary journeys and knew the disciples who traveled with Jesus and received the Holy Spirit. His goal was to present an historical account of the events since Jesus' resurrection.

You will love this book. It is full of action and drama. In it, you meet men and women intent on stomping out the Gospel of Jesus Christ and others who are willing to lay down their lives so that people everywhere can be saved and follow Jesus.

Directions for Acts Effect on Literature Chart

The Book of Acts has impacted Western literature and movies. In each chapter a story line/theme is given that is mirrored in later literature and movies. You will give the exact situation in Acts and then give an example of how it is repeated later on in literature and movies.

January Week Two Home

☐ Read The Book of Acts & Fill Out Chart

☐ Rewrite Parallel Lives Biographies

☐ Start Reading *City of God* by St. Augustine

Read The Book of Acts

Fill in the chart as you read *The Book of Acts* chapters 1-14. In each chapter a story line/theme is given that is mirrored in later literature and movies. You will give the exact situation in Acts and then give an example of how it is repeated later on in literature and movies.

Real Life Story in Acts	Theme	Same Story Line in Literature
Jesus Commissions Disciple v. 6 "You will be my witnesses, in Jerusalem, Judea, Samaria, and the whole world.	Leader who is about to leave or die commissions small group with an impossible task. Acts 1	
	An ordinary man is changed by the Power of God and able to influence/inspire thousands (or more) people Acts 2	
	Fulfillment of an Ancient Prophecy happening right now! Acts 2	
	Heroes: "We can't meet your felt meet, but we can meet your real need." Acts 3	

Real Life Story in Acts	Theme	Same Story Line in Literature
	Hero or Heroes arrested, tortured, or belittled, but refuse to give in. He/they will continue to do what is right. Obey God (or conscience) rather than man. Acts 4	
	Hypocrites are exposed and punished. Acts 5	
	Leaders are chosen based on character and commitment, not wealth, education, or talents. Acts 6	
	Hero, like Jesus, forgives those who persecute or put him to death. Acts 7	
	Hero is in the right place at the right time. A divine appointment type of situation. Acts 8	
	Damascus Road experience—blinded by the light. Hero's eyes are opened to the truth and his life is transformed. Acts 9	
	Outcasts are welcomed into the group rather reluctantly at first, but eventually warmly received. Acts 10	
	Mentor reaches out to someone with potential. Acts 11	
	After an arrest or capture, there is a miraculous escape. Acts 12	

Rewrite Parallel Lives Biographies

You have read your Parallel Lives Biographies to your peers or siblings, so now it's time to rewrite them. Tweak, craft, edit, and make it the best it can be.

Start Reading *City of God* by Saint Augustine

I know that you are reading the Book of Acts and filling out the chart, but I think you should start reading *City of God* by Saint Augustine this week. It is the longest book you have ever read.

Grading Rubric for Parallel Lives Biographies

With the input you received in group time, rewrite your plot evaluation paper, making corrections and adding any needed changes.

		Comments	Possible Points	Points
Subject	There are 2 different biographies; one is a person the author does know and one is of a person the author doesn't know.		10/10	/10
Character Trait	The character trait, or virtue, that unites them is clearly evident in both biographies		20/20	/20
Stories, Illustrations	Author "shows" you the two people through stories & illustrations		10/10	/10
Alike & Different	How are they alike? How different?			
Audience	The paper is enjoyable, easy-to-understand, and intersting		30/30	/30
Flow of Paper	Paragraphs and the sentences within those paragraphs flow into one another		20/20	/20
Grammar	Spelling/Grammar		10/10	/10
Grade			100/100	100/100

January Week Three Class

☐ Book Club: Discuss *The Book of Acts* & Acts' Impact on Literature

☐ Read Parallel Lives Biographies in Groups

☐ Turn in Parallel Lives

The Book of Acts Impact on Literature

You will see The Book of Acts stories show up in Western Literature.

"I don't have what you want, but I have what you really need." (Peter and John heal the lame man.)

"We have to obey God rather than man." (The disciples decide to continue sharing the Gospel when the authorities warn them to stop)

"I have seen the light!" "I'm now a changed man!" (Paul's encounter with Jesus as a bright light.)

Everyone share their charts with one another and come up with a list of literature and movie plot lines/messages that are adapted from the Book of Acts.

Now, keep in mind, most people don't purposely adapt their story line from the Bible or ancient Greeks works, but these story lines are such a part of our culture, that the story lines repeat over and over again.

Write the list here.

_____

_____

_____

_____

_____

_____

_____

_____

Read Rewritten Parallel Lives Biographies in Groups

You will read all your papers aloud to a partner or to a small group. This will help you to keep your audience in mind as you write. Your listener might be a parent or sibling or fellow students in a co-op class.

January Week Three & Four Home

☐ Read The Book of Acts & Fill Out Chart

☐ Read *City of God* by St. Augustine

Read The Book of Acts

Fill in the chart as you read *The Book of Acts* chapters 15-28.

Real Life Story in Acts	Theme	Same Story Line in Literature
Jesus Commissions Disciple v. 6 "You will be my witnesses, in Jerusalem, Judea, Samaria, and the whole world.	Leader who is about to leave or die commissions small group with an impossible task. Acts 1	
	Hero has a vision of someone asking for their help. Acts 16	
	Heroes arrested, tortured, or belittled and sing or rejoice in spite of suffering Acts 16	
	Hero meets people who are cautious, but still open to new ideas. They examine everything hero says and does carefully. Acts 17	
	Kind couple takes a zealous young person under their wing and helps them to discern truth from error. Acts 18	
	Changes that take place as a result of hero's words or actions cause someone's business to fail. Acts 19	

Real Life Story in Acts	Theme	Same Story Line in Literature
	Tearful good-bye by hero to his team as he heads off to face sure punishment or death. Acts 20.	
	A prophet tells hero he will be arrested, tortured, or killed Acts 21	
	Hero shares his testimony. Acts 22	
	Nephew (or other family member or friend) informs hero of a plot or conspiracy to kill him and he escapes. Acts 23	
	Judge sympathetic to hero while he is on trial Acts 25	
	During a shipwreck or other disaster, the hero keeps his head on straight and wins everyone's respect. Acts 27.	
	Something life-threatening happens to hero, but he survives. Acts 28	

February: Early Church Writings

Foundations of Western Literature

24 Constantine the Great, a Mosaic in Hagia Sophia

February Week One Class

- ☐ Book of Acts in Literature Discussion & Make a List
- ☐ Read & Discuss "Background on *City of God* by Saint Augustine"
- ☐ Read & Discuss "How to Write a Comparison Essay
- ☐ Come Up with Questions to Ask Yourself as You Read Pliny & London

The Book of Acts in Literature Discussion

Let's continue to talk about the Book of Acts and its impact on Western literature. Everyone share their charts with one another and come up with a list of literature and movie plot lines/messages that are adapted from the Book of Acts.

Write the list here.

_____

_____

_____

_____

_____

_____

_____

Background on *City of God* by St. Augustine

We are going to fast-forward almost 400 years to talk about St. Augustine of Hippo (354-430). Born in Tagaste, North Africa to a pagan father and a Christian mother, Augustine lived an immoral life for many years, even fathering a baby to a mistress. His mother, Monica, prayed for his conversion without ceasing.

Besides sinning up a storm, Augustine investigated all kinds of philosophies. Finally, he moved to Milan where he met Bishop Ambrose who led Augustine to Christ. Augustine repented, gave his life to Christ, and was baptized. He returned to Africa soon after his conversion and became a priest, eventually becoming the Bishop of Hippo.

Not only was St. Augustine a mighty man of God, he was a prolific writer. His writings have influenced the Church from his times until today. A theologian and philosopher, his two most famous works are *Confessions* and *City of God*.

Confessions is the story of Augustine's conversion to Christ. It starts with his childhood, teenage years, and time of rebellion. Augustine shares his conversion, baptism, and the role his mother's prayers had in his conversion. He goes on to share how Jesus changed his life and helped him to understand the Scriptures. He ends the book with great detail and explanation of Genesis chapter one, including the Trinity.

City of God was written in response to the Roman pagans' claim that Rome fell because Christians had led the Latins away from worshipping the idol/gods and idol/goddesses. He contrasts the earthly Roman Empire with the true Heavenly City.

St. Augustine's writings are not light reading, but well worth the effort to enjoy and understand.

How to Write a Compare & Contrast Essay

Pliny the Younger, born to a Roman knight, and adopted by his uncle, grew up to be a lawyer, magistrate, tribune, commissioner, quaestor, praetor, prefect of the military treasury, curator of the Tiber River and sewers of Rome, consul, and governor of Bithynia. As a wealthy man, he served his nation well in various offices as a politician and advisor. He was also a prolific writer.

Pliny the Younger witnessed the eruption of Vesuvius.

Eruption of Mt. Vesuvius

On August 24, in the year of our Lord 79, Mount Vesuvius erupted spewing molten ash and sulfuric gas straight up creating a firestorm of poisonous gases and debris that suffocated the surrounded area including Pompeii, Herculaneum, and Stabiae. These cities simply ceased to exist. When Pompeii was excavated centuries later in 1748, people, homes, animals, and furnishings were frozen in time. It was pretty creepy, but gave us a glimpse back in time.

Pliny the Younger described this natural disaster in two different letters. You can read his descriptions in the Resources section of the book.

San Francisco Earthquake

Another natural disaster happened in 1906, the San Francisco Earthquake. Jack London, a novelist and newspaperman described that natural disaster. You can read his description in the Resources section of this book too.

This week, you will be writing a comparison essay. You will compare Pliny the Younger's description of Mt. Vesuvius with Jack London's description of the San Francisco Earthquake of 1906.

How to Use Circles to Compare & Contrast

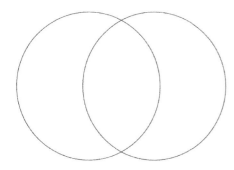

You can use overlapping circles to brainstorm for a comparison essay. Put things that are unique to Pliny the Younger's description in the left circle, things unique to Jack London's description in the right circle, and similarities in the overlapping section.

February Week One Home

☐ Read "Crash Course in History: Early Church to Vikings"

☐ Read *City of God* by Saint Augustine & Answer Questions

☐ Read Articles by Pliny the Younger and Jack London (in Resource section of this book)

☐ Underline & Write in Margins in Articles according to Directions

Crash Course in History: Early Church to Vikings

Constantine

Flavius Valerius Aurelius Constantinus, or Constantine I, was a Roman Emperor from 306 to 337. He rose through the ranks to become a military tribune under the emperor Diocletian and Galerius, and finally became an Emperor. During his reign, Constantine I made administrative, financial, social, and military reforms. He restructured the government and introduced a new gold coin to help bring financial stability.

During one of his campaigns, he saw a vision of a cross and a voice spoke to him telling him to conquer in the Name of Christ. He converted to Christianity and proclaimed the Edict of Milan, making it legal to be a Christian in the Roman Empire. He encouraged the Church to meet for the First Council of Nicaea in 325 where the Nicene Creed was penned because there was some squabbling in the Church.

Constantine defeated enemies on the Roman borders and even took back lands lost in earlier reigns. He moved his imperial residence to Byzantium, renaming it Constantinople. He had the Church of the Holy Sepulchre built in Jerusalem on the reported site of Jesus' tomb. It became the holiest place in Christendom in the Middle Ages.

St. Augustine

St. Augustine, Bishop of Hippo, after years of rebellion, gave His heart to Christ and spent his life loving the Lord with all His heart. He attended the Council of Nicaea, helping to draft the Nicene Creed. His most famous works are *City of God* and *Confessions*.

Fall of Rome

After 500 years as the world's superpower, the Western Roman Empire collapsed. Crippling taxation and the burden of running a welfare state caused the empire to crumble from within. There were also enemies without.

One enemy, the Visigoths, led by King Alaric, breached Rome's walls to plunder, pillage, and destroy the City of Rome in 410. King Alaric died shortly afterward. But the attacks continued.

Pope Leo was Pope in Rome when Attila the Hun decided to invade Rome. Pope Leo met with Attila and offered him money to turn back. Attila turned back. Pope Leo also helped rebuild the city after Vandels attacked the city in 455.

In 476 Romulus was overthrown by Odoacer, a Germanic leader. After Rome fell, the Roman Catholic Church stepped up and distributed food to the starving Romans, hiring armies to defend the city, and negotiating with the barbarians.

Over time, the Eastern and Western parts of the Empire had drifted apart from one another so that only the Western Roman Empire fell. The Western Roman Empire spoke Latin and worshipped in the Roman Catholic Church and the Eastern Roman Empire spoke Greek and worshipped in the Eastern Orthodox Church. The eastern half of the Roman Empire continued on for another 1000 years as the Byzantine Empire with its capital in Constantinople.

Missionaries from Rome

Though the Roman Empire was no longer a superpower, the Roman Catholic Church emerged stronger than ever. She sent missionaries to convert the pagans in Ireland, France, and England. The most famous of these was St. Patrick who went to Ireland to convert the Irish to Christianity.

When the Frankish King Clovis I (466-511), who conquered what had been Roman Gaul, gave his life to Jesus at the request of his wife, Clotilde, it caused widespread conversions to Christ across the Frankish Empire.

As rulers came to Christ, they would often pay to have churches and monasteries built. Monasteries became places of worship, prayer, fasting, and learning. Monks kept records, copied Bibles, and educated people.

All of the popes and many of the bishops before and after Pope Leo wrote numerous letters and books that influenced Christians at the time they were written and for years to come. Pope Gregory, though, was a more prolific writer than all the popes before him.

Pope Gregory

Gregorius Anicius (540-604) was born into a wealthy Roman family. His father served as a senator and Prefect of Rome. Well educated, Gregory became Prefect of Rome at the age of thirty-three. When his father died, he converted the family villa into a monastery and became a monk. In 579, Gregory was sent along with a Roman delegation to Constantinople to ask for help from the Byzantine Emperor. It was denied.

When he was elected pope, Gregory tried to reject the office, but eventually gave in. He lived a humble life, dressed plainly, and pursued righteousness. He sent Augustine of Canterbury to England to win the Angles and the Saxons to Christ. A singer and songwriter, he is credited with the creation of the Gregorian Chant. As Rome was still unstable, Pope Gregory distributed finances lavishly to the

25 Painting of Pope Gregory the Great
public domain.

destitute.

Even John Calvin thought highly of Pope Gregory, considering him to be the last good pope.

King Arthur

26 King Arthur and The Round Table experiences a vision of the Holy Grail. By Évrard d'Espinques c. 1475 public domain

A few centuries earlier, when the Roman Empire was expanding into England during the 100's, Christian missionaries were successfully making converts. **Celtic Christianity,** firmly established on the island, lived side by side with the paganism of Rome. When Germanic barbarians invaded Rome in the south, Germanic tribes also invaded England.

In the middle of the fifth century, **Anglo-Saxons (Angles, Saxons, Jutes)** conquered England and the Celtic Christians fled to the outskirts of civilization: Wales and Cornwall. Facing hunger and devastation, the Celts fought for their lives. They would have been wiped out, if not for the leadership of a great man named **King Arthur**.

In the fifth century, a post-Roman king lived and ruled, defending his nation against the ruthless Saxon invaders. This king was Arthurius, or King Arthur. Legendary tales have circulated for centuries about him. Arthur was a High-King of Britain and son of Uther Pendragon. He gathered the Briton tribes together to defend themselves against the Germanic tribes (Angles, Saxons, Jutes) invading their island home as Roman occupation was ending.

Centuries later, in the court of **Eleanor of Aquitaine** (1122-1204), in the 12th century (1100's), courtly manners and romance was cultivated to a high level. Along with all this romantic behavior, stories of the past were embellished to make them more romantic too. This happened to the tales of King Arthur. They grew more and more packed with the idealized romantic notions of the 12th century.

The following historical and fictional accounts of King Arthur contain his story.

- Gildas (mid-500's), *De Excidio et Conquest Britanniae*
- The Venerable Bede (731 AD), *Eccleisastical History of the English People*—mentions Ambrosius Aurelianus—is he King Arthur?
- Nennius (800 AD), *Historia Brittonum*—12 successful battles of King Arthur
- Geoffrey of Monmouth (Welsh cleric1130 AD), *History of the Kings of Britain*—mentions Arthur as a High-King, mentions Arthur's genealogy, conception, birth, childhood, ascension to the throne, military victories, and death in 542 BC.

- Maistre Wace (Anglo-French author 1155), *Roman de Brut*—mentions the knightly fellowship of the Round Table, introduces courtly love
- Cistercian monks in France (1215-1235), Vulgate Cycle—8 volumes of Arthur story, mentions Lancelot, Galahad, Tristan, chivalry, Knights of Round Table combat evil & right wrongs
- Robert de Boron (French Poet c. 1200), Arthurian Romances centered around Holy Grail, Merlin, mentions Sir Percival's Grail as the Last Supper Cup used by St. Joseph of Arimathea to collect blood of Christ from the cross
- Chretien de Troyes (French poet 1170-1185 AD), romanticized King Arthur story, frequented the court of Countess Marie, daughter of Eleanor of Aquitaine, wrote about conception & birth of King Arthur, mentions Camelot, Lancelot, Holy Grail, court of King Arthur as a place of chivalry, courtly love
- Gerald of Wales (Norman/Welsh author 1145-1235 AD), present at exhumation of King Arthur at Glastonbury Abbey
- Welsh Literature (8th – 12th Century), Arthur and his battle victories mentioned in poems and stories
- Sir Thomas Malory (1416-1470 AD), *Le Morte d'Arthur*—wrote 8 volumes, published by William Caxton in 1485 in 21 volumes
- John Leland (1545), *History & Antiquities*—visited many King Arthur locations and wrote about them in his book, collected many documents that would have been lost when monasteries were dissolved
- Alfred, Lord Tennyson (1809-1892), *Idylls of the King*
- T. H. White (1906-1964), *Once and Future King (Sword in the Stone, Queen of Air and Darkness, Ill-Made Knight, Book of Merlyn)*

Here is a summary of the legend of King Arthur. Arthur was the crown prince and heir to the throne, son of King Uther Pendragon. Because of the great terror of the Saxon invaders, Arthur was raised in a secret place by Sir Ector, a noble knight. When King Uther died, Arthur became king because he was the rightful heir and the only one able to pull a sword out of a special stone. He surrounded himself with the brave Knights of the Round Table who won many victories, halting the Saxon's advance into Briton territory.

King Arthur lived in **Camelot**, a lovely land, with a strong castle and beautiful queen named **Guinevere**, who loved him, but loved **Sir Lancelot** too. Arthur and his knights spend their time being chivalrous, rescuing damsels in distress, and fighting strange monsters. They searched for the Holy Grail, which they believed could cure all ills. Arthur obtained a special sword, Excalibur, that he used to defeat his foes. Eventually, Camelot experienced destruction due to Lancelot and Guinevere's deceit. King Arthur died on Good Friday.

Venerable Bede

Saint Bede (673-735) was an English monk at the Monastery of Saint Peter in the Kingdom of Northumbria in present day England. A skilled

27 Bede's Life of St Cuthbert, showing King Æthelstan (924–39) presenting a copy of the book to Bede public domain.

linguist and translator, he had access to a huge library of great works so he translated Latin and Greek works into the language of the Anglo-Saxons.

Written in 731, *Ecclesiastical History of the English People* is the most valuable source of historical information on the early Middle Ages in England. Bede details the history of the Christian Church in

England including accounts of supernatural miracles that took place to confirm the Gospel. He was helped by Albinus, abbot of St. Augustine's Abbey.

Bede was a prolific writer. He wrote about science, history, theology, music, and Scripture commentaries. His works were important to the "golden age" during Charlemagne's time. On his deathbed, Bede continued dictating works to his scribe and died singing praises to the Lord.

Byzantine Empire

Justinian I was the Byzantine Emperor from 527 to 565. He expanded the empire and made judicial reforms, completely revising Roman Law. A devoted Christian, he built the Hagia Sophia, one of the most beautiful churches in the world. Unfortunately, it was destroyed centuries later by invading Muslims. He upheld sound doctrine, including the Trinity, Incarnation, and other precious truths. Justinian and his wife, Theodora strengthened the Church and filled the land with bridges, churches, and impressive building projects.

Rise of Islam

Beginning in the seventh century (600s), Islam spread into Roman Syria, Roman Mesopotamia, Roman Palestine, Roman Egypt, Roman North Africa, and Persia. Soldiers spread Islam, forcing people to convert. The Christian kingdom of Iberia was invaded by Muslim Moors in 711. Muslims invaded Cyprus, Malta, Crete, Sicily, and Southern Italy. Eventually, Islam would be pushed out of Europe before the Middle Ages ended, but Palestine and the Middle East would be lost.

On a positive note, the works of Euclid and Archimedes, preserved by the Arabs, were translated to Latin in Spain when the Moors invaded. In addition, a notation for zero, developed by Hindu mathematicians in the fifth century, made its way to Europe through the Arabs.

Charlemagne

Charlemagne inherited the Frankish kingdom, expanding it to include present-day France, Germany, and northern Italy. Pope Leo III crowned Charlemagne Emperor on Christmas Day 800. During his reign, the arts, architecture, jurisprudence (law), literature, writing, and Bible study flourished. Literacy was encouraged. A common language and writing style was adopted for the whole empire. Illuminated manuscripts, sculptures, mosaics, frescoes, and altar triptychs were lovely, wholesome, and full of color.

Holy Roman Empire

King Otto I, a descendant of Charlemagne, was crowned "Emperor," an elected position. The German kings and princes would elect an emperor and the pope would crown him. The Holy Roman Empire started in 962 (though some say it started with Charlemagne in 800) and ended in 1806. That's a long time!

When the empire dissolved in 1806, it was replaced with the Dutch Republic, Kingdom of Prussia, Austrian Empire, Confederation of the Rhine (German states, Poland, Liechtenstein), and the Old Swiss Confederacy.

Vikings

From 800 to 1066 at the Battle of Hastings, the Vikings ruled the northern seas. Scandinavian warriors raided and explored Europe, Asia, northern African, and north-eastern North America. They looted, pillaged, and enslaved entire Christian cities. Feared by all, these tall blond warriors showed no mercy.

Read *City of God* by St. Augustine

I would encourage you to answer these questions about the story as you read. They are the questions you will be discussing in book club.

Augustine talks about the Roman Empire, a pagan and temporary city. What does he say about Rome?

_____
_____
_____
_____
_____

Augustine talks about the Kingdom of God, a holy and eternal city. What does he say about the Kingdom of God?

_____
_____
_____
_____
_____

Why is he comparing both cities? What is his purpose?

_____
_____
_____
_____
_____

What points is St. Augustine making to the Christian?

_____
_____
_____
_____
_____

What points is St. Augustine making to the Non-Christian?

_____
_____
_____
_____
_____

Read Pliny the Younger & Jack London

Read Pliny the Younger's Description of the Eruption of Mt. Vesuvius and Jack London's Description of the San Francisco Earthquake in 1906. As you are reading, use you pen and highlighter to underline and highlight various passages that will help to write your essay next week.

- Underline or highlight descriptive phrases of the natural disasters.
- Underline or highlight descriptive phrases of the results of these natural disasters.
- Underline or highlight descriptive phrases that show how life was different after the natural disasters.
- What was similar in Jack London's and Pliny the Younger's description of the natural disasters? Jot down in the margins.
- What was different in Jack London's and Pliny the Younger's description of the natural disasters? Jot down in the margins.

February Week Two Class

☐ Book Club Discussion: Ancient vs. Modern Descriptions of Natural Disasters

☐ Read & Discuss "Compare & Contrast Essay Directions"

☐ Brainstorm Compare & Contrast Essay Ideas—Everyone Share

Book Club Discussion: Ancient vs. Modern Descriptions of National Disasters

First, review the descriptions of Pliny the Younger and Jack London. Open to the pages in the back of this book that you have highlighted and underlined.

Let's talk about Pliny the Younger's and Jack London's descriptions of a natural disaster.

- Describe each natural disaster.
- What was the result of each disaster?
- How was life different after each disaster?

Write these similarities and differences down on a white board so everyone can see.

Now, let' talk about the essay you are going to write. You are going to compare how these two men, separated by centuries write about the disasters.

- How are the descriptions similar?
- How are they different?
- What stands out to you about their similarities?
- What stands out to you about their differences?
- What was similar in Jack London's and Pliny the Younger's description of the natural disasters?
- What was different in Jack London's and Pliny the Younger's description of the natural disasters?

Compare & Contrast Essay Directions

Start with a general point to establish the similarity of the two subjects you are comparing. Follow up with your thesis statement which should announce what you are comparing and your conclusion from comparing the subjects.

I suggest that you compare both subjects in each paragraph point by point with each point covered in a different paragraph. Although there are other ways to do it, they can be confusing for your reader.

Make sure that you compare the same subjects. Don't compare a nose to a tail unless you are comparing traits characters want to get rid of like Pinocchio's nose and Little Mermaid's tail. Don't compare color to size. Compare color to color, size to size, and usefulness to usefulness.

In your essay, compare word usage to word usage, descriptive phrases to descriptive phrases, and actual disaster to actual disaster.

If you were comparing two new girls at church. You would notice two things right off: They are new. They are girls.

Maybe you notice that there are differences in their appearance, interests, and language they speak. Each of those differences would be in your thesis and could be discussed in a paragraph.

Narrowing Down Focus of Paper

When you are writing an essay, it is important to keep your focus narrow. You cannot discuss everything. Instead, focus on your thesis, or the point you are trying to make. Use only examples that will help prove your thesis. You can summarize, paraphrase, or quote.

This is **NOT** a thesis statement: "I'm going to compare two descriptions of a natural disaster."

This **IS** a thesis statement: *Monk* and *The Mentalist* are both lighthearted mystery shows with a defective detective catching the murderer, but *Monk* is more appealing to an older crowd because the characters are older, the humor is clean, and the moral tone is stricter.

Little Women can be enjoyed by girls of all ages with younger children enjoying the warmth of happy family life, but missing the historical and economics aspects of the story that older readers pick up on.

While Publix and Winn Dixie are both great places for students to work, Publix offers more benefits for the future with stock options, opportunities for upward mobility, and free education.

Words You Might Use

While writing a comparison essay, you might want to use some of these words to help explain your points:

Like	Even though
Similar to	While
Also	Despite
Unlike	On the one hand….on the other hand
Similarly	Regardless
In the same way	Despite
Likewise	Even though
On the contrary	Nevertheless
Although	At the same time
Yet	

Comparing & Contrasting the Authors, not the Events

You will be analyzing the way the writers tell their story.

Both London and Pliny are watching a terrible disaster unfold. They both describe it. Pliny in a letter and London in a newspaper article.

You will analyze how they describe the event.

Are they personal or detached?

What words, phrases are sued and what do those words convey? What do they focus on and how does that impact the reader?

What is their tone?

Of course, the events themselves are different. Pliny writes about an earthquake that massively and abruptly destroys Pompeii. In San Francisco, an earthquake leads to a fire that blazes for days—a slower process. They also live in different times and places. All of these things will affect their telling of the event.

As you analyze this text, you will prove your point with the text only. Do not bring in quotes from other authors about these two articles. Simply read, reread, and reread the articles. Think about them. How do you feel when you read them. What do you picture in your mind? How are you affected emotionally? Now, try to figure out why?

Notice that you are going deeper into analysis with this paper. Isn't that exciting?

February Week Two Home

☐ Read *City of God* by St. Augustine

☐ Brainstorm and Answer Questions about Compare & Constrast Essay

☐ Write Compare & Contrast Essay

Continue Reading *City of God* by St. Augustine

I would encourage you to answer these questions about the story as you read. They are the questions you will be discussing in book club. You can answer these questions on Week One Home's page.

- Augustine talks about the Roman Empire, a pagan and temporary city. What does he say about Rome?
- Augustine talks about the Kingdom of God, a holy and eternal city. What does he say about the Kingdom of God?
- Why is he comparing both cities? What is his purpose?
- What points is St. Augustine making to the Christian?
- What points is St. Augustine making to the Non-Christian?

Write Compare & Contrast Essay on Pliny the Younger and Jack London

This week, you will be writing a comparison essay. You will compare Pliny the Younger's description of Mt. Vesuvius with Jack Wild's description of the San Francisco Earthquake of 1906.

How are the descriptions similar?

_____

How are they different?

_____

What stands out to you about their similarities?

_____
_____
_____
_____
_____

What stands out to you about their differences?

_____
_____
_____
_____
_____

My Thesis Statement:

_____
_____
_____
_____
_____

My First Point with Examples

_____
_____
_____
_____
_____

My Second Point with Examples

_____
_____
_____
_____
_____

My Third Point with Examples

_____
_____
_____
_____
_____
_____

Brainstorm your ideas using the overlapping circles on the next page. Write down things that are unique to Pliny the Younger's description in the left circle, things unique to Jack London's description in the right circle, and similarities in the overlapping section.

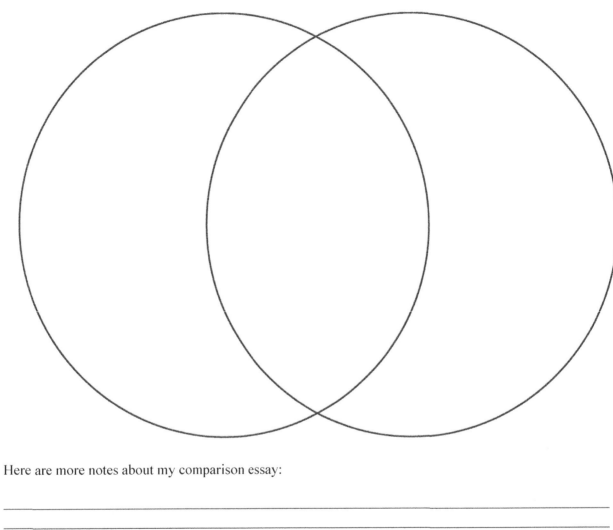

Here are more notes about my comparison essay:

_____
_____
_____
_____
_____
_____
_____
_____
_____
_____
_____
_____
_____

February Week Three Class

☐ Book Club Discussion: City of God vs. Roman Empire

☐ Read Compare & Contrast Essay in Groups

☐ Fill Out Peer Review for Comparison Essay

Book Club Discussion: City of God vs. Roman Empire

I know you aren't finished with *City of God* yet, but you've read enough to talk about what Augustine means by "City of God" and compare this to the Roman Republic & Roman Empire.

Today we will discuss the City of God and the Roman Republic.

- Augustine talks about the Roman Empire, a pagan and temporary city. What does he say about Rome?
- Augustine talks about the Kingdom of God, a holy and eternal city. What does he say about the Kingdom of God?
- Why is he comparing both cities? What is his purpose?
- What message is St. Augustine sending to the Christian reader?
- What is St. Augustine communicating to the Non-Christian?

Read Compare & Contrast Essay in Groups

You will read all your papers aloud to a partner or to a small group. This will help you to keep your audience in mind as you write. Your listener might be a parent or sibling or fellow students in a co-op class.

Peer Review for Compare & Contrast Essay

Let a peer review your compare & contrast essay as you read it aloud or as they read it on their own. You can use this information to rewrite your compare & contrast essay.

		Yes or No	Comments
Audience	Paper is interesting & enjoyable to read		
Thesis	Thesis compares & contrasts Pliny & London?		
Introductions	Introduction captures my attention and contains Thesis Statement		
Paragraphs	Do all the paragraphs prove the thesis statement? Does each paragraph compare and/or contrast? All paragraphs are clear, easy-to-understand, make a strong point and supported by the text? Is the argument convincing? Are you convinced? Are there points made not supported by text? (not good)		

Argument	Does the entire text support the claims of the thesis? Or are quotes taken out of context? Is the argument convincing? Is the Argument supported by the texts by Pliny & London?		
	Does the author compare London & Pliny's portrayal of events or just the events themselves? Does author show how similarities and differences in events themselves affect the way the articles were written? Are there good insights into the articles by Pliny & London? Does the author use lots of examples and quotes to support the claims being made?		
Flow of Paper	Paragraphs and the sentences within those paragraphs flow into one another		
Grammar	Spelling/Grammar		

February Week Three & Four Home

☐ Finish Reading *City of God* by Saint Augustine

☐ Rewrite Compare & Contrast Essay

Finish Reading *City of God* by St. Augustine

This week you will finish reading *City of God* by Saint Augustine. I would encourage you to answer these questions about the story as you finish reading it. They are the questions you will be discussing in book club.

- Augustine talks about the Roman Empire, a pagan and temporary city. What does he say about Rome?
- Augustine talks about the Kingdom of God, a holy and eternal city. What does he say about the Kingdom of God?
- Why is he comparing both cities? What is his purpose?
- What points is St. Augustine making to the Christian?
- What points is St. Augustine making to the Non-Christian?

Rewrite Compare & Contrast Essay

You will read all your Comparison Essay aloud to a partner or to a small group. This will help you to keep your audience in mind as you write. Your listener might be a parent or sibling or fellow students in a co-op class.

Grading Rubric for Comparison Essay

With the input you received in group time, rewrite your plot evaluation paper, making corrections and adding any needed changes.

		Comments	Possible Points	Points
Audience	Paper is interesting & enjoyable to read		5/5	/5
Thesis	Thesis compares & contrasts Pliny & London **using the 2 articles**		15/15	/15
Introductions	Introduction captures my attention and contains Thesis Statement		5/5	/5
Paragraphs	Do all the paragraphs prove the thesis statement? Does each paragraph compare and/or contrast? All paragraphs are clear, easy-to-understand, make a strong point and supported by the text? Is the argument convincing? Are you convinced? Are there points made not supported by text? (not good)		20/20	/20

		Comments	Possible Points	Points
Argument	Does the entire text support the claims of the thesis? Or are quotes taken out of context? Is the argument convincing? Is the Argument supported by the texts by Pliny & London?		15/15	15/15
Compare & Contrast	Does the author compare London & Pliny's portrayal of events or just the events themselves? Does the author show how similarities and differences in the events themselves affect the way the articles were written? Are there good insights into the articles by Pliny & London? Does the author use lots of examples and quotes to support the claims being made?		20/10	20/10
Flow of Paper	Paragraphs and the sentences within those paragraphs flow into one another		10/20	/10
Grammar	Spelling/Grammar		10/10	/10
Grade			100/100	/100

March: Middle Ages Literature

Foundations of Western Literature

28 Sack of Rome in 410

March Week One Class

☐ Book Club Discussion: *City of God* by Saint Augustine, using Discussion Questions

☐ Read & Discuss "Background on *1001 Arabian Nights*"

☐ Read & Discuss "Crafting Essays"

☐ Read & Discuss "How to Turn a Paper into a Blog Post"

☐ Turn in Compare & Contrast Essay

Book Club Discussion on *City of God* by St. Augustine

Here are some questions to discuss about *City of God*.

- Why is it wrong and foolish to worship demons by worshipping idols?
- What is the difference between good and bad angels?
- How is death related to Adam's sin?
- What is the history of the Heavenly City and what is its end?
- What is the history of the earthly city and what is its end?

Background on *1001 Arabian Nights*

Tales from Arabian Nights is a collection of Persian, Middle Eastern stories compiled during the Islamic Golden Age (900s)

The book begins with the story of two brothers who are both sultans, Shahrayer and Shahaman. They both learn that their wives have been unfaithful to them. Shahrayer has his wife executed and then decides that he will marry a new wife every evening and have her executed the following morning. His vizier must provide the wives for the sultan.

The vizier's daughter, Shahrazad, asks her daddy if she can marry the sultan. He is horrified, but eventually gives in. You see the young woman has a plan. On the wedding night, she begs the sultan to allow her sister to spend the night and the sister asks her for a story. She shares a story, but doesn't finish it. The sultan puts off her execution until the next day so he can hear the end of the story. She finishes the story the next day, but starts a new story and doesn't finish it. This continues for 1001 nights until finally the sultan declares that Shahrazad will not be executed.

The stories are fairy tales, love stories, adventures, and folk tales. Christians and Jews are portrayed horribly and the fatalistic Islam worldview is evident in each story, but these stories have been enjoyed for centuries.

Review of the Writing Process

Before we talk about crafting an essay, let's take a quick review of the writing process. The writing process involves five steps from the Trigger to Publish.

Trigger

The trigger is that initial spark that starts you writing.

You might get an idea that you want to write about. You might get an email or text that you want to respond to. Or you might get an assignment from your writing teacher like "Turn this essay into a blog post."

Pre-Writing

Everyone handles the pre-writing phase differently and it's important to discover what works for you.

You have an idea and you want to communicate that idea. How do you get ready to write?

I like to talk about the idea with others. As I talk, I formulate what I want to say. After all writing and talking are both forms of communication.

Other times I like to use an outline. It's such a clear way to list ideas. Some people like to take notes as they research and put those notes in some kind of order before they write. Some folks just free write. They just sit down and start typing. There are also the thinkers who spend hours sitting and thinking through what they want to say before sitting down to write.

Use whatever way works for you. It is best to try all the methods and see which one works best.

Writing

This step is where we sit down at the computer or with a pen and notebook and write. We write, write, and write some more.

Revising

Revising involves crafting and editing.

We will talk about crafting in more detail in the next section, but realize that crafting is basically putting everything you have written on the chopping block. You restructure the paper to make it more readable for your audience. You look at the focus and tone of your paper to see if it is consistent and if it is what you want. You might change whole paragraphs or move them around after asking yourself, "Are my paragraphs working?"

Editing is the final phase of crafting where you fix the formatting, grammar, and spelling.

Publish

This step is where you share your finished work with your audience. You can publish by sending an email, turning a paper into a teacher, posting a blog online, or having a publisher sell your book.

Crafting Essays

Why is crafting an essay so important? Writers spend over fifty percent of their time rewriting and crafting their stories. You might rewrite a paper to improve the writing, grammar, or readability. You might rewrite or craft a paper for a different audience. You could rewrite a women's article for an audience of teens. Today you are going to rewrite an earlier assignment, making it a blog post.

When you revise an essay or paper, you "go back again" and "view it again." This is a brutal undertaking if you are attached to certain words, phrases, and flow in your paper. The secret to successful crafting is to be willing to take all the pieces apart and put them back together again. Ouch!

What if you are in love with a sentence, but it could be stated better? Just write the sentence down and tuck it away for future use.

When you are crafting an essay, ask yourself, "What am I trying to say here?" Once you figure that out, ask yourself, "Can I say this more clearly and more powerfully?

One way to help yourself to craft your own paper is to do a reverse outline. You simply look at your essay objectively and write an outline from the essay, listing a sentence or point for every paragraph you wrote. Examine the outline to see if that is truly what you wanted to say.

How to Turn a Paper into a Blog Post

You will take your paper you wrote on the Love of God from the Prodigal Son parable and turn it into a blog post. Here are some tips to write a great blog post.

A blog post is a visual experience that includes text, spacing, photos, and titles. A reader will not just read your content, but experience your post visually. **Is your post visually attractive to your reader?**

A blog post gets right to the point. You can follow the post and find things in the post quickly. Blogs posts are short (between 500 and 800 words is best), so every word has to count. Blog readers have a short attention span so make every word, phrase, and sentence should make a significant impact on your reader. **Is your blog post between 500 and 800 words? Are the sentences short? Are the paragraphs short?**

You will be targeting a specific audience. Everything about your blog post should target that audience. The font, the photos, the words you choose, the message, and the examples/illustrations. **Does your post target a specific audience? Who is that audience? Does it connect with that audience? Do you speak directly to the audience throughout the whole blog?**

Hook your reader with your first sentence. It might be a thought-provoking question, a quote, a statistic, or a quick story.

End a blog by calling your reader to action. Does your final paragraph call your readers to action?

Tips for Your Blog Post on the Love of God from the Prodigal Son Parable

Keep your sentences short. Get rid of all your long sentences. Chop them up into two if you have to.

Use simple, but precise words.

Try to find a new way to describe the love of God.

Inform, inspire, and interact with your audience.

Ask questions.

Share a personal story or experience briefly.

End with calling the reader to some kind of action. Tell your reader how to respond to God's love.

Write Your Blog Post

Are you ready? Time to write your blog post!

March Week One Home

☐ Read "Crash Course in History: Middle Ages"

☐ Read *1001 Arabian Nights*

☐ Read "Turn your Prodigal Son Essay into a Blog Post"

☐ Write your Blog Post

Crash Course in History: Middle Ages

What an exciting time the Middle Ages were! Sturdy castles dotted the countryside and protective walls guarded cities. Monks copied Scripture creating beautiful illuminated manuscripts. Knights jousted in competitions hidden inside suits of armor, while archers competed with their bows. Everybody went to the same church—there was only one Roman Catholic Church and it was powerful, keeping rulers of nations in line.

Kings ruled nations with queens at their side. They relied on the nobles for help and advice when needed. In return, the nobles received lands. In turn, the nobles protected and provided for knights and peasants who fought and worked for them.

Bards traveled around the countryside spinning tales set to music. Traveling troupes of performers put on mystery plays and miracle plays. Everywhere, people worked hard. Disease was frightening. Hygiene was not the best.

Like today, people fell in love, got married, and had babies. Children squabbled with one another and grew up quickly. Some people loved Jesus with all their hearts and others lived lives that were in opposition to God. The Middle Ages lasted from the 5th Century A.D. (400s) to the end of the 15th Century (1400s). Let's learn about this exciting time in history!

Castles

A castle was a big, sturdy, fortified sanctuary owned by a king, queen, prince, princess, duke, duchess, count, earl, viscount, or lord. Castles were a combination of fort and home. People lived, worked, and slept in the castle, but if danger came, there was enough room for the family, servants, and nearby villagers to seek safety inside its walls.

29 Castle DeHaar in Holland, the Netherlands 2011.

Castles had walls and towers that were strong and sturdy, often made of stone. Sometimes there was a moat around a castle with a drawbridge that could be pulled up or down. Once everyone was safe inside the castle, the drawbridge was pulled up and no one could get in without swimming across the moat. Long banners, similar to flags, fluttered in the breeze at the top of the castle identifying the owners.

Heraldry

Today companies have logos. McDonald's® has the golden arches and when you see those golden arches, you know it represents McDonald's®. In the same way, every noble family had a family "coat of arms," or special symbol. This family crest had symbols, patterns, and colors. The colors and patterns are symbolic. A blue background symbolized truth. A silver background stood for peace and red symbolized warrior.

Heraldry started as a way to identify knights when they were in battle since they were covered from head to toe in their armor. A knight's coat of arms would be on his shield. Each knight had his own coat of arms and was passed down from father to son.

Feudalism

The king of a country ruled over it with the help and advice of the church leaders and his nobles. He gave "fiefs" to his nobles. What are fiefs? They are large portions of the country that included many manors. Each noble had to pledge loyalty to the king, pay taxes, and send troops if needed by the king.

In each fiefdom were several manors. The lord of the manor pledged his loyalty to the nobles, paid taxes, and provided troops if necessary. The nobles protected the lord and his manor. In turn, the lord protected the peasants and serfs on his manor.

30 Queen Tamar and King George III, Mural Painting 11th Century, Georgia public domain.

Nobility

Nobility was the highest social class in the Middle Ages. In the feudal system, nobles held a fief, or small estate and were responsible for all the people who lived within the estate, or nearby town. Nobles pledged allegiance to the King or ruler of the country and provided military and financial aid during times of crisis.

Titles were often hereditary.

Here is the listing in order of royal and noble ranks.

- Emperor
- King/Queen
- Archduke
- Grand Duke/Grand Prince
- Prince

- Duke/Duchess
- Sovereign Prince
- Marquees/Marquis/Margravee/Landgrave
- Count/Earl
- Viscount/Vidame
- Baron/Baroness
- Baronet/Hereditary Knight
- Knight
- Esquire
- Gentleman

Different nobles wore different crowns.

Crowns, Coronets, Nobility, & Titles

31 Crown worn by Prince of Wales in Middles Ages

Worn by royals, nobles, and even sometimes by local government officials, crowns are also called coronets. Initially crowns were a personal ornament used to keep hair out of the face because for hundreds of years it was considered fashionable for both men and women to wear their hair long. In England, the kings, queens, and their children have the fleurs-de-lis on their coronets as an emblem of the claim of the Kings of England to the throne of France. Additionally, strawberry leaves were used frequently on the coronets to remind nobles that though they may have attained a high station in society, they still needed to humble themselves under the reign and leadership of the Lord Jesus Christ.

As a group, royals, nobles, knights, lords, and ladies are referred to as the peerage. As part of their positions, they had specific duties, honors, and "uniforms." At special state functions, like a coronation of a new sovereign, they each wore a coronet styled particularly for their rank.

Manors

At the lowest rung of nobility was the lord. He lived in a big house in the village called the manor house. His job was to protect the villagers and to take care of them. In return, the peasants paid taxes to him for the use of his land in the form of food or money. The manor included the manor house, peasant homes, village, and a church.

Many manors supported the same noble. The noble might be a duke, baron, or count. If the noble needed fighting men, the lords would send soldiers to the nobles. If the manor needed protecting, the noble would send knights to the manor.

Vassals/Peasants

Vassals, or peasants owned their own homes and farms. Some peasants owned their own businesses. Many peasants lived in one-room huts with thatched roofs. Clothes were made of wool and held together with a rope tied around their waist. Peasants grew fruit trees, kept bees for honey, raised chickens, and kept a cow for milk and cheese.

Serfs

Serfs belonged to the land. Serfs were not slaves. Serfs could not be bought and sold. They rented the land from the lord of the manor. Though they could make some income, most of their labor went to support the manor house. In turn, the lord of the manor made sure they were provided for. Serfs also worked as blacksmiths, cooks, maids, and groomsmen in the manor house.

Knights & Squires & Pages

Knights were not the only soldiers who fought in the wars and skirmishes of the Middle Ages. Archers and foot soldiers made up the bulk of the king's army. But knights were dashing and chivalrous. Knights were rich nobles who wore heavy armor and rode strong horses. It was expensive to pay for the armor, the horses, and all the ceremonial responsibilities of knighthood. Each knight had a coat of arms on his shield and on his personal banner. There was a lot of pageantry when the knights and nobles arrived.

If you wanted to grow up to become a knight, you had to be born in a noble family. At the age of seven, your family would send you to a famous knight. You would live with him in his castle. (I would hate to say goodbye to my seven-year-old son.) The pages learned from the squires how to ride a horse, use weapons, and practice the protocol for interacting with nobility flawlessly. A page graduated to become a squire.

Squires were usually teenage boys who trained the pages and served the knights. A squire went to battle and fought at his knight's side. A squire proved himself on the battlefield. Once he was ready, he was knighted in a very special ceremony.

Chivalry

Knights in the Middle Ages had an elaborate code of conduct called chivalry. They promised to defend the honor of Christ, the church, their noble, and their king. Knight were to be faithful, loyal, brave, trustworthy, humble, merciful, and gracious. They were to be gentle and protective of women, children, and anyone in a weaker state.

There was an elaborate code of behavior followed by knights and nobility. You can think of it as good manners on steroids.

Walled Cities

From Ancient Times, people have built walls around their cities as a form of protection. Walled cities were common in the Middle Ages.

The Church in Charge!

Life in the Middle Ages revolved around the local church. Everyone from the local lord of the manor and the king in his palace to the peasant in the village and the monk in his monastery went to church on Sunday morning. Babies were baptized, funerals performed, and weddings celebrated in the churches. Local village churches and town churches were referred to as parishes and led by a priest. A diocese was made up of many parishes and ruled over by a bishop. Bishops often lived in fancy houses while parish priests lived more simply.

Cardinals oversaw all the bishops and dioceses in a nation. The Pope was in charge of the entire church.

Organs played festive music while people sang hymns and songs to Jesus. Gregorian chants were popular. The church hosted festivals to celebrate holy days such as Christmas, Easter, and saints days.

Many people tithed in the Middle Ages. Wealthy nobles left land or money to the church in their wills. While the church accumulated wealth, it was in the possession of the church itself, not individuals.

Some men and women wanted to devote their lives to serving God and to spending hours a day to prayer and worship. These men became monks and the women became nuns, moving to monasteries or abbeys.

Monasteries & Abbeys

Monasteries and abbeys were much more than homes for monks and nuns. An abbey was like a little village. There was a church, chapels, rooms for the monks or nuns, guest rooms, kitchen, cloisters, storehouses, workrooms, and an infirmary. A strong wall surrounded these buildings for protection. These were bustling centers of honorable work.

People visited abbeys and monasteries to receive education and hospitalization. Monks grew herbs and made medicines to administer to the sick. The poor received food and financial help. Visitors were never turned away. Monks and nuns spent hours in prayer. Scrolls and old writings were preserved in monasteries. They made beautiful illuminated copies of these old books. Most importantly, the Bible was preserved and meticulously copied for future generations to enjoy. These centers of education in the Middle Ages were filled with scholars and tutors. The best of what was happening in the Middle Ages took place inside the walls of a monastery or abbey.

32 Russian Cathedral of the Resurrection public domain.

Some monks, called friars, were part of an order, or group of monks, that went out into the world to minister to others.

Sacraments

While the monks and nuns ministered to practical needs, the priests led the church services week after week. These special celebrations called masses were a collection of prayers, songs, and Scripture readings. The church believed that God poured His grace out to His people in a special way through the sacraments. There were seven sacraments.

1. Baptism
2. Confirmation
3. Marriage
4. Penance
5. Communion
6. Holy Unction
7. Holy Orders

Cathedrals

With a desire to honor the Lord, people built beautiful churches in the Middles Ages. Very large churches were called cathedrals. Many times these cathedrals were built in the shape of a cross. People in a village or town would donate money to build these gorgeous buildings. Everyone chipped in. It took a long time to build a cathedral. Some took over a hundred years to build.

Cathedrals were filled with beautiful artwork. Stained glass windows often told stories from the Bible. These colored glass windows were illuminated by sunlight and sparkled.

Crusades

Jesus died, was buried, and rose from the dead in the city of Jerusalem. For centuries European Christians traveled to Jerusalem on pilgrimages to see the places they had heard or read about in the Bible. When the Turks conquered Jerusalem, they would not allow the Christians access to Jerusalem. In outrage, the pope called for the knights of Christendom to go to the Holy Land on a Crusade to win back the right to go on pilgrimages to Jerusalem.

The First Crusade lasted from 1095 to 1099. The European Christians drove the Turks out of Jerusalem. In the Second Crusade (1147-1149) the Christians lost some of their ground. In the Third Crusade (1187-1192), Saladin, sultan of Egypt and Syria recaptured the city of Jerusalem. The Fourth

33 1099 Fall of Jerusalem Painting public domain.

Crusader (1202-1204) never made it to the Holy Land; instead they pillaged Constantinople. The Children's Crusade (1212) was started by a child and thousands of children headed to the Holy Land, never to be seen again. The next five crusades were unsuccessful.

Holidays

The church year was celebrated by everyone in Christendom. The holidays kicked off at Christmas with the Twelve Days of Christmas starting with Christmas Day and ending on Epiphany, or Three Kings Day. For twelve days, everyone took a break from work and spent time relaxing with family. If nobles tried to make the peasants or serfs work, the Church would step in.

Here are some of the holidays.

Twelfth Night, or **Epiphany**, celebrated the visit of the Wise Men to baby Jesus (January).

Plough Sunday, celebrated the first Sunday after Epiphany, was a holiday that kicked off the beginning of plowing.

St. Valentine's Day was a saint's day that eventually turned into a celebration of love by dancing, singing, and pairing games.

Shrove Tuesday and **Ash Wednesday** kicked off the season of Lent.

Palm Sunday was a celebration of Jesus' triumphal entry to Jerusalem.

Good Friday and **Easter** often fell in March. Christians remembered the death and resurrection of Jesus.

All Fools' Day gave the jesters the chance to cause mischief with jokes and pranks. (April)

Whitsun, or Pentecost, celebrated seven weeks after Easter Sunday, remembered the outpouring of the Holy Spirit. **Trinity Sunday** was a week later, celebrating the Father, Son, and Holy Spirit. **The Feast of Corpus Christi** came the Thursday after Trinity Sunday. Mystery and Miracle Plays were performed on the Feast of Corpus Christi.

Michaelmas was a feast day in honor of the Archangel Michael on September 29.

All Saints' Day, celebrated the first day of November, remembered the heroes of the faith.

Advent was a season of preparation for Christmas and included four Sundays before Christmas.

December was time again for **Christmas**, celebrating Christ's birth.

St. Stephen's Day, or **Boxing Day** was celebrated the day after Christmas. Alms boxes were opened and distributed to the poor.

Festivals

Festivals were put on by the church for holy days such as Christmastide or saints' days. The Lord of the Manor would often cover the expenses, but the church hosted the festival. When a holy day festival arrived, everyone took off work. There might be a miracle play presenting the Gospel. Sometimes jugglers, musicians, or bards would perform. Dancing and singing was a big part of the festival. There would often be a jousting tournament or archery competition.

Bards

A bard was a singing poet who traveled from castle to castle singing his tales of adventure and romance. Most stories sung or recited, rather than written down. The bard was a skilled storyteller as well as a man with a pleasant singing voice. Bards memorized long poems and sometimes wrote their own ballads.

Miracle Plays

Since the church service, or mass, was in Latin, it was hard for uneducated peasants to understand the Bible passages that were read aloud. In an attempt to help the peasants love and understand the Word of God, the church put on plays.

Mystery plays brought Scripture alive! The performers acted out Bible stories.

Miracle plays were about the saints. The play would portray the saint's virtue and any miracles the saint performed. It would also inspire watchers to imitate the saint.

Morality plays were performed to inspire people to live good, upright lives to honor Christ. The play had an important moral or lesson.

Read Tales of Arabian Nights

I would encourage you to answer these questions about the story as you read. They are the questions you will be discussing in book club.

What role do genies play in these stories?

_____

_____

_____

_____

What timeless qualities do these stories possess?

_____

_____

_____

_____

How is "The Seven Voyages of Sinbad the Sailor" similar to Homer's Odyssey?

_____

_____

_____

_____

Many of the heroes in the stories are greedy. What are your thoughts on this?

_____

_____

_____

_____

How is justice defined in these stories?

_____

_____

_____

_____

Turn "Prodigal Son" Essay into a Blog Post

We talked about turning a paper into a blog post, so now it's time to do it. Remember to stop and read your sentences and paragraphs aloud. Make sure your sentences are brief, but clear, and the overall post is a quick read.

Here are some ingredients of a blog post to keep in mind:

Brevity

The overall length should be 500 to 800 words with short sentences and short paragraphs.

Visual Appeal

Photographs draw readers in. White space and an appealing font add to the overall visual effect. Use titles and subtitles—they are easy on the eye.

Audience

The intended audience should be obvious from reading your blog post. Words should fit the audience. Examples, stories, metaphors, and illustrations should be geared to the audience. Questions should connect to the audience.

Catchy & Clear

Your blog post should be clear with focused ideas and arguments. The title, photos, and introduction should draw the reader in. Sentences and paragraphs should be easy to understand. Subtitles should be catchy and clear. Remove all unnecessary sentences.

Engaging

You should interact with the audience through questions and you-statements. Use engaging stories and illustrations. Call the reader to action at the end, in the last paragraph.

Transformation from Essay

The blog post should have clear, purposeful differences from your original essay. It should relate to the original. All the revisions should be to make a better blog post.

March Week Two Class

- ☐ Play Scattegories®
- ☐ Read Blog Posts in Groups
- ☐ Do Peer Review for Someone's Blog Post

Play Scattegories®

It's time to relax and play some word games. You can play Scattegories®, Scrabble®, or Funglish®.

Read Blog Posts in Groups

You will read your blog post aloud to a partner or to a small group. This is very important and will help you to keep your audience in mind as you write. Your listener might be a parent or sibling or fellow students in a co-op class.

When you listen to each other's blogs, pretend you are reading a blog post online. Does it move quickly enough? Are the sentences brief? Does it call you to action at the end?

Do peer reviews.

Peer Review for Blog Post

Let a peer review your blog post as you read it aloud or as they read it on their own. You can use this information to rewrite your blog post.

		Yes or No	Comments
Audience	Does your post target a specific audience? Who is that audience? Does writer connect with that audience?		
Visual Attraction	Do photos, titles, subtitles, font, and white space combine to make blog pleasing to audience, visually attractive?		
Transform	Relates to original, but clear, purposeful differences		
Paragraphs	Is your blog post between 500 and 800 words? Are the sentences short? Are the paragraphs short? Does your final paragraph call your readers to action?		
Flow of Paper	Paragraphs and the sentences within those paragraphs flow into one another		
Grammar	Spelling/Grammar		

March Week Two Home

☐ Finish Reading *Tales of Arabian Nights*

☐ Rewrite Blog Post

Finish Reading *Tales of Arabian Nights*

I would encourage you to answer these questions about the story as you read in the space provided in Week One Home. They are the questions you will be discussing in book club.

- What role do genies play in these stories?
- What timeless qualities do these stories possess?
- How is "The Seven Voyages of Sinbad the Sailor" similar to Homer's Odyssey?
- Many of the heroes in the stories are greedy. What are your thoughts on this?
- How is justice defined in these stories?

Rewrite Blog Post

Using input you have received from friends and family members, rewrite your blog post to make it even better.

Grading Rubric for Blog Post

Here is the grading rubric for Mom or Teacher.

		Comments	Possible Points	Points
Audience	Does your post target a specific audience? Who is that audience? Does it connect with that audience?		20/20	/20
Visual Attraction	Do photos, titles, subtitles, font, and white space combine to make blog pleasing to audience, visually attractive?		20/20	/20
Transform	Does blog post related to original, but clear, purposeful differences		20/20	/20
Paragraphs	Is your blog post between 500 and 800 words? Are the sentences short? Are the paragraphs short? Does your final paragraph call your readers to action?		20/20	/20
Flow of Paper	Paragraphs and the sentences within those paragraphs flow into one another		20/20	/10
Grammar	Spelling/Grammar		10/10	/10
Grade			100/100	100/100

March Week Three Class

☐ Book Club Discussion on *1001 Tales from Arabian Nights* using discussion questions

☐ Read & Discuss "Background on *The Merry Adventures of Robin Hood*"

☐ Read & Discuss "How to Write A Literary Analysis" & "Characterization"

☐ Read Rewritten Blog Posts in Groups

☐ Turn in Blog Post

Book Club Discussion on Tales from Arabian Nights

Here are some questions to discuss about *1001 Tales from Arabian Nights*.

- What role do genies play in these stories?
- What timeless qualities do these stories possess?
- How is "The Seven Voyages of Sinbad the Sailor" similar to Homer's Odyssey?
- Many of the heroes in the stories are greedy. What are your thoughts on this?
- How is justice defined in these stories?

Background on *The Merry Adventures of Robin Hood* by Howard Pyle

There are many versions of the story of Robin Hood, the legendary hero who robbed from the rich to give to the poor. One of my favorites is the version by Howard Pyle with his beautiful illustrations.

Howard Pyle, born in my husband's home town of Wilmington, Delaware, was a teacher, author, and artist. He began work as a magazine illustrator and eventually started illustrating classic books. Howard married Anne Poole. God blessed them with seven children.

One of his most popular works was *The Merry Adventures of Robin Hood*. In the story, Robin runs away from life to hide out in Sherwood Forest to live a "merry life" with his best friends. His friends are not normal guys, though, they are practically super-heroes. Not only do we have an adventure set in the thrilling world of knights, castles, and archers, we get to celebrate Robin Hood's triumphs and mourn his defeats while we enjoy one exciting escapade after another.

Set in Medieval Times, we have a corrupt king on the throne with a beloved and brave son, Richard the Lionheart. The corruption is not just with the king. There is corruption and greed in the church and with other government officials. Taxes are causing a terrible burden on everyone, especially the peasants. This terrible time in history eventually led the nobles of England to force King John to sign the Magna Charta.

Here is a list of the main characters in Robin Hood.

Robin Hood

A likeable outlaw who is hiding out in Sherwood Forest with his band of friends

Sheriff of Nottingham

Local law enforcement. The story's bad guy

Little John

Amazing fighter and loyal supporter of Robin Hood

Will Scarlet

Robin's nephew. The strongest man in Robin's group

Alan a Dale

Singer, troubadour, ballad writer, who is a skilled musician

Queen Eleanor

Married to King Henry and friend to Robin Hood

King Henry

Wicked king who hates Robin Hood and seeks to kill him

Bishop of Hereford

Henry's advisor. Robin's enemy

34 King Richard the Lionheart Painting
public domain.

How to Write a Literary Analysis

This year we have been learning to analyze literature. In the past, you may have written books reviews or written essays about the plot, theme, characterization, or setting of a work of fiction. This year, we have gone a little deeper, especially in our group discussions.

We will read and analyze *The Merry Adventures of Robin Hood* to write a literary analysis paper.

Literary Analysis Assignment

The purpose of literary analysis assignments is to learn how to analyze literature, how to create an original argument about a literary work, and how to use and cite quotes and examples from a literary work as supporting evidence in an argument.

Directions for the Literary Analysis Assignment

Read the book with the idea in mind that you are analyzing it. Underline or dog ear spots that are very interesting to you or raise questions in your mind. The key is to ask yourself questions as you are reading about the characters, certain things in the story, aspects of the plot, and the role of symbols, if any are used.

Discuss the questions and possible answers with family or fellow students in co-op. Analyze all the possibilities.

The next step is to choose your favorite question that you feel you could best answer using evidence and examples from the book. Go back through the book and find quotes, examples, etc. that provide a possible answer to your questions. Dog ear them, write them down, or circle them in the book.

Thesis

The next step is to create a thesis (your answer to the question).

Introduction

Your introduction reveals your thesis to your audience. Your introduction should capture your reader's attention and introduce the focus, or subject of your paper. You want to "hook" the reader so that he will keep on reading.

Here are some creative ways to introduce your paper.

Summarize your book briefly with a "what" and "how" statement about the work of fiction you are analyzing.

> In her novel *The Winged Watchman*, Hilda van Stockum takes us back in time to World War II in idyllic Holland where peaceful Dutch country life is turned upside-down by the invading Nazis.

You can start your paper with a quote from the book.

> "Mother was silenced, but she felt sorry for the Schenderhans parents all the same. After the family rosary that night, she added a Hail Mary for them. Mother added so many Hail Marys that Joris

sometimes thought he would get holes in his knees. His mother prayed for Queen Wilhelmina in England and the princesses in Canada. She prayed for the Pope and for the Allies, but at first she would not pray for the Germans, though Father said that was wrong."

You could open your paper by explaining the author's purpose and telling your audience how well you think she achieves that purpose.

In *The Winged Watchman*, Hilda van Stockum set out to show the daily life of a typical family involved in the Dutch Resistance during World War II under Nazi occupation. The reader feels the tension the Dutch people felt as they made moral decisions that were influenced by the evil that surrounded them.

You might begin your paper with a few general statements about life that relate to the focus of your analysis.

The only thing it takes for evil to triumph is for good men to do nothing. In *The Winged Watchmen*, Hilda van Stockum introduces us to good men who push the tide of evil back with courage and fortitude.

Another way to introduce your analysis paper is to make a general statement about the genre of literature you are reading.

Good historical fiction makes the setting come alive for the reader. This is certainly true in *The Winged Watchman* by Hilda van Stockum.

Paragraphs

The paragraphs in the body of your paper will be proving your thesis using the examples and quotes you found in the book. Try to organize each paragraph around a specific idea or point to help your argument flow. Your thesis will guide the body of your paper.

In each paragraph, state the main point you are proving clearly and relate it to the thesis. Support this main point with quotes or details from the work of fiction you are analyzing. Explain how the detail or quote proves your point. Pretend you are proving that faith overcomes hate in your paper.

Mother's strong Catholic faith was tested by the cruel behavior of the Nazis so that it was hard for her to love them. At first she refused to pray for them, but Father challenged her to pray for them too. Her faith overcame her anger at the Germans.

Conclusions

Your conclusion should restate the thesis showing how the evidence you've used proved it. End in an interesting way by perhaps stating a new question or suggesting the value of understanding the book. Give your reader something to think about long after they finish reading your paper. You have proven your thesis that faith overcomes hatred toward evil men and now you begin your conclusion.

Though the Dutch were conquered quickly by the Nazis, they were never truly conquered because they continued to resist in every way they could, risking their lives. In *The Winged Watchman*, we meet a hidden Jewish child, an "underdiver," a downed RAF pilot, and a brave family who work together to overcome their evil conquerors. In the midst of this, they hold on to their faith, trusting Him even when things go wrong.

Characterization

When a reader likes a book, she is often fond of the characters in the book. These characters are real to her.

A writer introduces the reader to his characters through dialogue, interaction with other characters, actions, attitudes, thoughts, and things that other characters say about the character.

Choose a character you like in the book and focus on that character so that you can analyze him, or her.

How to Analyze Characterization

Howard Pyle does a great job of creating characters in this book. You will be analyzing these characters in a paper. Let's start by asking questions.

Here are some questions to get you started.

- Choose a character. How does that character change throughout the book? What aspects of the story cause this change?
- Choose a character. What forces, other characters, conflict, or circumstances make him, or her, act in a certain way?
- Choose a character. What do his, or her, words, thoughts, and actions reveal about a character trait in his, or her, life?
- Who is Robin Hood's confidant, the person he relies on and trusts? Is this person trustworthy?
- What effect does the setting have on the characters or on one specific character?
- Do the characters behave differently in different settings? Why or why not?
- Explore the conflict between Robin Hood and King Henry. How is it complicated by Queen Eleanor?
- Explore the conflict between Robin Hood and the Sheriff of Nottingham. Does it change, develop, or come to an end?

Now, come up with more questions. Brainstorm together.

_____
_____
_____
_____
_____
_____
_____
_____
_____

Read Rewritten Blog Posts in Groups

You will read all your papers aloud to a partner or to a small group. This will help you to keep your audience in mind as you write. Your listener might be a parent or sibling or fellow students in a co-op class.

Read your rewritten blog posts. Hopefully you get a thumbs up from everyone! Maybe you should post it. ☺

March Week Three & Four Home

☐ Read *Robin Hood* by Howard Pyle & Answer Discussion Questions While you Read

☐ Brainstorm Some Questions for Your Literary Analysis

Read *Robin Hood* by Howard Pyle

Answer these questions about the story as you read. They are the questions you will be discuss in book club.

What behavior is considered honorable in this book? How can you tell the author considers it honorable? Do you agree with the author's opinion about honorable behavior? Why or why not?

_____
_____
_____
_____

How does Little John become a part of Robin Hood's Band of Merry Men?

_____
_____
_____
_____

Why is Robin Hood considered a hero when he breaks the law?

_____
_____
_____
_____

Do you feel any sympathy for the Sheriff? Does the author do anything with the elements of the story to prevent you from sympathizing for the Sheriff?

_____
_____
_____
_____

How does the Sheriff view Robin Hood and his band? How does this impact the readers' view of Robin?

_____
_____
_____
_____

How do Robin Hood and his band of Merry Men view the Sheriff? How does this impact the readers' view of Robin Hood and his men?

_____
_____
_____
_____

Contrast King Henry's leadership style with Robin Hood's leadership style.

_____
_____
_____
_____

Describe King Richard. How is King Richard different from his father, King Henry?

_____
_____
_____
_____

Describe King John. How is he different from his brother, King Richard, and his father, King Henry?

_____
_____
_____
_____

Character Analysis Paper

Let's stop a minute and ask some questions before you read _Robin Hood_ about the characters in the book. What question have you decided to use in your paper?

_____
_____
_____
_____

April: Fairy Tales & Characterization Paper

Foundations of Western Literature

35 Eight Stages of The Song of Roland in One Painting

April Week One Class

☐ Book Club Discussion on *Robin Hood* using Discussion Questions

☐ Read & Discuss "Background on Grimm's Fairy Tales"

☐ Brainstorm about Literary Analysis Paper

Book Club Discussion on *Robin Hood* by Howard Pyle

Here are some questions to discuss about *The Merry Adventures of Robin Hood*.

- What behavior is considered honorable in this book? How can you tell the author considers it honorable? Do you agree with the author's opinion about honorable behavior? Why or why not?
- How does Little John become a part of Robin Hood's Band of Merry Men?
- Why is Robin Hood considered a hero when he breaks the law?
- Do you feel any sympathy for the Sheriff? Does the author do anything with the elements of the story to prevent you from sympathizing for the Sheriff?
- How does the Sheriff view Robin Hood and his band? How does this impact the readers' view of Robin?
- How do Robin Hood and his band of Merry Men view the Sheriff? How does this impact the readers' view of Robin Hood and his men?
- Contrast King Henry's leadership style with Robin Hood's leadership style.
- Describe King Richard. How is King Richard different from his father, King Henry?
- Describe King John. How is he different from his brother, King Richard, and his father, King Henry?

Background on Grimm's Fairy Tales

In the early 1800s, Jacob Grimm and Wilhelm Grimm collected 86 folk tales that were popular in Germany. The compilation of stories was beautifully illustrated. The brothers produced another volume of fairy tales with 70 more stories in 1815. The collection was updated several times. The seventh edition contained 211 fairy tales.

Jacob and Wilhelm lost their father at a young age and had to work hard to provide for their family. Devoted Christians, they both graduated at the top of their law classes, but later switched to medieval German literature and became librarians.

With a heart to see the German states united as one nation of Germany, the brothers collected these tales to give Germans a sense of national heritage.

Our beloved Cinderella, Snow White, Sleeping Beauty, Hansel and Gretel, and Rumpelstiltskin can all be found in the Grimm brother's collection of fairy tales. They have become a beloved part of our American heritage.

Brainstorm about Characterization Paper

Let's think about your question and the answers to your question. Everyone share their questions and answers, brainstorming how to turn that into a thesis statement and a paper. By the time class is over, everyone should have a plan for their paper.

Discuss possibilities of things from the book to use in your paper. For example....

The narrator tells us the people love Robin Hood (pg. 102)

Robin Hood picks fights (4 examples from book)

Did Robin Hood fight fair? (pag. 129-131)

Was it fighting fair to take revenge for the beggar or to blow his bugle for the men to help him fight (pg. 127)

Does Robin Hood really protect the weak? He endangers an old woman (pg. 122), takes from a poor man to give to his Merry Men (pg. 133) and a potter calls him out (pg. 135)

What about Robin Hood's pride in the Little John Scene (pg. 147-148)

Robin Hood shows humility. He apologizes (pg. 151) and admits wrong to potter (pg. 135)

King John: Is he an unjust ruler or an outlaw?

April Week One Home

☐ Read *Grimm's Fairy Tales* & Answer Discussion Questions

☐ Read "Things to Remember about Literary Analysis"

☐ Make Outline for Characterization Paper

☐ Start Characterization Paper

Read *Grimm's Fairy Tales*

I would encourage you to answer these questions about *Grimm's Fairy Tales* in the space in April Week One as you read. They are the questions you will be discussing in book club.

Which Grimm's fairy tale is your favorite? Why?

_____

_____

_____

_____

Do any of the Grimm's fairy tale creeps you out? Which ones? Why?

_____

_____

_____

_____

Take one of Grimm's fairy tales and contrast it with the Disney version. Why do you think Disney changed it?

_____

_____

_____

_____

Things to Remember about Literary Analysis

To analyze literature, you are like a television detective looking for clues, putting the pieces together, and coming up with a hypothesis.

You start by asking questions. Not "yes" or "no" questions, but throught-provoking questions that can lead you on a detective adventure through the pages of your book.

Thesis

Your thesis should answer a complex question. It should make the reader think. You need to make a clear argument.

Argument

Your argument must be clearly defined in your thesis statement. Your argument needs to be the focus of every paragraph in your paper. Make your argument unusual and interesting. Then fully prove it!

Argument $\implies$ Claims $\implies$ Evidence

Analysis in Body

You will dig into the novel to find interesting points to prove an unexpected conclusion.

Each paragraph should show good examples from *The Merry Adventures of Robin Hood.* These examples should be explored and explained so that they show and prove your claims in the thesis/

Please go below obvious and surface facts in the novel to discover hidden insights.

Textual Reference

You should use quotes and examples from the novel in every paragraph. After all this is a literary analysis paper. These well-chosen quotes and examples should prove your point.

Make sure you have enough evidence. Make sure you are convinced this novel truly says what you are claiming that it says.

Introduce and cite your quotes with quotation marks and footnotes or parenthetical references.

Make sure you have a Works Cited page.

Flow

Your paper should flow logically. The structure of your ideas and argument should make sense and be clear to the reader. Make sure you include good transitions so that your reader does not get lost in your argument.

Introduction

Your introduction should capture your readers interest, introduce your topic, and set up your thesis clearly. If you have a good introduction, your reader will want to keep reading.

Conclusion

In the conclusion, you should restate your argument clearly and soundly. Then, go further to end with a new or interesting idea that leaves the reader thinking.

Quoting Sources

You will want to give credit to your sources in your paper.

If you are using an exact quote, you will need to use quotation marks, as well as a footnote or parenthetical reference. If it is a paraphrase or just an idea that you found and expanded upon you will just need a footnote or parenthetical reference, or in-text.

You can use footnotes (easy to do on Word® from Microsoft® or you can credit your sources using parenthetical reference, or in-text, inside parenthesis right before the period at the end of your sentence.

A footnote looks like this:

Her brother tripped and fell on a beam. Clara took care of him for several months. This led to her becoming a nurse. [2] You can see what would appear at the bottom of your page, along with all your other footnotes.

A parenthetical reference looks like this:

Her brother tripped and fell on a beam. Clara took care of him for several months. This led to her becoming a nurse (Angel 53). Information on the book would appear at the end of your paper in a bibliography, or Works Cited page.

Bibliography, or Works Cited

At the end of your paper, you will need to have a bibliography, or works cited page. This page needs to be in alphabetical order, based on the authors last name.

Here are the ingredients of a Bibliography, or Works Cited page

- Alphabetical
- Authors Listed Last, First (first in entry)
- Title in Italics (second in entry)
- Publication Info: City, State, Publisher, Year Published, Print or Web (third in entry)
- Online information need to include Database (or Website Title) and Date Accessed

---

[2] Angel, Merci *Clara Barton, Angel of Mercy*, New York, NY, Christian Publishing; 2015; print, page 53.

Start Characterization Paper

Using the plan you came up with in class time, write your characterization paper. Don't forget to use quotes from the book in your paper.

My Thesis

_____
_____
_____
_____
_____
_____
_____
_____
_____
_____

My Essay Outline

Introduction

My Hook

_____
_____
_____
_____

My Thesis Statement

_____
_____
_____
_____

First Paragraph/First Point from My Thesis Statement

_____
_____
_____

Example

_____
_____
_____

Example

_____
_____
_____

Illustration

_____
_____
_____

Second Paragraph/Second Point from My Thesis Statement

_____
_____
_____

Example

_____
_____
_____

Example

_____
_____
_____

Illustration

_____
_____
_____

Third Paragraph/Third Point from My Thesis Statement

_____
_____
_____

Example

_____
_____
_____

Example

_____
_____
_____

Illustration

_____
_____
_____

Fourth Point (you may not have a 4th point!)

_____
_____
_____

Examples

_____
_____
_____

Illustration

_____
_____
_____

Fifth Point (you may not have a 5th point!)

_____
_____
_____

Example

_____
_____
_____

Example

_____
_____
_____

Illustration

_____

_____

_____

Conclusion

Restate My Thesis Statement

_____

_____

_____

Call Reader to Action

_____

_____

_____

April Week Two Class

- [ ] Read & Discuss "Background on *"Song of Roland"*
- [ ] Read sections of "Song of Roland" aloud
- [ ] Brainstorm about Characterization Paper

Background on *Song of Roland* and Battle of Roncevaux

The Battle of Roncevaux Pass was fought on August 1, 788. Charlemagne's Franks were retreating after a battle campaign in Spain. In the rear, Frankish soldiers were carrying a rich collection of war spoils home. The Basques attacked the Franks slaughtering every Frankish soldier.

In the poem, Roland is the nephew of Charlemagne. The Basques who attack the Franks become Muslim Saracens and Charlemagne returns to Spain to avenge the death of his knights. In the poem, Palestine is named Outremer, a Muslim land.

The plot of the poem begins with Charlemagne warring against the Muslim Saracens in Spain. The king of the one remaining Muslim stronghold promises to become Charlemagne's vassal so that Charlemagne will leave. But once Charlemagne is home in France, King Marsile breaks his promise.

Roland, nephew of Charlemagne and a brave knight, suggests that his stepfather, Ganelon, stays in Spain to negotiate with King Marsile. Deceitful Ganelon encourages King Marsile to attack the Franks on their way home, wanting to see his stepson Roland destroyed.

Archbishop Turpin fights alongside Roland in the ensuing battle where the Franks are massacred. Angels escort Roland's soul to Heaven. When Charlemagne hears the news, he returns to the battle scene where he and his men mourn the slain knights. The Lord holds the sun in place so that the Franks can destroy the Saracens. After they are destroyed, Ganelon is put on trial for treason and given a traitor's death.

The Poem Itself

Song of Roland is a French epic poem about the Battle of Roncevaux Pass. It is the oldest surviving piece of French literature.

The poem is written in stanzas (parts or chapters) of different length, but each line has ten syllables and the last vowel sound in each line is the same in each stanza.

The poem focuses on action and uses repetition and parallelism. Sometimes a scene is described several times, focusing on different perspectives.

The poem is written to be read aloud. Reading it silently would be like reading a movie script, so you won't get the same enjoyment. It's more fun to watch a movie than read a movie script.

Read *Song of Roland* Aloud

Poems are meant to be read aloud. Download the "Song of Roland" online and read it together aloud. Okay, you will need hours to read the whole thing aloud so just read it aloud for a set time. Take turns reading the poem. I have enclosed fourteen stanzas of "The Song of Roland" in the back of this book for you to read aloud.

Brainstorm about Characterization Paper

Bring your paper to class time and talk with others about what you have so far and where you are going with your paper.

Are you using and citing quotes from *The Merry Adventures of Robin Hood* in your paper?

Do you need to tweak your thesis?

Do you have enough evidence to prove your thesis?

Are you struggling with any part of your paper?

Be sure to give good advice to others too.

This is our time to brain storm and help each other.

April Week Two Home

☐ Finish Reading *Grimm's Fairy Tales*
☐ Finish Writing Characterization Analysis

Continue Reading *Grimm's Fairy Tales*

I would encourage you to answer these questions about *Grimm's Fairy Tales* in the space in April Week One as you read. They are the questions you will be discussing in book club.

- Which Grimm's fairy tale is your favorite? Why?
- Do any of the Grimm's fairy tale creeps you out? Which ones? Why?
- Take one of Grimm's fairy tales and contrast it with the Disney version. Why do you think Disney changed it?

Finish Characterization Analysis

Using the plan you came up with in class time, write your characterization paper. Don't forget to use quotes from the book in your paper.

Grading Rubric for Characterization Analysis

Turn in your Characterization Analysis Paper. Here is a Grading Rubric for Mom or Co-op Teacher.

		Comments	Possible Points	Points
Thesis	Does thesis answer a complex question, giving a clear argument?		10/10	/10
Argument	Is the argument clearly defined in the thesis? Is the argument fully proved in the essay? Does the argument make claims and give evidence for those claims?		20/20	/20
Textual References	Are quotes and examples from the novel used in every paragraph? Are quotes and examples clearly cited using footnotes or parenthetical references? Is there a works cited page?		20/20	/20
Analysis	Does writer dig into the novel, below the surface, and find interesting points to prove an unexpected conclusion?		20/20	/20

		Comments	Possible Points	Points
Flow of Paper	Is the argument presented in the paper logically and sequentially so that it makes sense to the reader? Are there good transitions so the reader doesn't get lost? Is the structure and order of ideas logical?		20/20	/20
Grammar	Spelling/Grammar		10/10	/10
Grade			100/100	100/100

April Week Three Class

Book Club Discussion on *Grimm's Fairy Tales* using discussion questions

☐ Read & Discuss "Background on Hans Christian Andersen's Fairy Tales"

☐ Read & Discuss "How to Write a Fairy Tale Paraphrase"

☐ Turn in your Characterization Analysis

Book Club Discussion: *Grimm's Fairy Tales*

Here are some questions to discuss about *Grimm's Fairy Tales*.

- Which Grimm's fairy tale is your favorite? Why?
- Do any of the Grimm's fairy tale creeps you out? Which ones? Why?
- Take one of Grimm's fairy tales and contrast it with the Disney version. Why do you think Disney changed it?

Background on Hans Christian Andersen's Fairy Tales

A Danish writer, Hans Christian Andersen, became famous around the world for his beautiful fairy tales like "The Ugly Duckling," "The Little Mermaid," "The Little Match Girl," "Thumbelina," "The Emperor's New Clothes," and "The Princess and the Pea." Educated and gifted in the arts, Hans is remember as a storyteller who loved Jesus. He believed that God is good and works all things together for our good. He never married, but lived a moral upright life.

Hans Christian Anderson's fairy tales often have a Christian message, or theme. These stories esteem love, generosity, truth, humility, and laying one's life down for others. They speak out against pride, foolishness, lying, and selfishness.

"The Jewish Girl" and "The Little Match Girl" promote the hope of Heaven and "The Red Shoes" address dealing with sin. These precious Danish fairy tales are part of our American heritage.

How to Paraphrase a Fairy Tale

Let's paraphrase a fairy tale. Here are the steps to paraphrase a fairy tale, or any other writing passage.

1. Skim the entire fairy tale
2. Read the fairy tale carefully. Note key words and phrases.
3. Try to list the main idea of each section without looking at the section.
4. Now go back and read each sentence, focusing on one paragraph at a time.
5. Summarize each idea (sentence by sentence) with clear writing.
6. When you finish one paragraph, go to the next one. (Use the pages in your book to make it easier)

April Week Three & Four Home

☐ Read *Hands Christian Andersen's Fairy Tales*

☐ Follow Directions to Write a Fairy Tale Paraphrase

Read *Hans Christian Andersen's Fairy Tales*

I would encourage you to answer these questions about the stories as you read. They are the questions you will be discussing in book club.

What is your favorite fairy tale and why?

_____
_____
_____

Name some ways that Hans Christian Andersen's faith is evident in his fairy tales?

_____
_____
_____

Name three fairy tales with a biblical theme. What are those three biblical themes?

_____
_____
_____

Is there a fairy tale that you would like to change the ending to? Which one and why?

_____
_____
_____

Fairy Tale Paraphrase Directions

We went over the fairy tale assignment in class time. So, now it's time to paraphrase a fairy tale.

The Hans Christian Andersen Tale I choose is _____.

Read the fairy tale through again. Summarize the plot in two sentences.

_____
_____
_____
_____
_____
_____
_____
_____

List the Characters in the story:

_____
_____
_____
_____
_____
_____
_____

Read the story again, paragraph by paragraph. After each paragraph, list key words from each sentence.

Paragraph One Key Words

_____
_____
_____
_____
_____

My own Paragraph One:

_____
_____
_____
_____
_____
_____
_____
_____
_____
_____

Paragraph Two Key Words

_____
_____
_____
_____
_____
_____

My own Paragraph Two:

_____
_____
_____
_____
_____
_____
_____
_____
_____
_____
_____
_____
_____
_____
_____

Paragraph Three Key Words

_____
_____
_____
_____
_____

My own Paragraph Three:

_____
_____
_____
_____
_____
_____
_____
_____
_____
_____
_____

Paragraph Four Key Words

My own Paragraph Four:

Paragraph Five Key Words

My own Paragraph Five:

Paragraph Six Key Words

_____
_____
_____
_____
_____

My own Paragraph Six:

_____
_____
_____
_____
_____
_____
_____
_____
_____
_____
_____
_____
_____
_____
_____
_____
_____
_____

Paragraph Seven Key Words

_____
_____
_____
_____
_____
_____

My own Paragraph Seven:

_____
_____
_____
_____
_____
_____
_____
_____
_____
_____
_____
_____
_____

Paragraph Eight Key Words

_____
_____
_____
_____
_____
_____

My own Paragraph Eight:

_____
_____
_____
_____
_____
_____
_____
_____
_____
_____
_____
_____
_____
_____
_____
_____
_____

Paragraph Nine Key Words

_____
_____
_____
_____
_____
_____

My own Paragraph Nine:

_____
_____
_____
_____
_____
_____
_____
_____
_____
_____
_____
_____
_____
_____

Paragraph Ten Key Words

_____
_____
_____
_____
_____
_____

My own Paragraph Ten:

_____
_____
_____
_____
_____
_____
_____
_____
_____
_____
_____
_____
_____
_____
_____

If you need more room, use notebook paper to finish your paragraphs. Now, put all the paragraph together and make sure they flow nicely into one another. You will need to add transitions and edit your sentences and paragraphs to make your paper enjoyable to read. Read it aloud to a family member and see if they like it.

Grading Rubric for Fairy Tale Paraphrase

Turn in your paraprhase

		Comments	Possible Points	Points
Audience	Is the paraphrase interesting & enjoyable to read?		10/10	/10
Relation to Original	Is the paraphrase the exact same as the original but in the writer's own words?		20/20	/20
Paragraph by Paragraph	Did writer summarize paragraph by paragraph so that it is true to the original story?		20/20	/20
Elements of Story	Are the plot, theme, characters, and setting in the paraphrase the same as the original?		20/20	/20
Flow of Paper	Paragraphs and the sentences within those paragraphs flow into one another		20/20	/20
Grammar	Spelling/Grammar		10/10	/10
Grade			100/100	100/100

May: Fairy Tales & Norse Mythology

Foundations of Western Literature

May Week One Class

- [ ] Book Club Discussion on Hans Christian Andersen's Fairy Tales
- [ ] Read & Discuss "Background on Norse Mythology" & "How the Vikings Embraced jesus"
- [ ] Read & Discuss "Ingredients of a Good Story" and "How to Write Your Own Fairy Tale"
- [ ] Turn in Fairy Tale Paraphrase

Book Club Discussion on Hans Christian Andersen's Fairy Tales

Here are some questions to discuss about *Han's Christian Anderson's Fairy Tales*.

- What is your favorite fairy tale and why?
- Name some ways that Hans Christian Andersen's faith is evident in his fairy tales?
- Name three fairy tales with a biblical theme. What are those three biblical themes?
- Is there a fairy tale that you would like to change the ending to? Which one and why?

Background on Norse Mythology

If you like to read J.R.R. Tolkien, you've probably wondered about the elfs, dwarfs, and hobbits. Where did those ideas come from? Well, Tolkien, a devout Christian, was also fascinated by Norse Mythology. He adapted some of it into his stories creating all kinds of non-human characters and lands.

You will also find Norse Mythology in some of the Marvel movies. Yes, Norse mythology still finds its way into modern culture.

The North men, Norsemen, or Vikings of Old, worshipped their own pagan idol/gods and idol/goddesses. These stories are quite a contrast to the Christian fairy tales of Hans Christian Anderson.

The Vikings of Norway, Sweden, Denmark, and Iceland were warriors who sailed to other nations, raided innocent villages, and took their plunder home. Like the Vikings, their idol/gods and idol/goddesses are strong, aggressive, and always itching for a fight.

We will read *D'Aulaires' Book of Norse Myths* by Ingri and Edgar Parin D'Aulaire. This version leaves out the sexual content of the original myths.

Six of our seven days of the week get their names from Norse idol/gods. God, of course established the seven days of the week at Creation and the Romans named them after the seven main heavenly bodies: Sun, Moon, Mars, Mercury, Jupiter, Venus, and Saturn. The English adapted these Viking names and we still use them today.

Sunday (Suna/sol/sun. The sun was worshipped)

Monday (Mani. Moon idol/god)

Tuesday (Tiw, or Tyr. A one-handed idol/god)

Wednesday (Odin or Wodin. Chief idol/god)

Thursday (Thor. The idol/god of thunder)

Friday (Frig. Idol/goddess and wife of Odin)

Saturday (Saturn, the name of a Roman god and the only non-Norse name)

Here is a list to keep everyone straight in the Norse Myths.

Valhalla

Their Heaven, a great hall in Asgard where Odin receives souls of heroes killed in battle

Valkyries

Beautiful blondes who escort Vikings who die in battle to Heaven

Asgard (Asgarth)

Where the idol/gods live

Aesir

Chief idol/gods of Asgard

Odin

Head of Aesir, creator of the world with his brothers Vili and Ve (is Wodan or Wotan in Teutonic mythology)

Frigg

Idol/goddess of sky, wife of Odin

Thor

Idol/god of thunder, oldest son of Odin (is Donar in Germanic mythology)

Sif

Wife of Thor

Tyr

Idol/god of war, son of Odin. (is Tiu in Teutonic mythology)

Frey

Idol/god of fertility and crops, son of Njorth

Freya

Idol/goddess of love and beauty sister or Frey

Sigi

Son of Odin, king of Huns

Rerir

King of Huns, son of Sigi

Ask (Aske, Askr)

First man, created by Odin, Hoenir, and Lothur

Regnarok

Final destruction of present world in battle between giants and idol/gods. Some minor gods will survive. Lif and Lifthrasir will repopulate the world

Lif and Lifthraisr

First man and woman after Ragnarok

Loki

God of evil and mischief

Fenrir

Wolf and offspring of Loki. Swallows Odin at Ragnarok and is slain by Vitharr

How the Vikings Embraced Jesus Christ

During the 800s and 900s (ninth century and tenth century), the Vikings plundered their way throughout Northern and Western Europe. They established settlements in Normandy, England, Scotland, Ireland, Greenland, and Russia.

In 783, the Vikings raided a Christian monastery in Lindisfarne, brutally butchering the priests. This filled believers with fear. While the Vikings were busy plundering, God put it on the heart of a young Christian named Ansgar to pray for the Vikings. He redeemed several Danish slaves and led them to Christ. Eventually, they were mentored to carry the Gospel to their own countrymen.

When King Harold of Denmark was driven from his court, he took refuge in the French court of Louis I, heard the Gospel, turned to Christ, and was baptized. When King Harold returned to Denmark, he and Ansgar partnered up to bring the Gospel to the Danes.

King Bjorn of Sweden actually called for Ansgar to come and preach to the Swedish Vikings. The missionaries were welcomed and a church was built. The Vikings got together to vote on the matter.

"Should missionaries be allowed to preach the Gospel?" they asked. "Wouldn't it anger the idol/gods?" they wondered aloud. When one old Viking stood up and declared, "The Christian God is stronger than Thor," the matter was decided. There is no one more powerful than our God!

In England, King Alfred the Saxon defeated the Danish Vikings who would not stop raiding the English coast. After his victory, King Alfred led the leader of the Vikings to Christ and stood as his sponsor in baptism.

The hardened Vikings were impressed by the powerful Jesus that triumphed over death itself and rose from the dead.

King Otto the Great, emperor of the Holy Roman Empire, sent missionaries to the Vikings, along with many other Saxon (Germanic) Christians.

King Canute of Denmark, and eventually England too, commanded his subjects to learn the Lord's Prayer and to take communion. The church in Denmark began to grow.

King Haakon of Norway who had been led to Christ and discipled in England, urged his people to give their hearts to Christ. Most of the men and women in his court were saved and baptized.

Let me tell you about one Swedish Viking who came to Christ. Olaf, tall and strong, led a fleet of 90 ships to pillage Holland, England, Scotland, Wales, and France. While off the coast of England, he heard of a prophet who could predict the future. He tracked the prophet down. The old prophet told Olaf that his crew would mutiny, Olaf would be wounded, recover, and be baptized as a Christian. When the mutiny, wounding, and healing happened as predicted, Olaf went to find the old man and ask for his gift. The man said that God had blessed him with the gift of prophecy, but he did not have the power to give this gift. Only Christ could give the gift of prophecy. Olaf repented and turned to Christ. After becoming a Christian, Olaf traveled to Norway to claim it for Christ. He burned heathen temples and destroyed idols.

Thankfully, human sacrifice to worship the Viking idol/gods stopped and the mighty Vikings began to serve the Lord. The also gave up raiding and pillaging.

Ingredients of a Good Story

All of us have stories that we love to reread or movies we have seen many times. What makes us love a good story?

We have been reading some amazing stories that have stood the test of time. What makes them so wonderful?

Here are some of the ingredients of a good story.

- Characters we can like and root for
- A setting that makes the story more believable
- A plot, or story line that starts with an inciting incident followed by action and conflict that intensifies until a climax, the final conflict. This is followed by a resolution, where bad guys are punished and good guys rewarded.
- A theme or message that builds us up

- Dialogue that is interesting and entertaining
- Descriptive writing that helps us to "see" what the author wants us to "see"
- Action that is exciting and suspenseful, yet believable

How to Write Your Own Fairy Tale

Now, it's time to put these ingredients into your own story. That may sound like a lot of things to keep track of, but I'm confident that you can do a great job on writing your own fairy tale.

Before you write your own fairy tale, we are going to brainstorm together with ideas for each of the ingredients that we just talked about.

Characters we can like and root for:

_____
_____
_____
_____

A setting that makes the story more believable:

_____
_____
_____
_____

A plot, or story line that starts with an inciting incident followed by action and conflict that intensifies until a climax, the final conflict. This is followed by a resolution, where bad guys are punished and good guys rewarded. Plot Ideas:

_____
_____
_____
_____
_____
_____
_____
_____

A theme or message that builds us up:

_____
_____
_____
_____

Dialogue that is interesting and entertaining:

_____
_____
_____
_____
_____

Descriptive writing that helps us to "see" what the author wants us to "see":

_____
_____
_____
_____
_____

Action that is exciting and suspenseful, yet believable:

_____
_____
_____
_____
_____

Read Fairy Tale Paraphrases in Groups

You will read all your papers aloud to a partner or to a small group. This is very important and will help you to keep your audience in mind as you write. Your listener might be a parent or sibling or fellow students in a co-op class.

Just read your paraphrases aloud for fun. You don't have to give or get input, except to say, "Well done!"

May Week One Home

☐ Read *D'Aulaires' Book of Norse Myths* by Ingri and Edgar Parin D'Aulaire.

☐ Brainstorm for your Fairy Tale by Completing All the Charts

☐ Write Your Own Fairy Tale

Read Norse Mythology

I would encourage you to answer these questions about *D'Aulaires' Book of Norse Myths* by Ingri and Edgar Parin D'Aulaire. They are the questions you will be discussing in book club.

Compare one of the Norse idol/gods to True God who created the heavens and the earth. How are they different?

_____

_____

_____

_____

Compare the Norse idea of the end of the world with the biblical end of the world.

_____

_____

_____

_____

What would be disappointing about worshipping these idol/gods and idol/goddesses?

_____

_____

_____

_____

Write Your Own Fairy Tale

We have talked about the ingredients of a good fairy tale. Using that information and the ideas you discussed in class, come up with your own fairy tale. Here are some charts to help you with brainstorming on your own.

Main Characters in My Fairy Tale

Stories almost always involve human or animal characters. They have personalities, likes and dislikes, physical appearance, and relationships to other characters. Authors must create their characters. Once the writer creates them, he must "show" them to the reader through actions, dialogue, and what other characters say about the character. A well-rounded character seems like a real person with strengths and flaws.

Main Characters Names	Age	Personality	Beliefs	Appearance	Likes/ Dislikes	Roles in Story/Relation to Other Characters

Minor Characters in My Fairy Tale

Minor characters might appear infrequently or play a less important role. Writers must create them, too, making sure they are well-rounded as well.

Supporting Characters Names	Age	Personality	Beliefs	Appearance	Likes/ Dislikes	Roles in Story/ Relation to Other Characters

The Setting in My Fairy Tale

The setting can often play a role in the plot and mood of the story. A dark stormy night is perfect for a mystery. Is the story set in present day or sometime in the past or future?

Settings in Story	Historical Time Period	Location	Any Significant Facts
Scene I			
Scene II			
Scene III			
Scene IV			

The Plot in My Fairy Tale

Plot is the story itself with an inciting incident, following by rising action, leading to the climax, and a resolution where the bad guys are punished and the good guys are rewarded.

Conflict in Story	Inciting Incident & Increasing Tension	Climax in Story	Resolution in Story

You've brainstormed. Now it's time to write your own fairy tale.

May Week Two Class

☐ Read & Discuss "Norse Mythology in Western Culture"

☐ Read Modern Fairy Tales Aloud in Groups & Peer Review

Norse Mythology in Western Culture

Brainstorm together ways in which Norse mythology plays a role in Western culture and literature. Write the list you come up with here:

_____

_____

_____

_____

_____

Read Your Own Fairy Tales Aloud in Groups

You will read all your papers and stories aloud to a partner or to a small group. This is very important and will help you to keep your audience in mind as you write. Your listener might be a parent or sibling or fellow students in a co-op class. Be sure to give helpful feedback to your siblings and friends.

Peer Review someone's story and make sure your story is reviewed by at least one peer.

Peer Review for Your Own Fairy Tale

Let a peer review your story as you read it aloud or as they read it on their own. You can use this information to rewrite your story.

		Yes or No	Comments
Audience	Story is enjoyable to read?		
Characters	Characters are well-rounded? Author "shows" characters through dialogue, actions, and what other characters think of character?		
Setting	The setting fits in with the plot, characters, and mood of the story?		
Plot	The plot, or storyline, has an inciting incident, rising action, climax, and resolution		
Story Flow	Story flows well from scene to scene and "makes sense"?		
Grammar	Spelling/Grammar		

May Week Two Home

☐ Finish Reading *D'Aulaires' Book of Norse Myths* by Ingri and Edgar Parin D'Aulaire

☐ Rewrite Your Own Fairy Tale

Finish Reading Norse Mythology

I would encourage you to answer these questions about *D'Aulaires' Book of Norse Myths* by Ingri and Edgar Parin D'Aulaire in the space provided in May Home Week One. They are the questions you will be discussing in book club.

Compare one of the Norse idol/gods to True God who created the heavens and the earth. How are they different?

Compare the Norse idea of the end of the world with the biblical end of the world.

What would be disappointing about worshipping these idol/gods and idol/goddesses?

Rewrite Your Own Fairy Tale

With the input you received from your peers and by rereading and evaluating it yourself, rewrite your own fairy tale. This is your last writing assignment of the year! ☺

Grading Rubric for Your Own Fairy Tale

With the input you received in group time, rewrite your own fairy tale, making corrections and adding any needed changes.

		Comments	Possible Points	Points
Audience	Story is enjoyable to read?		10/10	/10
Characters	Characters are well-rounded? Author "shows" characters through dialogue, actions, and what other characters think of character?		20/20	/20
Setting	The setting fits in with the plot, characters, and mood of the story?		10/10	/10
Plot	The plot, or storyline, has an inciting incident, rising action, climax, and resolution?		30/30	/30
Story Flow	Story flows well from scene to scene and "makes sense"?		20/20	/20
Grammar	Spelling/Grammar		10/10	/10
Grade			100/100	100/100

May Week Three Class

☐ Book Club Discussion on Norse Mythology

☐ Turn in Your Own Fairy Tale

☐ Celebrate! You are Finished!

Book Club Discussion on Norse Mythology

Here are some questions to discuss about *D'Aulaires' Book of Norse Myths* by Ingri and Edgar Parin D'Aulaire.

- Compare one of the Norse idol/gods to True God who created the heavens and the earth. How are they different?
- Compare the Norse idea of the end of the world with the biblical end of the world.
- What would be disappointing about worshipping these idol/gods and idol/goddesses?

Resources

36 Saint Augustine, Antonio Rodriguez

Sun Tzu on the Art of War

The Oldest Military Treatise in the World

I. LAYING PLANS

1. Sun Tzu said: The art of war is of vital importance to the State.
2. It is a matter of life and death, a road either to safety or to ruin. Hence it is a subject of inquiry which can on no account be neglected.
3. The art of war, then, is governed by five constant factors, to be taken into account in one's deliberations, when seeking to determine the conditions obtaining in the field.
4. These are: (1) The Moral Law; (2) Heaven; (3) Earth; (4)The Commander; (5) Method and discipline.
5. & 6. The Moral Law causes the people to be in complete accord with their ruler, so that they will follow him regardless of their lives, undismayed by any danger.
7. Heaven signifies night and day, cold and heat, times and seasons.
8. Earth comprises distances, great and small; danger and security; open ground and narrow passes; the chances of life and death.
9. The Commander stands for the virtues of wisdom, sincerely, benevolence, courage and strictness.
10. By method and discipline are to be understood the marshaling of the army in its proper subdivisions, the graduations of rank among the officers, the maintenance of roads by which supplies may reach the army, and the control of military expenditure.
11. These five heads should be familiar to every general: he who knows them will be victorious; he who knows them not will fail.
12. Therefore, in your deliberations, when seeking to determine the military conditions, let them be made the basis of a comparison, in this wise:--
13.   1.   Which of the two sovereigns is imbued with the Moral law?
       2.   Which of the two generals has most ability?
       3.   With whom lie the advantages derived from Heaven and Earth?
       4.   On which side is discipline most rigorously enforced?
       5.   Which army is stronger?
       6.   On which side are officers and men more highly trained?
       7.   In which army is there the greater constancy both in reward and punishment?
14. By means of these seven considerations I can forecast victory or defeat.
15. The general that hearkens to my counsel and acts upon it, will conquer: let such a one be retained in command! The general that hearkens not to my counsel nor acts upon it, will suffer defeat:--let such a one be dismissed!
16. While heading the profit of my counsel, avail yourself also of any helpful circumstances over and beyond the ordinary rules.
17. According as circumstances are favorable, one should modify one's plans.
18. All warfare is based on deception.
19. Hence, when able to attack, we must seem unable; when using our forces, we must seem inactive; when we are near, we must make the enemy believe we are far away; when far away, we must make him believe we are near.
20. Hold out baits to entice the enemy. Feign disorder, and crush him.
21. If he is secure at all points, be prepared for him. If he is in superior strength, evade him.
22. If your opponent is of choleric temper, seek to irritate him. Pretend to be weak, that he may grow arrogant.
23. If he is taking his ease, give him no rest. If his forces are united, separate them.
24. Attack him where he is unprepared, appear where you are not expected.
25. These military devices, leading to victory, must not be divulged beforehand.
26. Now the general who wins a battle makes many calculations in his temple ere the battle is fought. The general who loses a battle makes but few calculations beforehand. Thus do many calculations

lead to victory, and few calculations to defeat: how much more no calculation at all! It is by attention to this point that I can foresee who is likely to win or lose.

II. WAGING WAR

1. Sun Tzu said: In the operations of war, where there are in the field a thousand swift chariots, as many heavy chariots, and a hundred thousand mail-clad soldiers, with provisions enough to carry them a thousand li, the expenditure at home and at the front, including entertainment of guests, small items such as glue and paint, and sums spent on chariots and armor, will reach the total of a thousand ounces of silver per day. Such is the cost of raising an army of 100,000 men.
2. When you engage in actual fighting, if victory is long in coming, then men's weapons will grow dull and their ardor will be damped. If you lay siege to a town, you will exhaust your strength.
3. Again, if the campaign is protracted, the resources of the State will not be equal to the strain.
4. Now, when your weapons are dulled, your ardor damped, your strength exhausted and your treasure spent, other chieftains will spring up to take advantage of your extremity. Then no man, however wise, will be able to avert the consequences that must ensue.
5. Thus, though we have heard of stupid haste in war, cleverness has never been seen associated with long delays.
6. There is no instance of a country having benefited from prolonged warfare.
7. It is only one who is thoroughly acquainted with the evils of war that can thoroughly understand the profitable way of carrying it on.
8. The skillful soldier does not raise a second levy, neither are his supply-wagons loaded more than twice.
9. Bring war material with you from home, but forage on the enemy. Thus the army will have food enough for its needs.
10. Poverty of the State exchequer causes an army to be maintained by contributions from a distance. Contributing to maintain an army at a distance causes the people to be impoverished.
11. On the other hand, the proximity of an army causes prices to go up; and high prices cause the people's substance to be drained away.
12. When their substance is drained away, the peasantry will be afflicted by heavy exactions.
13. & 14. With this loss of substance and exhaustion of strength, the homes of the people will be stripped bare, and three-tenths of their income will be dissipated; while government expenses for broken chariots, worn-out horses, breast-plates and helmets, bows and arrows, spears and shields, protective mantles, draught-oxen and heavy wagons, will amount to four-tenths of its total revenue.
15. Hence a wise general makes a point of foraging on the enemy. One cartload of the enemy's provisions is equivalent to twenty of one's own, and likewise a single picul of his provender is equivalent to twenty from one's own store.
16. Now in order to kill the enemy, our men must be roused to anger; that there may be advantage from defeating the enemy, they must have their rewards.
17. Therefore in chariot fighting, when ten or more chariots have been taken, those should be rewarded who took the first. Our own flags should be substituted for those of the enemy, and the chariots mingled and used in conjunction with ours. The captured soldiers should be kindly treated and kept.
18. This is called, using the conquered foe to augment one's own strength.
19. In war, then, let your great object be victory, not lengthy campaigns.
20. Thus it may be known that the leader of armies is the arbiter of the people's fate, the man on whom it depends whether the nation shall be in peace or in peril.

III. ATTACK BY STRATAGEM

1. Sun Tzu said: In the practical art of war, the best thing of all is to take the enemy's country whole and intact; to shatter and destroy it is not so good. So, too, it is better to recapture an army entire than to destroy it, to capture a regiment, a detachment or a company entire than to destroy them.

2. Hence to fight and conquer in all your battles is not supreme excellence; supreme excellence consists in breaking the enemy's resistance without fighting.

3. Thus the highest form of generalship is to balk the enemy's plans; the next best is to prevent the junction of the enemy's forces; the next in order is to attack the enemy's army in the field; and the worst policy of all is to besiege walled cities.

4. The rule is, not to besiege walled cities if it can possibly be avoided. The preparation of mantlets, movable shelters, and various implements of war, will take up three whole months; and the piling up of mounds over against the walls will take three months more.

5. The general, unable to control his irritation, will launch his men to the assault like swarming ants, with the result that one-third of his men are slain, while the town still remains untaken. Such are the disastrous effects of a siege.

6. Therefore, the skillful leader subdues the enemy's troops without any fighting; he captures their cities without laying siege to them; he overthrows their kingdom without lengthy operations in the field.

7. With his forces intact, he will dispute the mastery of the Empire, and thus, without losing a man, his triumph will be complete. This is the method of attacking by stratagem.

8. It is the rule in war, if our forces are ten to the enemy's one, to surround him; if five to one, to attack him; if twice as numerous, to divide our army into two.

9. If equally matched, we can offer battle; if slightly inferior in numbers, we can avoid the enemy; if quite unequal in every way, we can flee from him.

10. Hence, though an obstinate fight may be made by a small force, in the end it must be captured by the larger force.

11. Now the general is the bulwark of the State; if the bulwark is complete at all points; the State will be strong; if the bulwark is defective, the State will be weak.

12. There are three ways in which a ruler can bring misfortune upon his army:--

13. (1) By commanding the army to advance or to retreat, being ignorant of the fact that it cannot obey. This is called hobbling the army.

14. (2) By attempting to govern an army in the same way as he administers a kingdom, being ignorant of the conditions which obtain in an army. This causes restlessness in the soldier's minds.

15. (3) By employing the officers of his army without discrimination, through ignorance of the military principle of adaptation to circumstances. This shakes the confidence of the soldiers.

16. But when the army is restless and distrustful, trouble is sure to come from the other feudal princes. This is simply bringing anarchy into the army, and flinging victory away.

17. Thus we may know that there are five essentials for victory:
    1. He will win who knows when to fight and when not to fight.
    2. He will win who knows how to handle both superior and inferior forces.
    3. He will win whose army is animated by the same spirit throughout all its ranks.
    4. He will win who, prepared himself, waits to take the enemy unprepared.
    5. He will win who has military capacity and is not interfered with by the sovereign.

18. Hence the saying: If you know the enemy and know yourself, you need not fear the result of a hundred battles. If you know yourself but not the enemy, for every victory gained you will also suffer a defeat. If you know neither the enemy nor yourself, you will succumb in every battle.

IV. TACTICAL DISPOSITIONS

1. Sun Tzu said: The good fighters of old first put themselves beyond the possibility of defeat, and then waited for an opportunity of defeating the enemy.
2. To secure ourselves against defeat lies in our own hands, but the opportunity of defeating the enemy is provided by the enemy himself.
3. Thus the good fighter is able to secure himself against defeat, but cannot make certain of defeating the enemy.
4. Hence the saying: One may know how to conquer without being able to do it.
5. Security against defeat implies defensive tactics; ability to defeat the enemy means taking the offensive.
6. Standing on the defensive indicates insufficient strength; attacking, a superabundance of strength.
7. The general who is skilled in defense hides in the most secret recesses of the earth; he who is skilled in attack flashes forth from the topmost heights of heaven. Thus on the one hand we have ability to protect ourselves; on the other, a victory that is complete.
8. To see victory only when it is within the ken of the common herd is not the acme of excellence.
9. Neither is it the acme of excellence if you fight and conquer and the whole Empire says, "Well done!"
10. To lift an autumn hair is no sign of great strength; to see the sun and moon is no sign of sharp sight; to hear the noise of thunder is no sign of a quick ear.
11. What the ancients called a clever fighter is one who not only wins, but excels in winning with ease.
12. Hence his victories bring him neither reputation for wisdom nor credit for courage.
13. He wins his battles by making no mistakes. Making no mistakes is what establishes the certainty of victory, for it means conquering an enemy that is already defeated.
14. Hence the skillful fighter puts himself into a position which makes defeat impossible, and does not miss the moment for defeating the enemy.
15. Thus it is that in war the victorious strategist only seeks battle after the victory has been won, whereas he who is destined to defeat first fights and afterwards looks for victory.
16. The consummate leader cultivates the moral law, and strictly adheres to method and discipline; thus it is in his power to control success.
17. In respect of military method, we have, firstly, Measurement; secondly, Estimation of quantity; thirdly, Calculation; fourthly, Balancing of chances; fifthly, Victory.
18. Measurement owes its existence to Earth; Estimation of quantity to Measurement; Calculation to Estimation of quantity; Balancing of chances to Calculation; and Victory to Balancing of chances.
19. A victorious army opposed to a routed one, is as a pound's weight placed in the scale against a single grain.
20. The onrush of a conquering force is like the bursting of pent-up waters into a chasm a thousand fathoms deep.

V. ENERGY

1. Sun Tzu said: The control of a large force is the same principle as the control of a few men: it is merely a question of dividing up their numbers.
2. Fighting with a large army under your command is nowise different from fighting with a small one: it is merely a question of instituting signs and signals.
3. To ensure that your whole host may withstand the brunt of the enemy's attack and remain unshaken-- this is effected by maneuvers direct and indirect.
4. That the impact of your army may be like a grindstone dashed against an egg--this is effected by the science of weak points and strong.
5. In all fighting, the direct method may be used for joining battle, but indirect methods will be needed in order to secure victory.
6. Indirect tactics, efficiently applied, are inexhaustible as Heaven and Earth, unending as the flow of rivers and streams; like the sun and moon, they end but to begin anew; like the four seasons, they pass away to return once more.
7. There are not more than five musical notes, yet the combinations of these five give rise to more melodies than can ever be heard.
8. There are not more than five primary colors (blue, yellow, red, white, and black), yet in combination they produce more hues than can ever been seen.
9. There are not more than five cardinal tastes (sour, acrid, salt, sweet, bitter), yet combinations of them yield more flavors than can ever be tasted.
10. In battle, there are not more than two methods of attack--the direct and the indirect; yet these two in combination give rise to an endless series of maneuvers.
11. The direct and the indirect lead on to each other in turn. It is like moving in a circle--you never come to an end. Who can exhaust the possibilities of their combination?
12. The onset of troops is like the rush of a torrent which will even roll stones along in its course.
13. The quality of decision is like the well-timed swoop of a falcon which enables it to strike and destroy its victim.
14. Therefore the good fighter will be terrible in his onset, and prompt in his decision.
15. Energy may be likened to the bending of a crossbow; decision, to the releasing of a trigger.
16. Amid the turmoil and tumult of battle, there may be seeming disorder and yet no real disorder at all; amid confusion and chaos, your array may be without head or tail, yet it will be proof against defeat.
17. Simulated disorder postulates perfect discipline, simulated fear postulates courage; simulated weakness postulates strength.
18. Hiding order beneath the cloak of disorder is simply a question of subdivision; concealing courage under a show of timidity presupposes a fund of latent energy; masking strength with weakness is to be effected by tactical dispositions.
19. Thus one who is skillful at keeping the enemy on the move maintains deceitful appearances, according to which the enemy will act. He sacrifices something, that the enemy may snatch at it.
20. By holding out baits, he keeps him on the march; then with a body of picked men he lies in wait for him.
21. The clever combatant looks to the effect of combined energy, and does not require too much from individuals. Hence his ability to pick out the right men and utilize combined energy.
22. When he utilizes combined energy, his fighting men become as it were like unto rolling logs or stones. For it is the nature of a log or stone to remain motionless on level ground, and to move when on a slope; if four-cornered, to come to a standstill, but if round-shaped, to go rolling down.
23. Thus the energy developed by good fighting men is as the momentum of a round stone rolled down a mountain thousands of feet in height. So much on the subject of energy.

VI. WEAK POINTS AND STRONG

1. Sun Tzu said: Whoever is first in the field and awaits the coming of the enemy, will be fresh for the fight; whoever is second in the field and has to hasten to battle will arrive exhausted.
2. Therefore, the clever combatant imposes his will on the enemy, but does not allow the enemy's will to be imposed on him.
3. By holding out advantages to him, he can cause the enemy to approach of his own accord; or, by inflicting damage, he can make it impossible for the enemy to draw near.
4. If the enemy is taking his ease, he can harass him; if well supplied with food, he can starve him out; if quietly encamped, he can force him to move.
5. Appear at points which the enemy must hasten to defend; march swiftly to places where you are not expected.
6. An army may march great distances without distress, if it marches through country where the enemy is not.
7. You can be sure of succeeding in your attacks if you only attack places which are undefended. You can ensure the safety of your defense if you only hold positions that cannot be attacked.
8. Hence that general is skillful in attack whose opponent does not know what to defend; and he is skillful in defense whose opponent does not know what to attack.
9. O divine art of subtlety and secrecy! Through you we learn to be invisible, through you inaudible; and hence we can hold the enemy's fate in our hands.
10. You may advance and be absolutely irresistible, if you make for the enemy's weak points; you may retire and be safe from pursuit if your movements are more rapid than those of the enemy.
11. If we wish to fight, the enemy can be forced to an engagement even though he be sheltered behind a high rampart and a deep ditch. All we need do is attack some other place that he will be obliged to relieve.
12. If we do not wish to fight, we can prevent the enemy from engaging us even though the lines of our encampment be merely traced out on the ground. All we need do is to throw something odd and unaccountable in his way.
13. By discovering the enemy's dispositions and remaining invisible ourselves, we can keep our forces concentrated, while the enemy's must be divided.
14. We can form a single united body, while the enemy must split up into fractions. Hence there will be a whole pitted against separate parts of a whole, which means that we shall be many to the enemy's few.
15. And if we are able thus to attack an inferior force with a superior one, our opponents will be in dire straits.
16. The spot where we intend to fight must not be made known; for then the enemy will have to prepare against a possible attack at several different points; and his forces being thus distributed in many directions, the numbers we shall have to face at any given point will be proportionately few.
17. For should the enemy strengthen his van, he will weaken his rear; should he strengthen his rear, he will weaken his van; should he strengthen his left, he will weaken his right; should he strengthen his right, he will weaken his left. If he sends reinforcements everywhere, he will everywhere be weak.
18. Numerical weakness comes from having to prepare against possible attacks; numerical strength, from compelling our adversary to make these preparations against us.
19. Knowing the place and the time of the coming battle, we may concentrate from the greatest distances in order to fight.
20. But if neither time nor place be known, then the left wing will be impotent to succor the right, the right equally impotent to succor the left, the van unable to relieve the rear, or the rear to support the van. How much more so if the furthest portions of the army are anything under a hundred LI apart, and even the nearest are separated by several LI!

21. Though according to my estimate the soldiers of Yueh exceed our own in number, that shall advantage them nothing in the matter of victory. I say then that victory can be achieved.
22. Though the enemy be stronger in numbers, we may prevent him from fighting. Scheme so as to discover his plans and the likelihood of their success.
23. Rouse him, and learn the principle of his activity or inactivity. Force him to reveal himself, so as to find out his vulnerable spots.
24. Carefully compare the opposing army with your own, so that you may know where strength is superabundant and where it is deficient.
25. In making tactical dispositions, the highest pitch you can attain is to conceal them; conceal your dispositions, and you will be safe from the prying of the subtlest spies, from the machinations of the wisest brains.
26. How victory may be produced for them out of the enemy's own tactics--that is what the multitude cannot comprehend.
27. All men can see the tactics whereby I conquer, but what none can see is the strategy out of which victory is evolved.
28. Do not repeat the tactics which have gained you one victory, but let your methods be regulated by the infinite variety of circumstances.
29. Military tactics are like unto water; for water in its natural course runs away from high places and hastens downwards.
30. So in war, the way is to avoid what is strong and to strike at what is weak.
31. Water shapes its course according to the nature of the ground over which it flows; the soldier works out his victory in relation to the foe whom he is facing.
32. Therefore, just as water retains no constant shape, so in warfare there are no constant conditions.
33. He who can modify his tactics in relation to his opponent and thereby succeed in winning, may be called a heaven-born captain.
34. The five elements (water, fire, wood, metal, earth) are not always equally predominant; the four seasons make way for each other in turn. There are short days and long; the moon has its periods of waning and waxing.

VII. MANEUVERING

1. Sun Tzu said: In war, the general receives his commands from the sovereign.
2. Having collected an army and concentrated his forces, he must blend and harmonize the different elements thereof before pitching his camp.
3. After that, comes tactical maneuvering, than which there is nothing more difficult. The difficulty of tactical maneuvering consists in turning the devious into the direct, and misfortune into gain.
4. Thus, to take a long and circuitous route, after enticing the enemy out of the way, and though starting after him, to contrive to reach the goal before him, shows knowledge of the artifice of DEVIATION.
5. Maneuvering with an army is advantageous; with an undisciplined multitude, most dangerous.
6. If you set a fully equipped army in march in order to snatch an advantage, the chances are that you will be too late. On the other hand, to detach a flying column for the purpose involves the sacrifice of its baggage and stores.
7. Thus, if you order your men to roll up their buff-coats, and make forced marches without halting day or night, covering double the usual distance at a stretch, doing a hundred LI in order to wrest an advantage, the leaders of all your three divisions will fall into the hands of the enemy.
8. The stronger men will be in front, the jaded ones will fall behind, and on this plan only one-tenth of your army will reach its destination.

9. If you march fifty LI in order to outmaneuver the enemy, you will lose the leader of your first division, and only half your force will reach the goal.

10. If you march thirty LI with the same object, two-thirds of your army will arrive.

11. We may take it then that an army without its baggage-train is lost; without provisions it is lost; without bases of supply it is lost.

12. We cannot enter into alliances until we are acquainted with the designs of our neighbors.

13. We are not fit to lead an army on the march unless we are familiar with the face of the country--its mountains and forests, its pitfalls and precipices, its marshes and swamps.

14. We shall be unable to turn natural advantage to account unless we make use of local guides.

15. In war, practice dissimulation, and you will succeed.

16. Whether to concentrate or to divide your troops, must be decided by circumstances.

17. Let your rapidity be that of the wind, your compactness that of the forest.

18. In raiding and plundering be like fire, is immovability like a mountain.

19. Let your plans be dark and impenetrable as night, and when you move, fall like a thunderbolt.

20. When you plunder a countryside, let the spoil be divided amongst your men; when you capture new territory, cut it up into allotments for the benefit of the soldiery.

21. Ponder and deliberate before you make a move.

22. He will conquer who has learnt the artifice of deviation. Such is the art of maneuvering.

23. The Book of Army Management says: On the field of battle, the spoken word does not carry far enough: hence the institution of gongs and drums. Nor can ordinary objects be seen clearly enough: hence the institution of banners and flags.

24. Gongs and drums, banners and flags, are means whereby the ears and eyes of the host may be focused on one particular point.

25. The host thus forming a single united body, is it impossible either for the brave to advance alone, or for the cowardly to retreat alone. This is the art of handling large masses of men.

26. In night-fighting, then, make much use of signal-fires and drums, and in fighting by day, of flags and banners, as a means of influencing the ears and eyes of your army.

27. A whole army may be robbed of its spirit; a commander-in-chief may be robbed of his presence of mind.

28. Now a soldier's spirit is keenest in the morning; by noonday it has begun to flag; and in the evening, his mind is bent only on returning to camp.

29. A clever general, therefore, avoids an army when its spirit is keen, but attacks it when it is sluggish and inclined to return. This is the art of studying moods.

30. Disciplined and calm, to await the appearance of disorder and hubbub amongst the enemy:--this is the art of retaining self-possession.

31. To be near the goal while the enemy is still far from it, to wait at ease while the enemy is toiling and struggling, to be well-fed while the enemy is famished:--this is the art of husbanding one's strength.

32. To refrain from intercepting an enemy whose banners are in perfect order, to refrain from attacking an army drawn up in calm and confident array:--this is the art of studying circumstances.

33. It is a military axiom not to advance uphill against the enemy, nor to oppose him when he comes downhill.

34. Do not pursue an enemy who simulates flight; do not attack soldiers whose temper is keen.

35. Do not swallow bait offered by the enemy. Do not interfere with an army that is returning home.

36. When you surround an army, leave an outlet free. Do not press a desperate foe too hard.

37. Such is the art of warfare.

VIII. VARIATION IN TACTICS

1. Sun Tzu said: In war, the general receives his commands from the sovereign, collects his army and concentrates his forces

2. When in difficult country, do not encamp. In country where high roads intersect, join hands with your allies. Do not linger in dangerously isolated positions. In hemmed-in situations, you must resort to stratagem. In desperate position, you must fight.

3. There are roads which must not be followed, armies which must be not attacked, towns which must be besieged, positions which must not be contested, commands of the sovereign which must not be obeyed.

4. The general who thoroughly understands the advantages that accompany variation of tactics knows how to handle his troops.

5. The general who does not understand these, may be well acquainted with the configuration of the country, yet he will not be able to turn his knowledge to practical account.

6. So, the student of war who is unversed in the art of war of varying his plans, even though he be acquainted with the Five Advantages, will fail to make the best use of his men.

7. Hence in the wise leader's plans, considerations of advantage and of disadvantage will be blended together.

8. If our expectation of advantage be tempered in this way, we may succeed in accomplishing the essential part of our schemes.

9. If, on the other hand, in the midst of difficulties we are always ready to seize an advantage, we may extricate ourselves from misfortune.

10. Reduce the hostile chiefs by inflicting damage on them; and make trouble for them, and keep them constantly engaged; hold out specious allurements, and make them rush to any given point.

11. The art of war teaches us to rely not on the likelihood of the enemy's not coming, but on our own readiness to receive him; not on the chance of his not attacking, but rather on the fact that we have made our position unassailable.

12. There are five dangerous faults which may affect a general:
    1. Recklessness, which leads to destruction;
    2. cowardice, which leads to capture;
    3. a hasty temper, which can be provoked by insults;
    4. a delicacy of honor which is sensitive to shame;
    5. over-solicitude for his men, which exposes him to worry and trouble.

13. These are the five besetting sins of a general, ruinous to the conduct of war.

14. When an army is overthrown and its leader slain, the cause will surely be found among these five dangerous faults. Let them be a subject of meditation.

IX. THE ARMY ON THE MARCH

1. Sun Tzu said: We come now to the question of encamping the army, and observing signs of the enemy. Pass quickly over mountains, and keep in the neighborhood of valleys.

2. Camp in high places, facing the sun. Do not climb heights in order to fight. So much for mountain warfare.

3. After crossing a river, you should get far away from it.

4. When an invading force crosses a river in its onward march, do not advance to meet it in mid-stream. It will be best to let half the army get across, and then deliver your attack.

5. If you are anxious to fight, you should not go to meet the invader near a river which he has to cross.

6. Moor your craft higher up than the enemy, and facing the sun. Do not move up-stream to meet the enemy. So much for river warfare.

7. In crossing salt-marshes, your sole concern should be to get over them quickly, without any delay.

8. If forced to fight in a salt-marsh, you should have water and grass near you, and get your back to a clump of trees. So much for operations in salt-marches.

9. In dry, level country, take up an easily accessible position with rising ground to your right and on your rear, so that the danger may be in front, and safety lie behind. So much for campaigning in flat country.

10. These are the four useful branches of military knowledge which enabled the Yellow Emperor to vanquish four several sovereigns.

11. All armies prefer high ground to low and sunny places to dark.

12. If you are careful of your men, and camp on hard ground, the army will be free from disease of every kind, and this will spell victory.

13. When you come to a hill or a bank, occupy the sunny side, with the slope on your right rear. Thus you will at once act for the benefit of your soldiers and utilize the natural advantages of the ground.

14. When, in consequence of heavy rains up-country, a river which you wish to ford is swollen and flecked with foam, you must wait until it subsides.

15. Country in which there are precipitous cliffs with torrents running between, deep natural hollows, confined places, tangled thickets, quagmires and crevasses, should be left with all possible speed and not approached.

16. While we keep away from such places, we should get the enemy to approach them; while we face them, we should let the enemy have them on his rear.

17. If in the neighborhood of your camp there should be any hilly country, ponds surrounded by aquatic grass, hollow basins filled with reeds, or woods with thick undergrowth, they must be carefully routed out and searched; for these are places where men in ambush or insidious spies are likely to be lurking.

18. When the enemy is close at hand and remains quiet, he is relying on the natural strength of his position.

19. When he keeps aloof and tries to provoke a battle, he is anxious for the other side to advance.

20. If his place of encampment is easy of access, he is tendering a bait.

21. Movement amongst the trees of a forest shows that the enemy is advancing. The appearance of a number of screens in the midst of thick grass means that the enemy wants to make us suspicious.

22. The rising of birds in their flight is the sign of an ambuscade. Startled beasts indicate that a sudden attack is coming.

23. When there is dust rising in a high column, it is the sign of chariots advancing; when the dust is low, but spread over a wide area, it betokens the approach of infantry. When it branches out in different directions, it shows that parties have been sent to collect firewood. A few clouds of dust moving to and fro signify that the army is encamping.

24. Humble words and increased preparations are signs that the enemy is about to advance. Violent language and driving forward as if to the attack are signs that he will retreat.

25. When the light chariots come out first and take up a position on the wings, it is a sign that the enemy is forming for battle.

26. Peace proposals unaccompanied by a sworn covenant indicate a plot.

27. When there is much running about and the soldiers fall into rank, it means that the critical moment has come.

28. When some are seen advancing and some retreating, it is a lure.

29. When the soldiers stand leaning on their spears, they are faint from want of food.

30. If those who are sent to draw water begin by drinking themselves, the army is suffering from thirst.

31. If the enemy sees an advantage to be gained and makes no effort to secure it, the soldiers are exhausted.

32. If birds gather on any spot, it is unoccupied. Clamor by night betokens nervousness.

33. If there is disturbance in the camp, the general's authority is weak. If the banners and flags are shifted about, sedition is afoot. If the officers are angry, it means that the men are weary.

34. When an army feeds its horses with grain and kills its cattle for food, and when the men do not hang their cooking-pots over the camp-fires, showing that they will not return to their tents, you may know that they are determined to fight to the death.

35. The sight of men whispering together in small knots or speaking in subdued tones points to disaffection amongst the rank and file.

36. Too frequent rewards signify that the enemy is at the end of his resources; too many punishments betray a condition of dire distress.

37. To begin by bluster, but afterwards to take fright at the enemy's numbers, shows a supreme lack of intelligence.

38. When envoys are sent with compliments in their mouths, it is a sign that the enemy wishes for a truce.

39. If the enemy's troops march up angrily and remain facing ours for a long time without either joining battle or taking themselves off again, the situation is one that demands great vigilance and circumspection.

40. If our troops are no more in number than the enemy, that is amply sufficient; it only means that no direct attack can be made. What we can do is simply to concentrate all our available strength, keep a close watch on the enemy, and obtain reinforcements.

41. He who exercises no forethought but makes light of his opponents is sure to be captured by them.

42. If soldiers are punished before they have grown attached to you, they will not prove submissive; and, unless submissive, then will be practically useless. If, when the soldiers have become attached to you, punishments are not enforced, they will still be unless.

43. Therefore soldiers must be treated in the first instance with humanity, but kept under control by means of iron discipline. This is a certain road to victory.

44. If in training soldiers commands are habitually enforced, the army will be well-disciplined; if not, its discipline will be bad.

45. If a general shows confidence in his men but always insists on his orders being obeyed, the gain will be mutual.

X. TERRAIN

1. Sun Tzu said: We may distinguish six kinds of terrain, to wit: (1) Accessible ground; (2) entangling ground; (3) temporizing ground; (4) narrow passes; (5) precipitous heights; (6) positions at a great distance from the enemy.

2. Ground which can be freely traversed by both sides is called accessible.

3. With regard to ground of this nature, be before the enemy in occupying the raised and sunny spots, and carefully guard your line of supplies. Then you will be able to fight with advantage.

4. Ground which can be abandoned but is hard to re-occupy is called entangling.

5. From a position of this sort, if the enemy is unprepared, you may sally forth and defeat him. But if the enemy is prepared for your coming, and you fail to defeat him, then, return being impossible, disaster will ensue.

6. When the position is such that neither side will gain by making the first move, it is called temporizing ground.
7. In a position of this sort, even though the enemy should offer us an attractive bait, it will be advisable not to stir forth, but rather to retreat, thus enticing the enemy in his turn; then, when part of his army has come out, we may deliver our attack with advantage.
8. With regard to narrow passes, if you can occupy them first, let them be strongly garrisoned and await the advent of the enemy.
9. Should the army forestall you in occupying a pass, do not go after him if the pass is fully garrisoned, but only if it is weakly garrisoned.
10. With regard to precipitous heights, if you are beforehand with your adversary, you should occupy the raised and sunny spots, and there wait for him to come up.
11. If the enemy has occupied them before you, do not follow him, but retreat and try to entice him away.
12. If you are situated at a great distance from the enemy, and the strength of the two armies is equal, it is not easy to provoke a battle, and fighting will be to your disadvantage.
13. These six are the principles connected with Earth. The general who has attained a responsible post must be careful to study them.
14. Now an army is exposed to six several calamities, not arising from natural causes, but from faults for which the general is responsible. These are: (1) Flight; (2) insubordination; (3) collapse; (4) ruin; (5) disorganization; (6) rout.
15. Other conditions being equal, if one force is hurled against another ten times its size, the result will be the flight of the former.
16. When the common soldiers are too strong and their officers too weak, the result is insubordination. When the officers are too strong and the common soldiers too weak, the result is collapse.
17. When the higher officers are angry and insubordinate, and on meeting the enemy give battle on their own account from a feeling of resentment, before the commander-in-chief can tell whether or no he is in a position to fight, the result is ruin.
18. When the general is weak and without authority; when his orders are not clear and distinct; when there are no fixes duties assigned to officers and men, and the ranks are formed in a slovenly haphazard manner, the result is utter disorganization.
19. When a general, unable to estimate the enemy's strength, allows an inferior force to engage a larger one, or hurls a weak detachment against a powerful one, and neglects to place picked soldiers in the front rank, the result must be rout.
20. These are six ways of courting defeat, which must be carefully noted by the general who has attained a responsible post.
21. The natural formation of the country is the soldier's best ally; but a power of estimating the adversary, of controlling the forces of victory, and of shrewdly calculating difficulties, dangers and distances, constitutes the test of a great general.
22. He who knows these things, and in fighting puts his knowledge into practice, will win his battles. He who knows them not, nor practices them, will surely be defeated.
23. If fighting is sure to result in victory, then you must fight, even though the ruler forbid it; if fighting will not result in victory, then you must not fight even at the ruler's bidding.
24. The general who advances without coveting fame and retreats without fearing disgrace, whose only thought is to protect his country and do good service for his sovereign, is the jewel of the kingdom.
25. Regard your soldiers as your children, and they will follow you into the deepest valleys; look upon them as your own beloved sons, and they will stand by you even unto death.
26. If, however, you are indulgent, but unable to make your authority felt; kind-hearted, but unable to enforce your commands; and incapable, moreover, of quelling disorder: then your soldiers must be likened to spoilt children; they are useless for any practical purpose.

27. If we know that our own men are in a condition to attack, but are unaware that the enemy is not open to attack, we have gone only halfway towards victory.
28. If we know that the enemy is open to attack, but are unaware that our own men are not in a condition to attack, we have gone only halfway towards victory.
29. If we know that the enemy is open to attack, and also know that our men are in a condition to attack, but are unaware that the nature of the ground makes fighting impracticable, we have still gone only halfway towards victory.
30. Hence, the experienced soldier, once in motion, is never bewildered; once he has broken camp, he is never at a loss.
31. Hence the saying: If you know the enemy and know yourself, your victory will not stand in doubt; if you know Heaven and know Earth, you may make your victory complete.

XI. THE NINE SITUATIONS

1. Sun Tzu said: The art of war recognizes nine varieties of ground: (1) Dispersive ground; (2) facile ground; (3) contentious ground; (4) open ground; (5) ground of intersecting highways; (6) serious ground; (7) difficult ground; (8) hemmed-in ground; (9) desperate ground.
2. When a chieftain is fighting in his own territory, it is dispersive ground.
3. When he has penetrated into hostile territory, but to no great distance, it is facile ground.
4. Ground the possession of which imports great advantage to either side, is contentious ground.
5. Ground on which each side has liberty of movement is open ground.
6. Ground which forms the key to three contiguous states, so that he who occupies it first has most of the Empire at his command, is a ground of intersecting highways.
7. When an army has penetrated into the heart of a hostile country, leaving a number of fortified cities in its rear, it is serious ground.
8. Mountain forests, rugged steeps, marshes and fens--all country that is hard to traverse: this is difficult ground.
9. Ground which is reached through narrow gorges, and from which we can only retire by tortuous paths, so that a small number of the enemy would suffice to crush a large body of our men: this is hemmed in ground.
10. Ground on which we can only be saved from destruction by fighting without delay, is desperate ground.
11. On dispersive ground, therefore, fight not. On facile ground, halt not. On contentious ground, attack not.
12. On open ground, do not try to block the enemy's way. On the ground of intersecting highways, join hands with your allies.
13. On serious ground, gather in plunder. In difficult ground, keep steadily on the march.
14. On hemmed-in ground, resort to stratagem. On desperate ground, fight.
15. Those who were called skillful leaders of old knew how to drive a wedge between the enemy's front and rear; to prevent co-operation between his large and small divisions; to hinder the good troops from rescuing the bad, the officers from rallying their men.
16. When the enemy's men were united, they managed to keep them in disorder.
17. When it was to their advantage, they made a forward move; when otherwise, they stopped still.
18. If asked how to cope with a great host of the enemy in orderly array and on the point of marching to the attack, I should say: "Begin by seizing something which your opponent holds dear; then he will be amenable to your will."

19. Rapidity is the essence of war: take advantage of the enemy's unreadiness, make your way by unexpected routes, and attack unguarded spots.

20. The following are the principles to be observed by an invading force: The further you penetrate into a country, the greater will be the solidarity of your troops, and thus the defenders will not prevail against you.

21. Make forays in fertile country in order to supply your army with food.

22. Carefully study the well-being of your men, and do not overtax them. Concentrate your energy and hoard your strength. Keep your army continually on the move, and devise unfathomable plans.

23. Throw your soldiers into positions whence there is no escape, and they will prefer death to flight. If they will face death, there is nothing they may not achieve. Officers and men alike will put forth their uttermost strength.

24. Soldiers when in desperate straits lose the sense of fear. If there is no place of refuge, they will stand firm. If they are in hostile country, they will show a stubborn front. If there is no help for it, they will fight hard.

25. Thus, without waiting to be marshaled, the soldiers will be constantly on the qui vive; without waiting to be asked, they will do your will; without restrictions, they will be faithful; without giving orders, they can be trusted.

26. Prohibit the taking of omens, and do away with superstitious doubts. Then, until death itself comes, no calamity need be feared.

27. If our soldiers are not overburdened with money, it is not because they have a distaste for riches; if their lives are not unduly long, it is not because they are disinclined to longevity.

28. On the day they are ordered out to battle, your soldiers may weep, those sitting up bedewing their garments, and those lying down letting the tears run down their cheeks. But let them once be brought to bay, and they will display the courage of a Chu or a Kuei.

29. The skillful tactician may be likened to the shuai-jan. Now the shuai-jan is a snake that is found in the Chung mountains. Strike at its head, and you will be attacked by its tail; strike at its tail, and you will be attacked by its head; strike at its middle, and you will be attacked by head and tail both.

30. Asked if an army can be made to imitate the shuai-jan, I should answer, Yes. For the men of Wu and the men of Yueh are enemies; yet if they are crossing a river in the same boat and are caught by a storm, they will come to each other's assistance just as the left hand helps the right.

31. Hence it is not enough to put one's trust in the tethering of horses, and the burying of chariot wheels in the ground

32. The principle on which to manage an army is to set up one standard of courage which all must reach.

33. How to make the best of both strong and weak--that is a question involving the proper use of ground.

34. Thus, the skillful general conducts his army just as though he were leading a single man, willy-nilly, by the hand.

35. It is the business of a general to be quiet and thus ensure secrecy; upright and just, and thus maintain order.

36. He must be able to mystify his officers and men by false reports and appearances, and thus keep them in total ignorance.

37. By altering his arrangements and changing his plans, he keeps the enemy without definite knowledge. By shifting his camp and taking circuitous routes, he prevents the enemy from anticipating his purpose.

38. At the critical moment, the leader of an army acts like one who has climbed up a height and then kicks away the ladder behind him. He carries his men deep into hostile territory before he shows his hand.

39. He burns his boats and breaks his cooking-pots; like a shepherd driving a flock of sheep, he drives his men this way and that, and nothing knows whither he is going.

40. To muster his host and bring it into danger:--this may be termed the business of the general.
41. The different measures suited to the nine varieties of ground; the expediency of aggressive or defensive tactics; and the fundamental laws of human nature: these are things that must most certainly be studied.
42. When invading hostile territory, the general principle is, that penetrating deeply brings cohesion; penetrating but a short way means dispersion.
43. When you leave your own country behind, and take your army across neighborhood territory, you find yourself on critical ground. When there are means of communication on all four sides, the ground is one of intersecting highways.
44. When you penetrate deeply into a country, it is serious ground. When you penetrate but a little way, it is facile ground.
45. When you have the enemy's strongholds on your rear, and narrow passes in front, it is hemmed-in ground. When there is no place of refuge at all, it is desperate ground.
46. Therefore, on dispersive ground, I would inspire my men with unity of purpose. On facile ground, I would see that there is close connection between all parts of my army.
47. On contentious ground, I would hurry up my rear.
48. On open ground, I would keep a vigilant eye on my defenses. On ground of intersecting highways, I would consolidate my alliances.
49. On serious ground, I would try to ensure a continuous stream of supplies. On difficult ground, I would keep pushing on along the road.
50. On hemmed-in ground, I would block any way of retreat. On desperate ground, I would proclaim to my soldiers the hopelessness of saving their lives.
51. For it is the soldier's disposition to offer an obstinate resistance when surrounded, to fight hard when he cannot help himself, and to obey promptly when he has fallen into danger.
52. We cannot enter into alliance with neighboring princes until we are acquainted with their designs. We are not fit to lead an army on the march unless we are familiar with the face of the country--its mountains and forests, its pitfalls and precipices, its marshes and swamps. We shall be unable to turn natural advantages to account unless we make use of local guides.
53. To be ignored of any one of the following four or five principles does not befit a warlike prince.
54. When a warlike prince attacks a powerful state, his generalship shows itself in preventing the concentration of the enemy's forces. He overawes his opponents, and their allies are prevented from joining against him.
55. Hence, he does not strive to ally himself with all and sundry, nor does he foster the power of other states. He carries out his own secret designs, keeping his antagonists in awe. Thus he is able to capture their cities and overthrow their kingdoms.
56. Bestow rewards without regard to rule, issue orders without regard to previous arrangements; and you will be able to handle a whole army as though you had to do with but a single man.
57. Confront your soldiers with the deed itself; never let them know your design. When the outlook is bright, bring it before their eyes; but tell them nothing when the situation is gloomy.
58. Place your army in deadly peril, and it will survive; plunge it into desperate straits, and it will come off in safety.
59. For it is precisely when a force has fallen into harm's way that is capable of striking a blow for victory.
60. Success in warfare is gained by carefully accommodating ourselves to the enemy's purpose.
61. By persistently hanging on the enemy's flank, we shall succeed in the long run in killing the commander-in-chief.
62. This is called ability to accomplish a thing by sheer cunning.
63. On the day that you take up your command, block the frontier passes, destroy the official tallies, and stop the passage of all emissaries.
64. Be stern in the council-chamber, so that you may control the situation.

65. If the enemy leaves a door open, you must rush in.
66. Forestall your opponent by seizing what he holds dear, and subtly contrive to time his arrival on the ground.
67. Walk in the path defined by rule, and accommodate yourself to the enemy until you can fight a decisive battle.
68. At first, then, exhibit the coyness of a maiden, until the enemy gives you an opening; afterwards emulate the rapidity of a running hare, and it will be too late for the enemy to oppose you.

XII. THE ATTACK BY FIRE

1. Sun Tzu said: There are five ways of attacking with fire. The first is to burn soldiers in their camp; the second is to burn stores; the third is to burn baggage trains; the fourth is to burn arsenals and magazines; the fifth is to hurl dropping fire amongst the enemy.
2. In order to carry out an attack, we must have means available. The material for raising fire should always be kept in readiness.
3. There is a proper season for making attacks with fire, and special days for starting a conflagration.
4. The proper season is when the weather is very dry; the special days are those when the moon is in the constellations of the Sieve, the Wall, the Wing or the Cross-bar; for these four are all days of rising wind.
5. In attacking with fire, one should be prepared to meet five possible developments:
6. (1) When fire breaks out inside to enemy's camp, respond at once with an attack from without.
7. (2) If there is an outbreak of fire, but the enemy's soldiers remain quiet, bide your time and do not attack.
8. (3) When the force of the flames has reached its height, follow it up with an attack, if that is practicable; if not, stay where you are.
9. (4) If it is possible to make an assault with fire from without, do not wait for it to break out within, but deliver your attack at a favorable moment.
10. (5) When you start a fire, be to windward of it. Do not attack from the leeward.
11. A wind that rises in the daytime lasts long, but a night breeze soon falls.
12. In every army, the five developments connected with fire must be known, the movements of the stars calculated, and a watch kept for the proper days.
13. Hence, those who use fire as an aid to the attack show intelligence; those who use water as an aid to the attack gain an accession of strength.
14. By means of water, an enemy may be intercepted, but not robbed of all his belongings.
15. Unhappy is the fate of one who tries to win his battles and succeed in his attacks without cultivating the spirit of enterprise; for the result is waste of time and general stagnation.
16. Hence the saying: The enlightened ruler lays his plans well ahead; the good general cultivates his resources.
17. Move not unless you see an advantage; use not your troops unless there is something to be gained; fight not unless the position is critical.
18. No ruler should put troops into the field merely to gratify his own spleen; no general should fight a battle simply out of pique.
19. If it is to your advantage, make a forward move; if not, stay where you are.
20. Anger may in time change to gladness; vexation may be succeeded by content.
21. But, a kingdom that has once been destroyed can never come again into being; nor can the dead ever be brought back to life.
22. Hence, the enlightened ruler is heedful, and the good general full of caution. This is the way to keep a country at peace and an army intact.

XIII. THE USE OF SPIES

1. Sun Tzu said: Raising a host of a hundred thousand men and marching them great distances entails heavy loss on the people and a drain on the resources of the State. The daily expenditure will amount to a thousand ounces of silver. There will be commotion at home and abroad, and men will drop down exhausted on the highways. As many as seven hundred thousand families will be impeded in their labor.

2. Hostile armies may face each other for years, striving for the victory which is decided in a single day. This being so, to remain in ignorance of the enemy's condition simply because one grudges the outlay of a hundred ounces of silver in honors and emoluments, is the height of inhumanity.

3. One who acts thus is no leader of men, no present help to his sovereign, no master of victory.

4. Thus, what enables the wise sovereign and the good general to strike and conquer, and achieve things beyond the reach of ordinary men, is foreknowledge.

5. Now this foreknowledge cannot be elicited from spirits; it cannot be obtained inductively from experience, nor by any deductive calculation.

6. Knowledge of the enemy's dispositions can only be obtained from other men.

7. Hence the use of spies, of whom there are five classes: (1) Local spies; (2) inward spies; (3) converted spies; (4) doomed spies; (5) surviving spies.

8. When these five kinds of spy are all at work, none can discover the secret system. This is called "divine manipulation of the threads." It is the sovereign's most precious faculty.

9. Having local spies means employing the services of the inhabitants of a district.

10. Having inward spies, making use of officials of the enemy.

11. Having converted spies, getting hold of the enemy's spies and using them for our own purposes.

12. Having doomed spies, doing certain things openly for purposes of deception, and allowing our spies to know of them and report them to the enemy.

13. Surviving spies, finally, are those who bring back news from the enemy's camp.

14. Hence, it is that which none in the whole army are more intimate relations to be maintained than with spies. None should be more liberally rewarded. In no other business should greater secrecy be preserved.

15. Spies cannot be usefully employed without a certain intuitive sagacity.

16. They cannot be properly managed without benevolence and straightforwardness.

17. Without subtle ingenuity of mind, one cannot make certain of the truth of their reports.

18. Be subtle! be subtle! and use your spies for every kind of business.

19. If a secret piece of news is divulged by a spy before the time is ripe, he must be put to death together with the man to whom the secret was told.

20. Whether the object be to crush an army, to storm a city, or to assassinate an individual, it is always necessary to begin by finding out the names of the attendants, the aides-de-camp, and door-keepers and sentries of the general in command. Our spies must be commissioned to ascertain these.

21. The enemy's spies who have come to spy on us must be sought out, tempted with bribes, led away and comfortably housed. Thus they will become converted spies and available for our service.

22. It is through the information brought by the converted spy that we are able to acquire and employ local and inward spies.

23. It is owing to his information, again, that we can cause the doomed spy to carry false tidings to the enemy.

24. Lastly, it is by his information that the surviving spy can be used on appointed occasions.

25. The end and aim of spying in all its five varieties is knowledge of the enemy; and this knowledge can only be derived, in the first instance, from the converted spy. Hence, it is essential that the converted spy be treated with the utmost liberality.

26. Of old, the rise of the Yin dynasty was due to I Chih who had served under the Hsia. Likewise, the rise of the Chou dynasty was due to Lu Ya who had served under the Yin.

27. Hence, it is only the enlightened ruler and the wise general who will use the highest intelligence of the army for purposes of spying and thereby they achieve great results. Spies are a most important element in water, because on them depends an army's ability to move.
    [Tu Mu closes with a note of warning: "Just as water, which carries a boat from bank to bank, may also be the means of sinking it, so reliance on spies, while production of great results, is oft-times the cause of utter destruction."]
    Spies are a most important element in water, because on them depends an army's ability to move.
    [Chia Lin says that an army without spies is like a man with ears or eyes.]

Rhetoric by Aristotle

Part 1

Rhetoric is the counterpart of Dialectic. Both alike are concerned with such things as come, more or less, within the general ken of all men and belong to no definite science. Accordingly, all men make use, more or less, of both; for to a certain extent, all men attempt to discuss statements and to maintain them, to defend themselves, and to attack others. Ordinary people do this either at random or through practice and from acquired habit. Both ways being possible, the subject can plainly be handled systematically, for it is possible to inquire the reason why some speakers succeed through practice and others spontaneously; and every one will at once agree that such an inquiry is the function of an art.

Now, the framers of the current treatises on rhetoric have constructed but a small portion of that art. The modes of persuasion are the only true constituents of the art: everything else is merely accessory. These writers, however, say nothing about enthymemes, which are the substance of rhetorical persuasion, but deal mainly with non-essentials. The arousing of prejudice, pity, anger, and similar emotions has nothing to do with the essential facts, but is merely a personal appeal to the man who is judging the case. Consequently if the rules for trials which are now laid down some states—especially in well-governed states-were applied everywhere, such people would have nothing to say. All men, no doubt, think that the laws should prescribe such rules, but some, as in the court of Areopagus, give practical effect to their thoughts and forbid talk about non-essentials. This is sound law and custom. It is not right to pervert the judge by moving him to anger or envy or pity-one might as well warp a carpenter's rule before using it. Again, a litigant has clearly nothing to do but to show that the alleged fact is so or is not so, that it has or has not happened. As to whether a thing is important or unimportant, just or unjust, the judge must surely refuse to take his instructions from the litigant: he must decide for himself all such points as the law-giver has not already defined for him.

Now, it is of great moment that well-drawn laws should themselves define all the points they possibly can and leave as few as may be to the decision of the judges; and this for several reasons. First, to find one man, or a few men, who are sensible persons and capable of legislating and administering justice is easier than to find a large number. Next, laws are made after long consideration, whereas decisions in the courts are given at short notice, which makes it hard for those who try the case to satisfy the claims of justice and expediency. The weightiest reason of all is that the decision of the lawgiver is not particular but perspective and general, whereas members of the assembly and the jury find it their duty to decide on definite cases brought before them. They will often have allowed themselves to be so much influenced by feelings of friendship or hatred or self-interest that they lose any clear vision of the truth and have their judgement obscured by considerations of personal pleasure or pain. In general, then, the judge should, we say, be allowed to decide as few things as possible. But questions as to whether something has happened or not happened, will be or will not be, is or is not, must of necessity be left to the judge, since the lawgiver cannot foresee them. If this is so, it is evident that anyone who lays down rules about other matters, such as wheat must be the contents of the 'introduction' or the 'narration' or any of the other divisions of a speech, is theorizing about non-essentials as if they belonged to the art. The only question with which these writers here deal is how to put the judge into a given frame of mind. About the orator's proper modes of persuasion they have nothing to tell us; nothing, that is, about how to gain skill in enthymemes.

Hence it comes that, although the same systematic principles apply to political as to forensic oratory, and although the former is a nobler business, and fitter for a citizen, than that which concerns the relations of private individuals, these authors say nothing about political oratory, but try, one and all, to write treatises on the way to plead in court. The reason for this is that in political oratory there is less inducement to talk about nonessentials. Political oratory is less given to unscrupulous practices than forensic, because it treats of wider issues. In a political debate the man who is forming a judgement is making a decision about his own vital interests. There is not need, therefore, to prove anything except that the facts are what the supporter of a measure maintains they are. In forensic oratory this is not enough; to conciliate the listener is what pays here. It is other people's affairs that are to be decided, so that the judges, intent on their own satisfaction and listening with partiality, surrender themselves to the disputants instead of judging between them. Hence in many places as we have said already, irrelevant speaking is forbidden in the law-courts: in the public assembly those who have to form a judgement are themselves well able to guard against that.

It is clear, then, that rhetorical study, in its strict sense, is concerned with the modes of persuasion. Persuasion is clearly a sort of demonstration, since we are most fully persuaded when we consider a thing to have been demonstrated. The orator's demonstration is an enthymeme, and this is, in general, the most effective of the modes of persuasion. The enthymeme is a sort of syllogism, and the consideration of syllogisms of all kinds, without distinction, is the business of dialectic, either of dialectic as a whole or of one of its branches. It follows plainly, therefore, that he who is best able to see how and from what elements a syllogism is produced will also be best skilled in the enthymeme, when he has further learnt what its subject-matter is and in what respects it differs from the syllogism of strict logic. The true and the approximately true are apprehended by the same facility; it may also be noted that men have a sufficient natural instinct for what is true, and usually do arrive at the truth. Hence, the man who makes a good guess at truth is likely to make a good guess at probabilities.

It has now been shown that ordinary writers on rhetoric treat of non-essentials; it has also been shown why they have inclined more toward the forensic branch of oratory.

Rhetoric is useful (1) because things that are true and things that are just have a natural tendency to prevail over their opposites, so that if the decisions of judges are not what they ought to be, the defeat must be due to the speakers themselves, and they must be blamed accordingly. Moreover, (2) before some audiences not even the possession of the exactest knowledge will make it easy for what we say to produce conviction. For argument based on knowledge implies instruction, and there are people whom one cannot instruct. Here, then, we must use, as our modes of persuasion and argument, notions possessed by everybody, as we observed in the Topics when dealing with the way to handle a popular audience. Further (3) we must be able to employ persuasion, just as strict reasoning can be employed, on opposite sides of a question, not n order that we may in practice employ it in both ways (for we must not make people believe what is wrong), but in order that we may see clearly what the facts are, and that, if another man argues unfairly, we on our part may be able to confute him. No other other arts draws opposite conclusions: dialectic and rhetoric alone do theis. Both these arts draw opposite conclusions impartially. Nevertheless, the underlying facts do not lend themselves equally well to the contrary views. No; things that are true and things that are better are, by their nature, practically always easier to prove and easier to believe in. Again, (4) it is absurd to hold that a man ought to be ashamed of being unable to defend himself with his limbs, but not of being unable to defend himself with speech and reason, when the use of rational speech is more distinctive of a human being than the use of his limbs. And if it be objected that one who uses such power of speech unjustly might do great harm, that is a charge which may be made in common against all good things except virtue, and above all against the things that are most useful, as strength, health, wealth, generalship. A man can confer the greatest of benefits by a right use of these, and inflict the greatest of injuries by using them wrongly.

It is clear, then, that rhetoric is not bound up with a single definite class of subjects, but is as universal as dialectic; it is clear, also, that it is useful. It is clear, further, that its function is not simply to succeed in persuading, but rather to discover the means of coming as near such success as the circumstances of each particular case allow. In this it resembles all other arts. For example, it is not the function of medicine simply to make a man quite healthy, but to put him as far as may be on the road to health; it is possible to give excellent treatment even to those who can never enjoy sound health. Furthermore, it is plain that it is the function of one and the same art to discern the real and the apparent means of persuasion, just as it is the function of dialectic to discern the real and the apparent syllogism. What makes a man a 'sophist' is not his faculty, but his moral purpose. In rhetoric, however, the term 'rhetorician' may describe either the speaker's knowledge or the art, or his moral purpose. In dialectic it is different: a man is a 'sophist' because he has a certain kind of moral purpose, a 'dialectician' in respect, not of his moral purpose, but of his faculty.

Let us know try to give some account of the systematic principles of Rhetoric itself-of the right method and means of succeeding in the object we set before us. We must make as it were a fresh start, and before going further define what rhetoric is.

Part 2

Rhetoric may be defined as the faculty of observing in any given case the available means of persuasion. This is not a function of any other art. Every other art can instruct or persuade about its own particular subject-matter; for instance, medicine about what is healthy and unhealthy, geometry about the properties of magnitudes, arithmetic about numbers, and the same is true of the other arts and sciences. But rhetoric we look up on as the power of observing the means of persuasion on almost any subject presented to us; and that is why we say that, in its technical character, it is not concerned with any special or definite class of subjects.

Of the modes of persuasion, some belong strictly to the art of rhetoric and some do not. By the latter, I mean such things that are not supplied by the speaker but are there at the outset-witnesses, evidence given under torture, written contracts, and so on. By the former, I mean such as we can ourselves construct by means of the principles of rhetoric. The one kind has merely to be used, the other has to be invented.

Of the modes of persuasion furnished by the spoken word there are three kinds. The first kind depends on the personal character of the speaker; the second on putting the audience into a certain from of mind; the third on the proof, or apparent proof, provided by the words of the speech itself. Persuasion is achieved by the speaker's personal character when the speech is so spoken as to make us think him credible. We believe good men more fully and more readily than others: this is true generally whatever the question is, and absolutely true where exact certainty is impossible and opinions are divided. This kind of persuasion, like the others, should be achieved by what the speaker says, not by what people think of his character before he beings to speak. It is not true, as some writers assume in their treatises on rhetoric, that the personal goodness revealed by the speaker contributes nothing to his power of persuasion; on the contrary, his character may almost be called the most effective means of persuasion he possesses. Secondly, persuasion may come through the hearers, when the speech stirs their emotions. Our judgements when we are pleased and friendly are not the same as when we are pained and hostile. It is towards producing these effects, as we maintain, that present-day writers on rhetoric direct the whole of their efforts. This subject shall be treated in detail when we come to speak of the emotions. Thirdly, persuasion is effected through the speech itself when we have proved a truth or an apparent truth by means of the persuasive arguments suitable to the case in question.

There are, then, these three means of effecting persuasion. The man who is to be in command of them must, it is clear, be able (1) to reason logically, (2) to understand human character and goodness in their various forms, and (3) to understand the emotions-that is, to name them and describe them, to know their causes and the way in in which they are excited. It thus appears that rhetoric is an offshoot of dialectic and also of ethical studies. Ethical studies may fairly be called political; and for this reason rhetoric masquerades as political science, and the professors of it as political experts-sometimes from want of education, sometimes from ostentation, sometimes owing to other human failings. As a matter of fact, it is a branch of dialectic and similar to it, as we said at the outset. Neither rhetoric nor dialectic is the scientific study of any one separate subject: both are faculties for providing arguments. This is perhaps a sufficient account of their scope and of how they are related to each other.

With regard to the persuasion achieved by proof or apparent proof: just as in dialectic there is induction on the one hand and syllogism or apparent syllogism on the other, so it is in rhetoric. The example is an induction, the enthymeme is a syllogism, and the apparent enthymeme is an apparent syllogism. I call the enthymeme a rhetorical syllogism, and the example a rhetorical induction. Everyone who effects persuasion through proof does in fact use either enthymemes or examples: there is no other way. And since everyone who proves anything at all is bound ot use either syllogisms or inductions. The difference between example and enthymeme is made plain by the passages in the Topics where induction and syllogism have already been discussed. When we base the proof of a proposition on a number of similar cases, this is induction in dialectic, example in rhetoric; when it is shown that, certain propositions being true, a further and quite proposition must also be true in consequence, whether invariably or usually, this is called syllogism in dialectic, enthymeme in rhetoric. It is plain also that each of these types of oratory has its advantages. Types of oratory, I say: for what has been said in the Methodics applies equally well here; in some oratorical styles examples prevail, in others enthymemes; and in like manner, some orators are better at the former and some at the latter. Speeches that rely on examples are as persuasive as the other kind, but those which rely on enthymemes excite the louder applause. The sources of examples and enthymemes, and their proper uses, we will discuss later. Our next step is to define the processes themselves more clearly.

A statement is persuasive and credible either because it is directly self-evident or because it appears to be proved form other statements that are so. In either case, it is persuasive because there is somebody whom it persuades. But, none of the arts theorize about individual cases. Medicine, for instance, does not theorize about what will help to cure Socrates or Callias, but only about what will help to cure any or all of a given class of patients: this alone is business: individual cases are so infinitely various that no systematic knowledge of them is possible. In the same way, the theory of rhetoric is concerned not with what seems probable to a given individual like Socrates or Hippias, but with what seems probable to men of a given type; and this is true of dialectic also. Dialectic does not construct its syllogisms out of any haphazard materials, such as the fancies of crazy people, but out of materials that call for discussion; and rhetoric, too, draws upon the regular subjects of debate. The duty of rhetoric is to deal with such matters as we deliberate upon without arts or systems to guide us, in the hearing of persons who cannot take in at a glance a complicated argument, or follow a long chain of reasoning. The subjects of our deliberation are such as seem to present us with the alternative possibilities: about things that could not have been, and cannot now or in the future be, other than they are, nobody who takes them to be of this nature wastes his time in deliberation.

It is possible to form syllogisms and draw conclusions form the results of previous syllogism; or, on the other hand, from premises which have not been thus proved, and at the same times are so little accepted that they call for proof. Reasonings of the former kind will necessarily be hard to follow owing to their length, for we assume an audience of untrained thinkers; those of the latter kind will fail to win assent, because they are based on premises that are not generally admitted or believed.

The enthymeme and the example must, then, deal with what is in the main contingent the example being an induction, and the enthymeme a syllogism, about such matters. The enthymeme must consist of few propositions, few often than those which make up the normal syllogism. For if any of these propositions is a familiar fact, there is no need even to mention it; the hearer adds it himself. Thus, to show that Dorieus has been victor in a contest for which the price is a crown, it is enough to say 'For he has been victor in the Olympic games', without adding 'And in the Olympic games the prize is a crown', a fact which everybody knows.

There are few facts of the 'necessary' type that can form the basis of rhetorical syllogisms. Most of the things about which we make decisions, and into which therefore we inquire, present su with alternative possibilities. For it is about our actions that we deliberate and inquire, and all our actions have been a contingent character; hardly any of them are determined by necessity. Again, conclusions that state what is merely usual or possible must be drawn from 'necessary' premises; this too is clear to us from the Analytics. It is evident, therefore, that the propositions forming the basis of enthymemes, though some of them may be 'necessary', will most of them be only usually true. Now the materials of enthymemes are Probabilities and Signs, which we can see must correspond respectively with the propositions that are generally and those that are not necessarily true. A Probability is a thing that usually happens; not, however, as some definitions would suggest, anything whatever that usually happens, but only if it belongs ot the class of the 'contingent' or 'variable'. It bears the same relation to that in respect of which it is probable as the universal bears ot the particular. Of Signs, one kind bears the same relation to the statement it supports as the particular bears to the universal, the other the same as the universal bears to the particular. The infallible kind is a 'complete proof' (tekmerhiou); the fallible kind has no specific name. By infallible signs, I mean those on which syllogisms proper may be based: and this shows us why this kind of Sign is called 'complete proof': when people think that what they have said cannot be refuted, they then think that they are bringing forward a 'complete proof', meaning that the matter has now been demonstrated and completed (perperhasmeuou); for the word 'perhas' has the same meaning (of 'end' or 'boundary') as the word 'tekmarh' in the ancient tongue. Now the one kind of Sign (that which bears to the proposition it supports the relation of particular to universal) may be illustrated thus. Suppose it were said, 'The fact that

Socrates was a wise and just is a sign that the wise are just'. Here we certainly have a Sign; but even though the proposition be true, the argument is refutable, since it does not forma syllogism. Suppose, on the other hand, it were said, 'The fact that he has a fever is a sign that he is ill', or, 'The fact that she is giving milk is a sign that she has lately borne a child'. Here we have the infallible kind of Sign, the only kind that constitutes a complete proof, since it is the only kind that, if the particular statement is true, is irrefutable. The other kind of Sign, that which bears to the proposition it supports the relation of universal to particular, might be illustrated by saying, 'The fact that he breathes fast is a sign that he has a fever'. This argument also is refutable, even if the statement about fast breathing be true, since a man may breathe hard without having a fever.

It has, then, been stated above what is the nature of a Probability, of a Sign, and of a complete proof, and what are the differences between them. In the Analytics a more explicit description has been given of these points; it is there shown why some of the reasonings can be put into syllogisms and some cannot.

The 'example' has already been described as one kind of induction; and the special nature of the subject-matter that distinguishes it from the other kinds has also been stated above. Its relation to the proposition it supports is not that of part to whole, nor whole to part, nor whole to whole, but of part of part, or like to like. When two statements are of the same order, but one is more familiar than the other, the former is an 'example'. The argument may, for instance, be that Dionysius, in asking as he does for a bodyguard, is scheming to make himself a despot. For in the past Peisistratus kept asking for a bodyguard in order to carry out such a scheme, and did make himself a despot as soon as he got it; and so did Theagenes at Megara; and in the same way all other instances known to the speaker are made into examples, in order to show what is not yet known, that Dionysius has the same purpose in making the same request; all these being instances of the one general principle, that a man who asks for a bodyguard is scheming to make himself a despot. We have now described the sources of those means of persuasion which are popularly supposed to be demonstrative.

There is an important distinction between two sorts of enthymemes that has been wholly overlooked by almost everybody-one that also subsists between the syllogisms treated of in dialectic. One sort of enthymeme really belongs to rhetoric, as one sort of syllogism really belongs to dialectic; but the other sort really belongs to other arts and faculties, whether to those we already exercise or to those we have not yet acquired. Missing this distinction, people fail to notice that he more correctly they handle their particular subject the further they are getting away from pure rhetoric or dialectic. This statement will be clearer if expressed more fully. I mean that he proper subjects of dialectical and rhetorical syllogisms are the things with which we say the regular or universal Lines of Argument are concerned, that is to say those lines of argument that apply equally to questions of right conduct, natural science, politics, and many other things that have nothing to do with one another. Take, for instance, the line of argument concerned with 'the more or less'. On this line of argument it is equally easy to base a syllogism or enthymeme about any of what nevertheless are essentially disconnected subjects-right conduct, natural science, or anything else whatever. But, there are also those special Lines of Argument which are based on such propositions as apply only to particular groups or classes of things. Thus, there are propositions about natural science on which it is impossible to base any enthymeme or syllogism about ethics, and other propositions about ethics on which nothing can be based about natural science. The same principle applies throughout. The general Lines of Argument have no special subject-matter, and therefore will not increase our understanding of any particular class of things. On the other hand, the better the selection one makes of propositions suitable for Lines of Argument, the nearer one comes, unconsciously, to setting up a science that is distinct from dialectic and rhetoric. One may succeed in stating the required principles, but one's science will be no longer dialectic or rhetoric, but the science to which the principles thus discovered belong. Most enthymemes are in fact based upon these particular or special Lines of Argument; comparatively few on the common or general kind. As in the therefore, so in this work, we must distinguish, in dealing with enthymemes, the special and the general Lines of Argument on which they are to be founded. By special Lines of Argument, I mean the propositions peculiar to each several class of things, by general those common to all classes alike We may begin with the special Lines of Argument. But, first of all, let us classify rhetoric into its varieties. Having distinguished these we may deal with them one by one, and try to discover the elements of which each is composed, and the propositions each must employ.

Part 3

Rhetoric falls into three divisions, determined by the three classes of listeners to speeches. For of all the elements in speech-making—speaker, subject, and person addressed—it is the last one, the hearer, that determines the speech's end and object. The hearer must be either a judge, with a decision to make about things past or future, or an observer. A member of the assembly decides about future events, a juryman about past events: while those who merely decide on the orator's skills are observers. From this it follows that there are three divisions of oratory-(1) political, (2) forensic, and (3) the ceremonial oratory of display.

Political speaking urges us either to do or not to do something: one of these two courses is always taken by private counsellors, as well as by men who address public assemblies. Forensic speaking either attacks or defends somebody: one or other of these two things must always be done by the parties in a case. The ceremonial oratory of display either praises or censures somebody. These three kinds of rhetoric refer to three different kinds of time. The political orator is concerned with the future: it is about things to be done hereafter that he advises, for or against. The party in a case at law is concerned with the past; one man accuses the other, and the other defends himself, with reference to things already done. The ceremonial orator is, properly speaking, concerned with the present, since all men praise or blame in view of the state of things existing at the time, though they often find it useful also to recall the past and to make guesses at the future.

Rhetoric has three distinct ends in view, one for each of its three kinds. The political orator aims at establishing the expediency or the harmfulness of a proposed course of action; if he urges its acceptance, he does so on the ground that it will do good; if he urges its rejection, he does so on the ground that it will do harm; and all other points such as whether the proposal is just or unjust, honorable, or dishonorable, he brings in as a subsidiary and relative ot this main consideration. Parties in a law-case aim at establishing the justice or injustice of some action, and they too bring in all other points as subsidiary and relative to this one. Those who praise or attack a man aim at proving him worthy or honor or the reverse, and they too treat all other considerations with reference to this one.

That the three kinds of rhetoric do aim respectively at the three ends we have mentioned is shown by the fact that speakers will sometimes not try to establish anything else. Thus, the litigant will sometimes not deny that a thing has happened or that he has done harm. But that he is guilty of injustice he will never admit; otherwise there would be no need of a trial. So too, political orators often make any concession short of admitting that they are recommending their hearers to take an inexpedient course or not to take an expedient one. The question whether it is not unjust for a city to enslave its innocent neighbors often does not trouble them at all. In like manner those who praise or censure a man do not consider whether his acts have been expedient or not, but often make it a ground of actual praise that he has neglected his own interest to do what was honorable. Thus, they praise Achilles because he championed his fallen friend Patroclus, though he knew that this meant death, and that otherwise he need not die: yet while to die thus was the nobler thing for him to do, the expedient thing was to live on.

It is evident from what has been said that it is these three subjects, more than any other, about which the orator must be able to have propositions at his command. Now the propositions of Rhetoric are Complete Proofs, Probabilities, and Signs. Every kind of syllogism is composed of propositions, and the enthymeme is a particular kind of syllogism composed of the aforesaid propositions.

Since only possible actions, and not impossible ones, can ever have been done in the past or the present, and since things which have not occurred, or will not occur, also cannot have been done or be going to be done, it is necessary for the political, the forensic, and the ceremonial speaker alike to be able to have at their command propositions about the possible and the impossible, and about whether a thing has or has not occurred, will or will not occur. Further all men, in giving praise or blame, in urging us to accept or reject proposals for action, in accusing others or defending themselves, attempt not only to prove the points mentioned but also to show that the good or the harm, the honor, or disgrace, the justice or injustice, is great or small either absolutely or relatively; and therefore it is plain that we must also have at our command propositions about greatness or smallness and the greater or the lesser-propositions both universal and particular. Thus, we must be able to say which is the greater or lesser good, the greater or lesser act of justice or injustice; and so on.

Such, then, are the subjects regarding which we are inevitably bound to master the propositions relevant to them. We must now discuss each particular class of these subjects in turn, namely those dealt with in political, in ceremonial, and lastly in legal oratory.

Part 4

First, then, we must ascertain what are the kinds of things, good or bad, about which the political orator offers counsel. For he does not deal with all things, but only with such as may or may not take place. Concerning things which exist or will exist inevitably, or which cannot possibly exist or take place, no counsel can be given. Nor, again, can counsel be given about the whole class of things which may or may not take place; for this class includes some good things which may or may not take place; for this class includes some good things that occur naturally, and some that occur by accident; and about these it is useless to offer counsel. Clearly, counsel can only be given on matters about which people deliberate; matters, namely, that ultimately depend on ourselves, and which we have it in our power to set going. For we turn a thing over in our mind until we have reached the point of seeing whether we can do it or not.

Now to enumerate and classify accurately the usual subjects of public business, and further to frame, as far as possible, true definitions of them is a task which we must not attempt on the present occasion. For it does not belong to the art of rhetoric, but to a more instructive art and a more real branch of knowledge; and as it is, rhetoric has been given a far wider subject-matter than strictly belongs to it. The truth is, as indeed we have said already, that rhetoric is a combination of the science of logic and of the ethical branch of politics; and it is partly like dialectic, partly like sophistical reasoning. But the more we try to make either dialectic rhetoric not, what they really are, practical faculties, but sciences, the more we shall inadvertently be destroying their true nature; for we shall be re-fashioning them and shall be passing into the region of sciences dealing with definite subjects rather than simply with words and forms of reasoning. Even here, however, we will mention those points which it is of practical importance to distinguish, their fuller treatment falling naturally to political science.

The main matters on which all men deliberate and on which political speakers make speeches are some five in number: ways and means, war and peace, national defense, imports and exports, and legislation.

As to Ways and Means, then, the intending speaker will need to know the number and extent of the country's sources of revenue, so that, if any is being overlooked, it may be added, and, if any is defective, it may be increased. Further, he should know all the expenditure of the country, in order that, if any part of it is superfluous, it may be abolished, or, if any is too large, it may be reduced. For men become richer not only by increasing their existing wealth but also by reducing their expenditure. A comprehensive view of these questions cannot be gained solely from experience in home affairs; in order to advise on such matters a man must be keenly interested in the methods worked out in other lands.

As to Peace and War, he must know the extent of the military strength of his country, both actual and potential, and also the nature of that actual and potential strength; and further, what wars his country has waged and how it has waged them. He must know these facts not only about his own country, but also about neighboring countries; and also about countries with which war is likely, in order that peace may be maintained with those stronger than his own, and that his own may have power to make war or not against those who are weaker. He should know, too, whether the military power of another country is like or unlike that of his own; for this is a matter that may affect their relative strength. With the same end in view he must, besides, have studied the wars of other countries as well as those of his own, and the way they ended; similar causes are likely to have similar results.

With regard to National Defense; he ought to know all about the methods of defense in actual use, such as the strength and character of the defensive force and the positions of the forts-this last means that he must be well acquainted with the lie of the country-in order that a garrison may be increased if it is too small or removed if it is not wanted, and that the strategic points may be guarded with special care.

With regard to the Food Supply: he must know what outlay will meet the needs of his country; what kinds of food are produced at home and what imported; and what articles must be exported or imported. This last he must know in order that agreements and commercial treaties may be made with the countries concerned. There are, indeed, two sorts of state to which he must see that his countrymen give no cause for offense, states stronger than his own, and states with which it is advantageous to trade.

But, while he must, for security's sake, be able to take all this into account, he must before all things understand the subject of legislation; for it is on a country's laws that its whole welfare depends. He must, therefore, know how many different forms of constitution there are; under what conditions each of these will prosper and by what internal developments or external attacks each of them tends to be destroyed.

When I speak of destruction through internal developments, I refer to the fact the all constitutions, except the best one of all, are destroyed both by not being pushed far enough and by being pushed too far. Thus, democracy loses its vigor, and finally passes into oligarchy, not only when it is not pushed far enough, but also when it is pushed a great deal too far; just as the aquiline and the snub nose not only turn into normal noses by not being aquiline or snub enough, but also by being too violently aquiline or snub arrive at a condition in which they no longer look like noses at all. It is useful, in framing laws, not only to study the past history of one's own country, in order to understand which constitution is desirable for it now, but also to have a knowledge of the constitutions of other nations, and so to learn for what kinds of nation the various kinds of constitution are suited. From this, we can see that books of travel are useful aids to legislation, since from these we may learn the laws and customs of different races. The political speaker will also find the researches of historians useful. But, all this is the business of political science and not of rhetoric.

These, then, are the most important kinds of information which the political speaker must possess. Let us now go back and state the premises from which he will have to argue in favor of adopting or rejecting measures regarding these and other matters.

David & Goliath

(I Samuel 17:1-58 NASB)

Now the Philistines gathered their armies for battle; and they were gathered at Socoh which belongs to Judah, and they camped between Socoh and Azekah, in Ephes-dammim. Saul and the men of Israel were gathered and camped in the valley of Elah, and drew up in battle array to encounter the Philistines. The Philistines stood on the mountain on one side while Israel stood on the mountain on the other side, with the valley between them. Then a champion came out from the armies of the Philistines named Goliath, from Gath, whose height was six cubits and a span. *He had* a bronze helmet on his head, and he was clothed with scale-armor which weighed five thousand shekels of bronze. *He* also *had* bronze greaves on his legs and a bronze javelin *slung* between his shoulders. The shaft of his spear was like a weaver's beam, and the head of his spear *weighed* six hundred shekels of iron; his shield-carrier also walked before him. He stood and shouted to the ranks of Israel and said to them, "Why do you come out to draw up in battle array? Am I not the Philistine and you servants of Saul? Choose a man for yourselves and let him come down to me. If he is able to fight with me and kill me, then we will become your servants; but if I prevail against him and kill him, then you shall become our servants and serve us." Again the Philistine said, "I defy the ranks of Israel this day; give me a man that we may fight together." When Saul and all Israel heard these words of the Philistine, they were dismayed and greatly afraid.

Now David was the son of the Ephrathite of Bethlehem in Judah, whose name was Jesse, and he had eight sons. And Jesse was old in the days of Saul, advanced *in years* among men. The three older sons of Jesse had gone after Saul to the battle. And the names of his three sons who went to the battle were Eliab the firstborn, and the second to him Abinadab, and the third Shammah. David was the youngest. Now the three oldest followed Saul, but David went back and forth from Saul to tend his father's flock at Bethlehem. The Philistine came forward morning and evening for forty days and took his stand.

Then Jesse said to David his son, "Take now for your brothers an ephah of this roasted grain and these ten loaves and run to the camp to your brothers. Bring also these ten cuts of cheese to the commander of *their* thousand, and look into the welfare of your brothers, and bring back news of them. For Saul and they and all the men of Israel are in the valley of Elah, fighting with the Philistines."

David Accepts the Challenge

So David arose early in the morning and left the flock with a keeper and took *the supplies* and went as Jesse had commanded him. And he came to the circle of the camp while the army was going out in battle array shouting the war cry. Israel and the Philistines drew up in battle array, army against army. Then David left his baggage in the care of the baggage keeper, and ran to the battle line and entered in order to greet his brothers. As he was talking with them, behold, the champion, the Philistine from Gath named Goliath, was coming up from the army of the Philistines, and he spoke these same words; and David heard *them*.

When all the men of Israel saw the man, they fled from him and were greatly afraid. The men of Israel said, "Have you seen this man who is coming up? Surely, he is coming up to defy Israel. And it will be that the king will enrich the man who kills him with great riches and will give him his daughter and make his father's house free in Israel."

Then David spoke to the men who were standing by him, saying, "What will be done for the man who kills this Philistine and takes away the reproach from Israel? For who is this uncircumcised Philistine, that he should taunt the armies of the living God?" The people answered him in accord with this word, saying, "Thus it will be done for the man who kills him."

Now Eliab his oldest brother heard when he spoke to them; and Eliab's anger burned against David and he said, "Why have you come down? And with whom have you left those few sheep in the wilderness? I know your insolence and the wickedness of your heart; for you have come down in order to see the battle." But David said, "What have I done now? Was it not just a question?" Then he turned away from him to another and said the same thing; and the people answered the same thing as before.

David Kills Goliath

When the words which David spoke were heard, they told *them* to Saul, and he sent for him. David said to Saul, "Let no man's heart fail on account of him; your servant will go and fight with this Philistine." Then Saul said to David, "You are not able to go against this Philistine to fight with him; for you are *but* a youth while he has been a warrior from his youth." But David said to Saul, "Your servant was tending his father's sheep. When a lion or a bear came and took a lamb from the flock, I went out after him and attacked him, and rescued *it* from his mouth; and when he rose up against me, I seized *him* by his beard and struck him and killed him. Your servant has killed both the lion and the bear; and this uncircumcised Philistine will be like one of them, since he has taunted the armies of the living God." And David said, "The LORD who delivered me from the paw of the lion and from the paw of the bear, He will deliver me from the hand of this Philistine." And Saul said to David, "Go, and may the LORD be with you." Then Saul clothed David with his garments and put a bronze helmet on his head, and he clothed him with armor. David girded his sword over his armor and tried to walk, for he had not tested *them*. So David said to Saul, "I cannot go with these, for I have not tested *them*." And David took them off. He took his stick in his hand and chose for himself five smooth stones from the brook, and put them in the shepherd's bag which he had, even in *his* pouch, and his sling was in his hand; and he approached the Philistine.

Then the Philistine came on and approached David, with the shield-bearer in front of him. When the Philistine looked and saw David, he disdained him; for he was *but* a youth, and ruddy, with a handsome appearance. The Philistine said to David, "Am I a dog that you come to me with sticks?" And the Philistine cursed David by his gods. The Philistine also said to David, "Come to me, and I will give your flesh to the birds of the sky and the beasts of the field." Then David said to the Philistine, "You come to me with a sword, a spear, and a javelin, but I come to you in the name of the LORD of hosts, the God of the armies of Israel, whom you have taunted. This day the LORD will deliver you up into my hands, and I will strike you down and remove your head from you. And I will give the dead bodies of the army of the Philistines this day to the birds of the sky and the wild beasts of the earth, that all the earth may know that there is a God in Israel, and that all this assembly may know that the LORD does not deliver by sword or by spear; for the battle is the LORD's and He will give you into our hands."

Then it happened when the Philistine rose and came and drew near to meet David, that David ran quickly toward the battle line to meet the Philistine. And David put his hand into his bag and took from it a stone and slung *it*, and struck the Philistine on his forehead. And the stone sank into his forehead, so that he fell on his face to the ground.

Thus David prevailed over the Philistine with a sling and a stone, and he struck the Philistine and killed him; but there was no sword in David's hand. Then David ran and stood over the Philistine and took his sword and drew it out of its sheath and killed him, and cut off his head with it. When the Philistines saw that their champion was dead, they fled. The men of Israel and Judah arose and shouted and pursued the Philistines as far as the valley, and to the gates of Ekron. And the slain Philistines lay along the way to Shaaraim, even to Gath and Ekron. The sons of Israel returned from chasing the Philistines and plundered their camps. Then David took the Philistine's head and brought it to Jerusalem, but he put his weapons in his tent.

Now when Saul saw David going out against the Philistine, he said to Abner the commander of the army, "Abner, whose son is this young man?" And Abner said, "By your life, O king, I do not know." The king said, "You inquire whose son the youth is." So when David returned from killing the Philistine, Abner took him and brought him before Saul with the Philistine's head in his hand. Saul said to him, "Whose son are you, young man?" And David answered, "*I am* the son of your servant Jesse the Bethlehemite."

The Prodigal Son

(Luke 15:11-32 NASB)

And He said, "A man had two sons. The younger of them said to his father, 'Father, give me the share of the estate that falls to me.' So he divided his wealth between them. And not many days later, the younger son gathered everything together and went on a journey into a distant country, and there he squandered his estate with loose living. Now when he had spent everything, a severe famine occurred in that country, and he began to be impoverished. So he went and hired himself out to one of the citizens of that country, and he sent him into his fields to feed swine. And he would have gladly filled his stomach with the pods that the swine were eating, and no one was giving *anything* to him. But when he came to his senses, he said, 'How many of my father's hired men have more than enough bread, but I am dying here with hunger! I will get up and go to my father, and will say to him, "Father, I have sinned against heaven, and in your sight; I am no longer worthy to be called your son; make me as one of your hired men."' So he got up and came to his father. But while he was still a long way off, his father saw him and felt compassion *for him*, and ran and embraced him and kissed him. And the son said to him, 'Father, I have sinned against heaven and in your sight; I am no longer worthy to be called your son.' But the father said to his slaves, 'Quickly bring out the best robe and put it on him, and put a ring on his hand and sandals on his feet; and bring the fattened calf, kill it, and let us eat and celebrate; for this son of mine was dead and has come to life again; he was lost and has been found.' And they began to celebrate.

"Now his older son was in the field, and when he came and approached the house, he heard music and dancing. And he summoned one of the servants and *began* inquiring what these things could be. And he said to him, 'Your brother has come, and your father has killed the fattened calf because he has received him back safe and sound.' But he became angry and was not willing to go in; and his father came out and *began* pleading with him. But he answered and said to his father, 'Look! For so many years I have been serving you and I have never neglected a command of yours; and *yet* you have never given me a young goat, so that I might celebrate with my friends; but when this son of yours came, who has devoured your wealth with prostitutes, you killed the fattened calf for him.' And he said to him, 'Son, you have always been with me, and all that is mine is yours. But we had to celebrate and rejoice, for this brother of yours was dead and *has begun* to live, and *was* lost and has been found.'"

The Sower and His Seed

(Luke 8:4-15 NASB)

When a large crowd was coming together, and those from the various cities were journeying to Him, He spoke by way of a parable: "The sower went out to sow his seed; and as he sowed, some fell beside the road, and it was trampled underfoot and the birds of the air ate it up. Other *seed* fell on rocky *soil*, and as soon as it grew up, it withered away, because it had no moisture. Other *seed* fell among the thorns; and the thorns grew up with it and choked it out. Other *seed* fell into the good soil, and grew up, and produced a crop a hundred times as great." As He said these things, He would call out, "He who has ears to hear, let him hear."

His disciples *began* questioning Him as to what this parable meant. And He said, "To you it has been granted to know the mysteries of the kingdom of God, but to the rest *it is* in parables, so that SEEING THEY MAY NOT SEE, AND HEARING THEY MAY NOT UNDERSTAND.

"Now the parable is this: the seed is the word of God. Those beside the road are those who have heard; then the devil comes and takes away the word from their heart, so that they will not believe and be saved. Those on the rocky *soil are* those who, when they hear, receive the word with joy; and these have no *firm* root; they believe for a while, and in time of temptation fall away. The *seed* which fell among the thorns, these are the ones who have heard, and as they go on their way they are choked with worries and riches and pleasures of *this* life, and bring no fruit to maturity. But the *seed* in the good soil, these are the ones who have heard the word in an honest and good heart, and hold it fast, and bear fruit with perseverance.

(Matthew 13:1-23)

That day Jesus went out of the house and was sitting by the sea. And large crowds gathered to Him, so He got into a boat and sat down, and the whole crowd was standing on the beach.

And He spoke many things to them in parables, saying, "Behold, the sower went out to sow; and as he sowed, some *seeds* fell beside the road, and the birds came and ate them up. Others fell on the rocky places, where they did not have much soil; and immediately they sprang up, because they had no depth of soil. But when the sun had risen, they were scorched; and because they had no root, they withered away. Others fell among the thorns, and the thorns came up and choked them out. And others fell on the good soil and yielded a crop, some a hundredfold, some sixty, and some thirty. He who has ears, let him hear."

And the disciples came and said to Him, "Why do You speak to them in parables?" Jesus answered them, "To you it has been granted to know the mysteries of the kingdom of heaven, but to them it has not been granted. For whoever has, to him *more* shall be given, and he will have an abundance; but whoever does not have, even what he has shall be taken away from him. Therefore, I speak to them in parables; because while seeing they do not see, and while hearing they do not hear, nor do they understand. In their case the prophecy of Isaiah is being fulfilled, which says,

'YOU WILL KEEP ON HEARING, BUT WILL NOT UNDERSTAND;
YOU WILL KEEP ON SEEING, BUT WILL NOT PERCEIVE;
FOR THE HEART OF THIS PEOPLE HAS BECOME DULL,
WITH THEIR EARS THEY SCARCELY HEAR,
AND THEY HAVE CLOSED THEIR EYES,
OTHERWISE THEY WOULD SEE WITH THEIR EYES,

Hear with their ears,
And understand with their heart and return,
And I would heal them.'

But blessed are your eyes, because they see; and your ears, because they hear. For truly I say to you that many prophets and righteous men desired to see what you see, and did not see *it*, and to hear what you hear, and did not hear *it*.

"Hear then the parable of the sower. When anyone hears the word of the kingdom and does not understand it, the evil *one* comes and snatches away what has been sown in his heart. This is the one on whom seed was sown beside the road. The one on whom seed was sown on the rocky places, this is the man who hears the word and immediately receives it with joy; yet he has no *firm* root in himself, but is *only* temporary, and when affliction or persecution arises because of the word, immediately he falls away. And the one on whom seed was sown among the thorns, this is the man who hears the word, and the worry of the world and the deceitfulness of wealth choke the word, and it becomes unfruitful. And the one on whom seed was sown on the good soil, this is the man who hears the word and understands it; who indeed bears fruit and brings forth, some a hundredfold, some sixty, and some thirty."

The Destruction of Pompeii

On August 24, 79 Mount Vesuvius literally blew its top, spewing tons of molten ash, pumice and sulfuric gas miles into the atmosphere. A "firestorm" of poisonous vapors and molten debris engulfed the surrounding area suffocating the inhabitants of the neighboring Roman resort cities of Pompeii, Herculaneum and Stabiae. Tons of falling debris filled the streets until nothing remained to be seen of the once thriving communities. The cities remained buried and undiscovered for almost 1700 years until excavation began in 1748. These excavations continue today and provide insight into life during the Roman Empire.

An ancient voice reaches out from the past to tell us of the disaster. This voice belongs to Pliny the Younger whose letters describe his experience during the eruption while he was staying in the home of his Uncle, Pliny the Elder. The elder Pliny was an official in the Roman Court, in charge of the fleet in the area of the Bay of Naples and a naturalist. Pliny the Younger's letters were discovered in the 16th century.

Wrath of the Gods

A few years after the event, Pliny wrote a friend, Cornelius Tacitus, describing the happenings of late August 79 AD when the eruption of Vesuvius obliterated Pompeii, killed his Uncle and almost destroyed his family. At the time, Pliney was eighteen and living at his Uncle's villa in the town of Misenum. We pick up his story as he describes the warning raised by his mother:

"My uncle was stationed at Misenum, in active command of the fleet. On 24 August, in the early afternoon, my mother drew his attention to a cloud of unusual size and appearance. He had been out in the sun, had taken a cold bath, and lunched while lying down, and was then working at his books. He called for his shoes and climbed up to a place which would give him the best view of the phenomenon. It was not clear at that distance from which mountain the cloud was rising (it was afterwards known to be Vesuvius); its general appearance can best be expressed as being like an umbrella pine, for it rose to a great height on a sort of trunk and then split off into branches, I imagine because it was thrust upwards by the first blast and then left unsupported as the pressure subsided, or else it was borne down by its own weight so that it spread out and gradually dispersed. In places it looked white, elsewhere blotched and dirty, according to the amount of soil and ashes it carried with it.

My uncle's scholarly acumen saw at once that it was important enough for a closer inspection, and he ordered a boat to be made ready, telling me I could come with him if I wished. I replied that I preferred to go on with my studies, and as it happened he had himself given me some writing to do.

As he was leaving the house he was handed a message from Rectina, wife of Tascus whose house was at the foot of the mountain, so that escape was impossible except by boat. She was terrified by the danger threatening her and implored him to rescue her from her fate. He changed his plans, and what he had begun in a spirit of inquiry he completed as a hero. He gave orders for the warships to be launched and went on board himself with the intention of bringing help to many more people besides Rectina, for this lovely stretch of coast was thickly populated.

He hurried to the place which everyone else was hastily leaving, steering his course straight for the danger zone. He was entirely fearless, describing each new movement and phase of the portent to be noted down exactly as he observed them. Ashes were already falling, hotter and thicker as the ships drew near, followed by bits of pumice and blackened stones, charred and cracked by the flames: then suddenly they were in shallow water, and the shore was blocked by the debris from the mountain.

For a moment my uncle wondered whether to turn back, but when the helmsman advised this he refused, telling him that Fortune stood by the courageous and they must make for Pomponianus at Stabiae. He was cut off there by the breadth of the bay (for the shore gradually curves round a basin filled by the sea) so that he was not as yet in danger, though it was clear that this would come nearer as it spread. Pomponianus had therefore already put his belongings on board ship, intending to escape if the contrary wind fell. This wind was of course full in my uncle's favour, and he was able to bring his ship in. He embraced his terrified friend, cheered and encouraged him, and thinking he could calm his fears by showing his own composure, gave orders that he was to be carried to the bathroom. After his bath, he lay down and dined; he was quite cheerful, or at any rate he pretended he was, which was no less courageous.

Meanwhile on Mount Vesuvius broad sheets of fire and leaping flames blazed at several points, their bright glare emphasized by the darkness of night. My uncle tried to allay the fears of his companions by repeatedly declaring that these were nothing but bonfires left by the peasants in their terror, or else empty houses on fire in the districts they had abandoned. Then he went to rest and certainly slept, for as he was a stout man his breathing was rather loud and heavy and could be heard by people coming and going outside his door. By this time the courtyard giving access to his room was full of ashes mixed with pumice stones, so that its level had risen, and if he had stayed in the room any longer he would never have got out. He was wakened, came out and joined Pomponianus and the rest of the household who had sat up all night.

They debated whether to stay indoors or take their chance in the open, for the buildings were now shaking with violent shocks, and seemed to be swaying to and fro as if they were torn from their foundations. Outside, on the other hand, there was the danger of failing pumice stones, even though these were light and porous; however, after comparing the risks they chose the latter. In my uncle's case one reason outweighed the other, but for the others it was a choice of fears. As a protection against falling objects they put pillows on their heads tied down with cloths.

Elsewhere there was daylight by this time, but they were still in darkness, blacker and denser than any ordinary night, which they relieved by lighting torches and various kinds of lamp. My uncle decided to go down to the shore and investigate on the spot the possibility of any escape by sea, but he found the waves still wild and dangerous. A sheet was spread on the ground for him to lie down, and he repeatedly asked for cold water to drink.

Then the flames and smell of sulphur which gave warning of the approaching fire drove the others to take flight and roused him to stand up. He stood leaning on two slaves and then suddenly collapsed, I imagine because the dense, fumes choked his breathing by blocking his windpipe which was constitutionally weak and narrow and often inflamed. When daylight returned on the 26th - two days after the last day he had been seen - his body was found intact and uninjured, still fully clothed and looking more like sleep than death.

Shrieks of the People

In a second letter to Tacitus, Pliny describes what happened to him and to his mother during the second day of the disaster:

Ashes were already falling, not as yet very thickly. I looked round: a dense black cloud was coming up behind us, spreading over the earth like a flood.' Let us leave the road while we can still see, 'I said,' or we shall be knocked down and trampled underfoot in the dark by the crowd behind.' We had scarcely sat down to rest when darkness fell, not the dark of a moonless or cloudy night, but as if the lamp had been put out in a closed room.

You could hear the shrieks of women, the wailing of infants, and the shouting of men; some were calling their parents, others their children or their wives, trying to recognize them by their voices. People bewailed their own fate or that of their relatives, and there were some who prayed for death in their terror of dying. Many besought the aid of the gods, but still more imagined there were no gods left, and that the universe was plunged into eternal darkness for evermore.

There were people, too, who added to the real perils by inventing fictitious dangers: some reported that part of Misenum had collapsed or another part was on fire, and though their tales were false they found others to believe them. A gleam of light returned, but we took this to be a warning of the approaching flames rather than daylight. However, the flames remained some distance off; then darkness came on once more and ashes began to fall again, this time in heavy showers. We rose from time to time and shook them off, otherwise we should have been buried and crushed beneath their weight. I could boast that not a groan or cry of fear escaped me in these perils, but I admit that I derived some poor consolation in my mortal lot from the belief that the whole world was dying with me and I with it."

The Story of an Eyewitness

by Jack London

1906

The earthquake shook down in San Francisco hundreds of thousands of dollars worth of walls and chimneys. But the conflagration that followed burned up hundreds of millions of dollars' worth of property. There is no estimating within hundreds of millions the actual damage wrought. Not in history has a modern imperial city been so completely destroyed. San Francisco is gone. Nothing remains of it but memories and a fringe of dwelling-houses on its outskirts. Its industrial section is wiped out. Its business section is wiped out. Its social and residential section is wiped out. The factories and warehouses, the great stores and newspaper buildings, the hotels and the palaces of the nabobs, are all gone. Remains only the fringe of dwelling houses on the outskirts of what was once San Francisco.

Within an hour after the earthquake shock, the smoke of San Francisco's burning was a lurid tower visible a hundred miles away. And for three days and nights this lurid tower swayed in the sky, reddening the sun, darkening the day, and filling the land with smoke.

On Wednesday morning at a quarter past five came the earthquake. A minute later, the flames were leaping upward. In a dozen different quarters south of Market Street, in the working-class ghetto, and in the factories, fires started. There was no opposing the flames. There was no organization, no communication. All the cunning adjustments of a twentieth century city had been smashed by the earthquake. The streets were humped into ridges and depressions, and piled with the debris of fallen walls. The steel rails were twisted into perpendicular and horizontal angles. The telephone and telegraph systems were disrupted. And the great water-mains had burst. All the shrewd contrivances and safeguards of man had been thrown out of gear by thirty seconds' twitching of the earth-crust.

The Fire Made its Own Draft

By Wednesday afternoon, inside of twelve hours, half the heart of the city was gone. At that time I watched the vast conflagration from out on the bay. It was dead calm. Not a flicker of wind stirred. Yet from every side wind was pouring in upon the city. East, west, north, and south, strong winds were blowing upon the doomed city. The heated air rising made an enormous suck. Thus did the fire of itself build its own colossal chimney through the atmosphere. Day and night, this dead calm continued, and yet, near to the flames, the wind was often half a gale, so mighty was the suck.

Wednesday night saw the destruction of the very heart of the city. Dynamite was lavishly used, and many of San Francisco's proudest structures were crumbled by man himself into ruins, but there was no withstanding the onrush of the flames. Time and again successful stands were made by the fire-fighters, and every time the flames flanked around on either side or came up from the rear, and turned to defeat the hard-won victory.

An enumeration of the buildings destroyed would be a directory of San Francisco. An enumeration of the buildings undestroyed would be a line and several addresses. An enumeration of the deeds of heroism would stock a library and bankrupt the Carnegie medal fund. An enumeration of the dead will never be made. All vestiges of them were destroyed by the flames. The number of the victims of the earthquake will never be known. South of Market Street, where the loss of life was particularly heavy, was the first to catch fire.

Remarkable as it may seem, Wednesday night while the whole city crashed and roared into ruin, was a quiet night. There were no crowds. There was no shouting and yelling. There was no hysteria, no disorder. I passed Wednesday night in the path of the advancing flames, and in all those terrible hours, I saw not one woman who wept, not one man who was excited, not one person who was in the slightest degree panic-stricken.

Before the flames, throughout the night, fled tens of thousands of homeless ones. Some were wrapped in blankets. Others carried bundles of bedding and dear household treasures. Sometimes a whole family was harnessed to a carriage or delivery wagon that was weighted down with their possessions. Baby buggies, toy wagons, and go-carts were used as trucks, while every other person was dragging a trunk. Yet everybody was gracious. The most perfect courtesy obtained. Never in all San Francisco's history, were her people so kind and courteous as on this night of terror.

A Caravan of Trunks

All night these tens of thousands fled before the flames. Many of them, the poor people from the labor ghetto, had fled all day as well. They had left their homes burdened with possessions. Now and again they lightened up, flinging out upon the street clothing and treasures they had dragged for miles.

They held on longest to their trunks, and over these trunks, many a strong man broke his heart that night. The hills of San Francisco are steep, and up these hills, mile after mile, were the trunks dragged. Everywhere were trunks with across them lying their exhausted owners, men and women. Before the march of the flames were flung picket lines of soldiers. And a block at a time, as the flames advanced, these pickets retreated. One of their tasks was to keep the trunk-pullers moving. The exhausted creatures, stirred on by the menace of bayonets, would arise and struggle up the steep pavements, pausing from weakness every five or ten feet.

Often, after surmounting a heart-breaking hill, they would find another wall of flame advancing upon them at right angles and be compelled to change anew the line of their retreat. In the end, completely played out, after toiling for a dozen hours like giants, thousands of them were compelled to abandon their trunks. Here the shopkeepers and soft members of the middle class were at a disadvantage. But the working-men dug holes in vacant lots and backyards and buried their trunks.

The Doomed City

At nine o'clock Wednesday evening, I walked down through the very heart of the city. I walked through miles and miles of magnificent buildings and towering skyscrapers. Here was no fire. All was in perfect order. The police patrolled the streets. Every building had its watchman at the door. And yet it was doomed, all of it. There was no water. The dynamite was giving out. And at right angles two different conflagrations were sweeping down upon it.

At one o'clock in the morning, I walked down through the same section. Everything still stood intact. There was no fire. And yet there was a change. A rain of ashes was falling. The watchmen at the doors were gone. The police had been withdrawn. There were no firemen, no fire-engines, no men fighting with dynamite. The district had been absolutely abandoned. I stood at the corner of Kearney and Market, in the very innermost heart of San Francisco. Kearny Street was deserted. Half a dozen blocks away it was burning on both sides. The street was a wall of flame. And against this wall of flame, silhouetted sharply, were two United States cavalrymen sitting their horses, calmly watching. That was all. Not another person was in sight. In the intact heart of the city two troopers sat their horses and watched.

Spread of the Conflagration

Surrender was complete. There was no water. The sewers had long since been pumped dry. There was no dynamite. Another fire had broken out further uptown, and now from three sides conflagrations were sweeping down. The fourth side had been burned earlier in the day. In that direction stood the tottering walls of the Examiner building, the burned-out Call building, the smoldering ruins of the Grand Hotel, and the gutted, devastated, dynamited Palace Hotel.

The following will illustrate the sweep of the flames and the inability of men to calculate their spread. At eight o'clock Wednesday evening, I passed through Union Square. It was packed with refugees. Thousands of them had gone to bed on the grass. Government tents had been set up, supper was being cooked, and the refugees were lining up for free meals.

At half past one in the morning, three sides of Union Square were in flames. The fourth side, where stood the great St. Francis Hotel was still holding out. An hour later, ignited from top and sides the St. Francis was flaming heavenward. Union Square, heaped high with mountains of trunks, was deserted. Troops, refugees, and all had retreated.

A Fortune for a Horse!

It was at Union Square that I saw a man offering a thousand dollars for a team of horses. He was in charge of a truck piled high with trunks from some hotel. It had been hauled here into what was considered safety, and the horses had been taken out. The flames were on three sides of the Square and there were no horses.

Also, at this time, standing beside the truck, I urged a man to seek safety in flight. He was all but hemmed in by several conflagrations. He was an old man and he was on crutches. Said he: "Today is my birthday. Last night I was worth thirty thousand dollars. I bought five bottles of wine, some delicate fish and other things for my birthday dinner. I have had no dinner, and all I own are these crutches."

I convinced him of his danger and started him limping on his way. An hour later, from a distance, I saw the truck-load of trunks burning merrily in the middle of the street.

On Thursday morning at a quarter past five, just twenty-four hours after the earthquake, I sat on the steps of a small residence on Nob Hill. With me sat Japanese, Italians, Chinese, and negroes--a bit of the cosmopolitan flotsam of the wreck of the city. All about were the palaces of the nabob pioneers of Forty-nine. To the east and south at right angles, were advancing two mighty walls of flame.

I went inside with the owner of the house on the steps of which I sat. He was cool and cheerful and hospitable. "Yesterday morning," he said, "I was worth six hundred thousand dollars. This morning this house is all I have left. It will go in fifteen minutes. He pointed to a large cabinet. "That is my wife's collection of china. This rug upon which we stand is a present. It cost fifteen hundred dollars. Try that piano. Listen to its tone. There are few like it. There are no horses. The flames will be here in fifteen minutes."

Outside the old Mark Hopkins residence, a palace was just catching fire. The troops were falling back and driving the refugees before them. From every side came the roaring of flames, the crashing of walls, and the detonations of dynamite.

The Dawn of the Second Day

I passed out of the house. Day was trying to dawn through the smoke-pall. A sickly light was creeping over the face of things. Once only the sun broke through the smoke-pall, blood-red, and showing quarter its usual size. The smoke-pall itself, viewed from beneath, was a rose color that pulsed and fluttered with lavender shades Then it turned to mauve and yellow and dun. There was no sun. And so dawned the second day on stricken San Francisco.

An hour later, I was creeping past the shattered dome of the City Hall. Than it there was no better exhibit of the destructive force of the earthquake. Most of the stone had been shaken from the great dome, leaving standing the naked framework of steel. Market Street was piled high with the wreckage, and across the wreckage lay the overthrown pillars of the City Hall shattered into short crosswise sections.

This section of the city, with the exception of the Mint and the Post-Office, was already a waste of smoking ruins. Here and there through the smoke, creeping warily under the shadows of tottering walls, emerged occasional men and women. It was like the meeting of the handful of survivors after the day of the end of the world.

Beeves Slaughtered and Roasted

On Mission Street lay a dozen steers, in a neat row stretching across the street just as they had been struck down by the flying ruins of the earthquake. The fire had passed through afterward and roasted them. The human dead had been carried away before the fire came. At another place on Mission Street, I saw a milk wagon. A steel telegraph pole had smashed down sheer through the driver's seat and crushed the front wheels. The milk cans lay scattered around.

All day Thursday and all Thursday night, all day Friday and Friday night, the flames still raged on.

Friday night saw the flames finally conquered, though not until Russian Hill and Telegraph Hill had been swept and three-quarters of a mile of wharves and docks had been licked up.

The Last Stand

The great stand of the fire-fighters was made Thursday night on Van Ness Avenue. Had they failed here, the comparatively few remaining houses of the city would have been swept. Here were the magnificent residences of the second generation of San Francisco nabobs, and these, in a solid zone, were dynamited down across the path of the fire. Here and there the flames leaped the zone, but these fires were beaten out, principally by the use of wet blankets and rugs.

San Francisco, at the present time, is like the crater of a volcano, around which are camped tens of thousands of refugees At the Presidio alone are at least twenty thousand. All the surrounding cities and towns are jammed with the homeless ones, where they are being cared for by the relief committees. The refugees were carried free by the railroads to any point they wished to go, and it is estimated that over one hundred thousand people have left the peninsula on which San Francisco stood. The Government has the situation in hand, and, thanks to the immediate relief given by the whole United States, there is not the slightest possibility of a famine. The bankers and business men have already set about making preparations to rebuild San Francisco.

Song of Roland

Charles the King, our Lord and Sovereign,
Full seven years hath sojourned in Spain,
Conquered the land, and won the western main,
Now no fortress against him doth remain,
No city walls are left for him to gain,
Save Sarraguce, that sits on high mountain.
Marsile its King, who feareth not God's name,
Mahumet's man, he invokes Apollin's aid,
Nor wards off ills that shall to him attain.

II

King Marsilies he lay at Sarraguce,
Went he his way into an orchard cool;
There on a throne he sate, of marble blue,
Round him his men, full twenty thousand, stood.
Called he forth then his counts, also his dukes:
"My Lords, give ear to our impending doom:
That Emperour, Charles of France the Douce,
Into this land is come, us to confuse.
I have no host in battle him to prove,
Nor have I strength his forces to undo.
Counsel me then, ye that are wise and true;
Can ye ward off this present death and dule?"
What word to say no pagan of them knew,
Save Blancandrin, of th' Castle of Val Funde.

III

Blancandrins was a pagan very wise,
In vassalage he was a gallant knight,
First in prowess, he stood his lord beside.
And thus he spoke: "Do not yourself affright!
Yield to Carlun, that is so big with pride,
Faithful service, his friend and his ally;
Lions and bears and hounds for him provide,
Thousand mewed hawks, sev'n hundred camelry;
Silver and gold, four hundred mules load high;
Fifty wagons his wrights will need supply,
Till with that wealth he pays his soldiery.
War hath he waged in Spain too long a time,
To Aix, in France, homeward he will him hie.
Follow him there before Saint Michael's tide,
You shall receive and hold the Christian rite;
Stand honour bound, and do him fealty.

Send hostages, should he demand surety,
Ten or a score, our loyal oath to bind;
Send him our sons, the first-born of our wives;—
An he be slain, I'll surely furnish mine.
Better by far they go, though doomed to die,
Than that we lose honour and dignity,
And be ourselves brought down to beggary."

IV

Says Blancandrins: "By my right hand, I say,
And by this beard, that in the wind doth sway,
The Frankish host you'll see them all away;
Franks will retire to France their own terrain.
When they are gone, to each his fair domain,
In his Chapelle at Aix will Charles stay,
High festival will hold for Saint Michael.
Time will go by, and pass the appointed day;
Tidings of us no Frank will hear or say.
Proud is that King, and cruel his courage;
From th' hostage he'll slice their heads away.
Better by far their heads be shorn away,
Than that ourselves lose this clear land of Spain,
Than that ourselves do suffer grief and pain."
"That is well said. So be it." the pagans say.

V

The council ends, and that King Marsilie
Calleth aside Clarun of Balaguee,
Estramarin and Eudropin his peer,
And Priamun and Guarlan of the beard,
And Machiner and his uncle Mahee,
With Jouner, Malbien from over sea,
And Blancandrin, good reason to decree:
Ten hath he called, were first in felony.
"Gentle Barons, to Charlemagne go ye;
He is in siege of Cordres the city.
In your right hands bear olive-branches green
Which signify Peace and Humility.
If you by craft contrive to set me free,
Silver and gold, you'll have your fill of me,
Manors and fiefs, I'll give you all your need."
"We have enough," the pagans straight agree.

VI

King Marsilies, his council finishing,
Says to his men: "Go now, my lords, to him,

Olive-branches in your right hands bearing;
Bid ye for me that Charlemagne, the King,
In his God's name to shew me his mercy;
Ere this new moon wanes, I shall be with him;
One thousand men shall be my following;
I will receive the rite of christening,
Will be his man, my love and faith swearing;
Hostages too, he'll have, if so he will."
Says Blancandrins: "Much good will come of this."

VII

Ten snow-white mules then ordered Marsilie,
Gifts of a King, the King of Suatilie.
Bridled with gold, saddled in silver clear;
Mounted them those that should the message speak,
In their right hands were olive-branches green.
Came they to Charle, that holds all France in fee,
Yet cannot guard himself from treachery.

VIII

Merry and bold is now that Emperour,
Cordres he holds, the walls are tumbled down,
His catapults have battered town and tow'r.
Great good treasure his knights have placed in pound,
Silver and gold and many a jewelled gown.
In that city there is no pagan now
But he been slain, or takes the Christian vow.
The Emperour is in a great orchard ground
Where Oliver and Rollant stand around,
Sansun the Duke and Anseis the proud,
Gefreid d'Anjou, that bears his gonfaloun;
There too Gerin and Geriers are found.
Where they are found, is seen a mighty crowd,
Fifteen thousand, come out of France the Douce.
On white carpets those knights have sate them down,
At the game-boards to pass an idle hour;—
Chequers the old, for wisdom most renowned,
While fence the young and lusty bachelours.
Beneath a pine, in eglantine embow'red,
l Stands a fald-stool, fashioned of gold throughout;
There sits the King, that holds Douce France in pow'r;
White is his beard, and blossoming-white his crown,
Shapely his limbs, his countenance is proud.
Should any seek, no need to point him out.
The messengers, on foot they get them down,
And in salute full courteously they lout.

IX

The foremost word of all Blancandrin spake,
And to the King: "May God preserve you safe,
The All Glorious, to Whom ye're bound to pray!
Proud Marsilies this message bids me say:
Much hath he sought to find salvation's way;
Out of his wealth meet presents would he make,
Lions and bears, and greyhounds leashed on chain,
Thousand mewed hawks, sev'n hundred dromedrays,
Four hundred mules his silver shall convey,
Fifty wagons you'll need to bear away
Golden besants, such store of proved assay,
Wherewith full tale your soldiers you can pay.
Now in this land you've been too long a day
Hie you to France, return again to Aix;
Thus saith my Lord, he'll follow too that way."
That Emperour t'wards God his arms he raised
Lowered his head, began to meditate.

X

That Emperour inclined his head full low;
Hasty in speech he never was, but slow:
His custom was, at his leisure he spoke.
When he looks up, his face is very bold,
He says to them: "Good tidings have you told.
King Marsilies hath ever been my foe.
These very words you have before me told,
In what measure of faith am I to hold?"
That Sarrazin says, "Hostages he'll show;
Ten shall you take, or fifteen or a score.
Though he be slain, a son of mine shall go,
Any there be you'll have more nobly born.
To your palace seigneurial when you go,
At Michael's Feast, called in periculo;
My Lord hath said, thither will he follow
Ev'n to your baths, that God for you hath wrought;
There is he fain the Christian faith to know."
Answers him Charles: "Still may he heal his soul."

XI

Clear shone the sun in a fair even-tide;
Those ten men's mules in stall he bade them tie.
Also a tent in the orchard raise on high,
Those messengers had lodging for the night;
Dozen serjeants served after them aright.
Darkling they lie till comes the clear daylight.

That Emperour does with the morning rise;
Matins and Mass are said then in his sight.
Forth goes that King, and stays beneath a pine;
Barons he calls, good counsel to define,
For with his Franks he's ever of a mind.   .

XII

That Emperour, beneath a pine he sits,
Calls his barons, his council to begin:
Oger the Duke, that Archbishop Turpin,
Richard the old, and his nephew Henry,
From Gascony the proof Count Acolin,
Tedbald of Reims and Milun his cousin:
With him there were Gerers, also Gerin,
And among them the Count Rollant came in,
And Oliver, so proof and so gentil.
Franks out of France, a thousand chivalry;
Guenes came there, that wrought the treachery.
The Council then began, which ended ill.   .

XIII

"My Lords Barons," says the Emperour then, Charles,
"King Marsilies hath sent me his messages;
Out of his wealth he'll give me weighty masses.
Greyhounds on leash and bears and lions also,
Thousand mewed hawks and seven hundred camels,
Four hundred mules with gold Arabian charged,
Fifty wagons, yea more than fifty drawing.
But into France demands he my departure;
He'll follow me to Aix, where is my Castle;
There he'll receive the law of our Salvation:
Christian he'll be, and hold from me his marches.
But I know not what purpose in his heart is."
Then say the Franks: "Beseems us act with caution!"   .

XIV

That Emperour hath ended now his speech.
The Count Rollanz, he never will agree,
Quick to reply, he springs upon his feet;
And to the King, "Believe not Marsilie.
Seven years since, when into Spain came we,
I conquer'd you Noples also Commibles,
And took Valterne, and all the land of Pine,
And Balaguet, and Tuele, and Sezilie.
Traitor in all his ways was Marsilies;
Of his pagans he sent you then fifteen,

Bearing in hand their olive-branches green:
Who, ev'n as now, these very words did speak.
You of your Franks a Council did decree,
Praised they your words that foolish were in deed.
Two of your Counts did to the pagan speed,
Basan was one, and the other Basilie:
Their heads he took on th' hill by Haltilie.
War have you waged, so on to war proceed,
To Sarraguce lead forth your great army.
All your life long, if need be, lie in siege,
Vengeance for those the felon slew to wreak."

Powerline Productions

Being World Changers!

Raising World Changers!

Powerline Productions exists to serve you! We want you to grow in your relationship with Jesus, experience joy and success in your homeschooling journey, and fulfill the Great Commission with your family in your home, church, and community. We offer Homeschooling books, unit studies, curriculum, one-credit high school classes, ladies Bible studies, God's Girls Bible studies, Real Men Bible studies, audios, and cookbooks just for you!

Our Websites

joyfulandsuccessfulhomeschooling.com/

jshomeschooling.com/

finishwellcon.com/

powerlineprod.com/

meredithcurtis.com/

E-books Available at powerlineprod.com/

currclick.com/browse/pub/247/Powerline-Productions

Print Books Available @ amazon.com/ **(look up Books by Title)**

You can find our books here: https://www.amazon.com/Meredith-Curtis/e/B01GOEMVUC

Contact Us: Laura@powerlinecc.com **&** Meredith@powerlinecc.com **&** PastorMike@powerlinecc.com

Powerline Productions
251 Brightview Drive Lake Mary, FL 32746

High School Classes

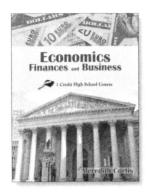
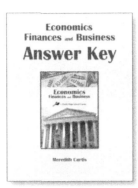

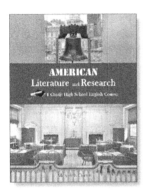

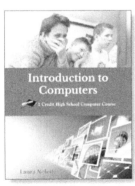

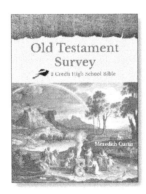

Real Men Discipleship Manuals

God calls fathers to impart life to their sons, passing the baton in the race of faith. These Bible studies were created for fathers (or mentors) to go through this material with their sons. Pastor Mike Curtis used these materials to mentor his own son and other young men in the church. These manuals cover tough issues that fathers and sons need to talk about and live out in their lives.

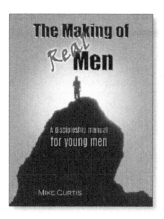  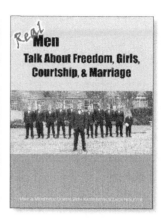

Real Men Classes

Do you want to prepare your sons to become godly husbands, fathers, church leaders, and pillars in their communities? These one-credit high school life skills classes build character and prepare young men for the future. Using living books, Scripture, and practical assignments, young men will learn to become the man God has called them to be.

God's Girls Bible Studies & Courses

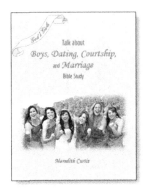

Maggie King Mysteries

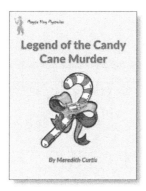
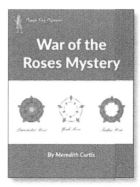
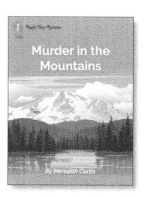

Ladies Bible Studies

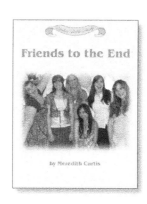

More Books from Powerline Production

 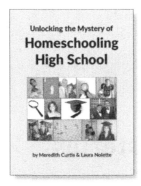 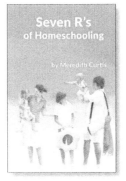 

 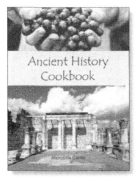  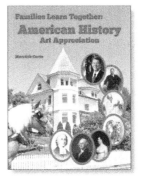

 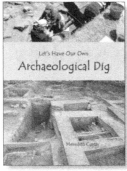  

 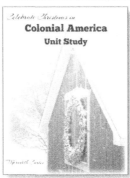  

About the Author

Meredith Curtis, a pastor's wife and homeschooling mom of five children, leads worship, mentors ladies, and, sometimes, even cooks dinner. Her passion is to equip people to love Jesus, raise godly children, and change the world around them with the power of the Gospel. "Lives are changed in the context of relationships," Meredith often says, as well as, "Be a world changer! Raise world changers!" She enjoys speaking to small and large groups.

All inquiries can be made to the author, Meredith Curtis, through email: Meredith@powerlinecc.com or contact her through her websites: joyfulandsuccessfulhomeschooling.com/

meredithcurtis.com/
finishwellcon.com/
powerlineprod.com/

Meredith is the author of several books.
Joyful and Successful Homeschooling
Seven R's of Homeschooling
Quick & EZ Unit Study Fun
Unlocking the Mysteries of Homeschooling High School (with Laura Nolette)
Celebrate Thanksgiving
Celebrate Our Christian Heroes
HIS Story of the 20th Century

Meredith is the author of several cozy mysteries: The Maggie King Mysteries series.
Drug Dealers Deadly Disguise
Legend of the Candy Cane Murder
War of the Roses Mystery
Murder in the Mountains

Meredith is the author of several Bible studies.
Lovely to Behold
A Wise Woman Builds
Jesus, Fill My Heart & Home
Welcome Inn: Practicing the Art of Hospitality in Jesus" Name
Friends to the End
God's Girls Beauty Secrets (with Sarah Jeffords)
God's Girls Friends to the End (with Katie-Beth Nolette & Sarah Jeffords)
God's Girls Talk about Boys, Dating, Courtship, & Marriage

Meredith is the author of several unit studies, timelines, and cookbooks.
Celebrate Christmas in Colonial America
Celebrate Christmas with Cookies
Travel to London Unit Study

Celebrate Thanksgiving with the Pilgrims
American History Cookbook
Ancient History Cookbook
Travel God's World Cookbook
Families Learning Together American History Art Appreciation
American History Timeline (with Laura Nolette)
Ancient History Timeline (with Laura Nolette)
Let's Have Our Own Medieval Banquet (with Laura Nolette)
Let's Have Our Archaeological Dig
Let's Have Our Own Olympic Games

Meredith is the author of several high school courses.
HIS Story of the 20th Century High School Workbook
HIS Story of the 20th Century High School Workbook Answer Key
American Literature and Research
British Literature and Writing
Who Dun It: Murder Mystery Literature & Writing
Communication 101: Essays and Speeches
Foundations of Western Literature
Economics, Finances, and Business
Economics, Finances, and Business Answer Key
Government: God's Blueprint/Man's Agenda
Worldview 101: Understand the Times
New Testament Survey
Old Testament Survey
Great Commission
Career Choices and The College Decision
Real Men 101: Godly Manhood
Real Men 102: Freedom, Courtship, Marriage, and Family
Real Men 103: Leadership
Real Men 104: Pass the Torch
God's Girls 101: Grow in Christ
God's Girls 102: Virtuous Womanhood
God's Girls 103: Courtship, Marriage, and the Christian Family
God's Girls 104: Motherhood
God's Girls 105: Homemaking
God's Girls 106: Friendship, Hospitality, and Celebrations
God's Girls 107: How to Homeschool
Drama 101: Act it Out! (with Laura Nolette)

Meredith is the author of several middle school courses.
Americana News Reporting
HIS Story of the 20th Century Middle School Workbook
HIS Story of the 20th Century Middle School Workbook Answer Key